Left-Handed Teaching

LEFT-HANDED TEACHING

Lessons in Affective Education

Second Edition

GLORIA A. CASTILLO

*Consultant in Confluent Education, Confluent
Education Program, Department of Education,
Manitoba, Canada; Resource Teacher, Learning
Assistant Center, Winnipeg School Division #1,
Winnipeg, Manitoba, Canada*

Holt, Rinehart and Winston

New York   Chicago   San Francisco
Dallas   Montreal   Toronto   London   Sydney

Library of Congress Cataloging in Publication Data
Castillo, Gloria A.
 Left-handed teaching.

 Bibliography: p. 231
 1. Education of children.   2.   Education—Aims and objectives.   I.   Title
LB1115.C34   1978   372.1′3   77-85508
ISBN 0-03-040266-2

Printed in the United States of America
890   090 987654321

To my human teachers

Janet Lederman
Robin Montz
Aaron Hillman
Sherry Carty
and all the children

PREFACE AND
ACKNOWLEDGMENTS

Traditionally, public schools have had as their main focus the development of cognitive skills. But today many experts in education as well as in a growing number of other fields insist that the development of cognitive skills is not enough. They say that we also need to deal with the affective dimensions of students—their interests, concerns, fears, anxieties, joys, and other personal and emotional reactions they bring to the learning situation. When students are made to feel that their experiences, their emotional being, the affective parts of them have nothing to do with the "worthwhile knowledge" the school system intends to set before them, they are being told that they are of secondary importance to the curriculum. In order to teach students in meaningful and relevant ways, it is necessary to blend the cognitive with the affective domain and to seek continually ways of developing the emotional issues that are a part of every cognitive learning experience.

But when I undertook such a search, I soon discovered that there was very little material available on how to incorporate the student's affective dimensions into the cognitive work of the classroom. According to Richard Jones, one of the few who had done practical work in blending the cognitive and affective domains, "The arrangement of opportunities for these coordinative events to take place in schoolrooms is, of course, work for the teacher's 'left hand.' "[1] He and others had developed the af-

[1] Richard M. Jones, *Fantasy and Feeling in Education* (New York: New York University Press, 1968), p. 199.

fective domain within the confines of a particular curriculum. But that curriculum was not available in my classroom. Even more frustrating, I could not imagine or develop ways to adapt those affective lessons to the curriculum I *did* have in my classroom. They were too interwoven with the curriculum to be used separately. A way had to be found to deal with the affective dimensions of students with *any* given curriculum. So I began to work out my own "left-handed" style of teaching.

After two years of experimentation, I developed a model in order to allow systematically and predictably for the growth and development of the whole student. This meant developing the affective as well as the cognitive dimensions of learning. For me this also meant being concerned with the readiness/awareness level of the student as well as attending to what each one was to be responsible for in terms of cognitive and affective development. That model is described in detail in Part I of this book.

While developing the model for teaching lessons that fostered the growth of the whole student, I became aware of the need to have affective lessons—lessons specifically designed to elicit affective responses from students—explicitly available so that I could use them again as well as share them with others. The students spontaneously created affective lessons, which I wrote down after they had worked through them. Other teachers offered more ideas. Gradually the collection grew. It has now been brought together in Part II of this book.

Few attempts have been made to relate these lessons to particular cognitive content. Each teacher in using them will have to make arrangements for coordinating them with the cognitive content that will emerge from the students' participation in the affective domain. Each teacher will then have multiple opportunities to work with his or her "left hand."

In Part III, the cognitive domain becomes more central. Each lesson is designed to develop or enhance a cognitive skill while simultaneously developing or enhancing the student's affective domain. This is primarily done by revising standardized textbook lessons to include some way to deal with the student's interest, concerns, fears, anxieties, and joys. Each lesson allows the student to share some part of him or herself within the context of a cognitive skill.

Ideally all learning should be a blending of the cognitive and affective domains. When such blending occurs, we have "confluent education" —education that allows students to develop their emotional abilities along with their intellectual abilities. In the final section of this book, one lesson from the affective domain is developed in several cognitive contexts to show how confluent lessons can be developed. The goal of this book is not to have teachers use their right or their left hands exclusively in teaching but to equip them to use both with equal skill; not to teach cognitive *or* affective lessons, but to have cognitive *and* affective dimensions available in each and every learning situation.

Many, many people helped me in writing this book.

First were those who gave me support and guidance along the way: my principal, Robert Pearce, who allowed me opportunities for experimentation; Bud Robinson who offered much needed encouragement and valuable feedback on the effects of new lessons; and Dr. George I. Brown who offered his own personal and professional encouragement as well as made the Ford-Esalen Project available to me.

Then there have been all the teachers and students who were willing to field-test these lessons and give me their suggestions on how to improve them. Many freely shared their own ideas. Carolyn Bogad developed the original "Make Me" lesson (p. 99). Susie McCall gave me the idea for "The Angry Sock" (p. 155). Beverly Galyean suggested a framework for developing the unit on Language. Others gave me the beginnings of a new idea or helped me work out an idea to a creative ending.

Most recently there has been Keven Van Camp and the entire staff of the Confluent Education Program in Manitoba. With them, I have been able to use my model in a wide variety of situations as well as continue to have opportunities to explore and experiment to learn and grow professionally and personally.

Finally there have been my editors at Praeger Publishers. Without their guidance and support I would have never written down my ideas for making teaching more meaningful and enjoyable.

G. A. C.

CONTENTS

Left-Handed Teaching

A Personal Approach to Confluent Education

When I began teaching, I was sure I had all the answers on how to become a great teacher. I was young and energetic, and had just been graduated from a reputable "teacher training" college. I knew how to teach, which at that time meant that I could pick up a teachers' manual on any subject, read explicit directions, and, by following those directions, teach the students. I was sure of what to teach, for there were adequate guidelines set by the state and the local school district. All I had to do was teach from the books. I did, and I did it very well according to all those who evaluated my work.

And yet, at the end of that year I had a vague, empty feeling about what had gone on in that class. The highlights of the year, upon reflection, had been the days when we broke away from the prescribed activities and went off exploring something spontaneously, as we did on the day we had a discussion on policemen after one boy told us that the police had come to his house to take his father to jail. Of course, we didn't stay off course very long because there was always the material that had to be covered by June, and the only way to cover it was to march through the textbooks page by page. There wasn't much time for anything else.

Each year the empty feeling grew. Something had gone wrong on my way to becoming a great teacher. All I had were questions. Where do I want to go in teaching, and how do I get there? What do I want my students—for these students are mine for the time they are with me—to come to value? What do I want them to understand about themselves,

1

about me, about other people and other things in their world? How do I want them to relate to their total universe? To what do I want them to be inclined to commit themselves?

Of course, I did not have the answers to these questions, but at least now I realized that my empty feeling, my concerns, centered upon students and not the curriculum. Knowing this, I explored ways of using more of what the students brought into the classroom with them. I rearranged the schedule in order to provide a time when no curriculum would be presented. This was to be the time for them to direct and control their learning activities.

Again, something went wrong. The students and I were very uncomfortable in this time period. For one thing, I kept expecting the principal to drop in and ask me to account for what was—or was not—going on. I'm sure the students kept expecting me to "drop in" on them and demand the same thing. We tried different things, such as having small group discussions, listening to records, or reading stories. Nothing very interesting or exciting seemed to happen. I imagine I had a harder time with the period than the students did, because even though I wanted it to be a time for them—their development, their growth, their pleasure—I kept wanting to put it all into some kind of structure. But the students had a double standard to work under. The period had to be free and open and structured and constructive at the same time. After a month of this double bind, we were all relieved when I admitted that I was not ready yet to give them much time away from curriculum or in student-directed activities.

I took over again. This time I began each session with a program. I set the theme of the motivation and gave the students a way to follow through with it. For example, when we studied plants in science, I used that time period to read them a story about leaves and give a lesson on how to make a leaf print. This led to how to do art "rubbings"—coloring over various textures in the room. When a student finished a print he or she was pleased with, he or she was encouraged to write a story about it.

I realized that in order for me to let the students work on their own, every one had to be doing something. So I set out to teach or allow them to do all kinds of things—run the tape recorder, play a record, set up an art project, take the roll. Some were so obvious and easy it is ridiculous to speak of teaching them, but until then I had always thought I had to do these things. Little by little, I could allow for more transaction and interaction between myself and the students, letting them know how I felt as they moved around in the room, asking them how they felt about what was going on in the room. Everything was centered on the materials and experiences that collectively could be called the curriculum. For the first time, when the students failed to develop and grow as I expected they would, I looked for the shortcomings or errors in the structure of the class, not in the innards of the students.

That experience was a time of discovering my own expectations and demands as a teacher. I learned more about myself and how I was in the classroom. I discovered my need for structure, boundaries, control. I also discovered ways to give it up once in a while. Little by little, I gave more of that time back to the students. It was also a time for the development of a commitment to the equal worth of all the students and hence to the importance of each student's development and growth, whatever his or her so-called native capacities. I found that this time period led to much personal growth for me and the students. I also became aware of an urgent need to learn so much more—everything and anything I could about how to teach.

Through the books I read, I realized that the whole educational world was dealing with the very issues I was struggling with in my classroom—namely, the ultimate goals of education: What understandings, values, and commitments do we want to teach our students? I gained support and drew ideas from leaders in the field of humanistic psychology, such as Rollo May, Abraham Maslow, Carl Rogers, and Sidney Jourard.

At the same time I became involved in the Ford-Esalen project. Esalen Institute was founded to explore the potential of human existence. It does this through a program of workshops and seminars, drawing from humanistic psychology as well as from modern dance, sensitivity training, Eastern religions, and physical education. The Fund for the Advancement of Education of the Ford Foundation provided Dr. George I. Brown, Professor of Education at the University of California at Santa Barbara, and Esalen Institute with a grant for a "pilot project to explore ways to adapt approaches in the affective domain to the school curriculum." The project was thus an attempt to renew the central tradition of Western education— education for the whole person. Its focus was on assembling various approaches to affective learning from the activities in Esalen's unique workshops, conversations with people attending Esalen, reading published materials, and examining them to determine which of these approaches might be appropriate for the classroom. The staff members of the project would then try out the most promising affective approaches with our classes in an appropriate curriculum context and report our results at the monthly meetings. From that year-long examination of affective experiences and experiments in blending them into the cognitive curriculum already available in the classroom, we began to approach curriculum in new ways. The term "confluent education" emerged from our experience, meaning "the integration or flowing together of the affective and cognitive elements in individual and group learning—sometimes called humanistic or psychological education."[1] Confluent education allows for intellectual, emotional, and physical learning.

Although it was not necessarily anticipated beforehand, the tech-

[1] George I. Brown, *Human Teaching for Human Learning: An Introduction to Confluent Education* (New York: Viking Press, 1971), p. 3.

niques and methodology of Gestalt therapy were to play a very important part in the Ford-Esalen project. Both Dr. Brown, the project director, and Janet Lederman, one of the staff, were experienced Gestalt therapists. The late Dr. Frederick ("Fritz") Perls, the founder of Gestalt therapy (or "refinder of Gestalt therapy," as he called himself), was also in residence at Esalen during that time. He would often talk to us informally and expressed great interest in what we were doing. We spent time with him in actual Gestalt therapy sessions, and then he supervised as members of the staff took over the leadership role and conducted Gestalt therapy techniques with other members of the group.

Although we experienced the role of Gestalt therapist, it was the technique and methodology of Gestalt therapy, not the role of being a therapist, that we took back to the classroom settings. Gestalt therapy starts with *what is*. It relates the context to the content. Together they form the Gestalt, the whole. The Gestalt approach pays attention to the obvious, to the utmost surface. What was obvious was that we were all teachers in our classrooms even though we were other things in other places.

For example, one tenet of Gestalt therapy that I found especially useful in the class was that of awareness, of myself, my world, my feelings, my fantasies. Awareness leads to being in touch with the environment. Awareness can also lead to new cognition. When I become aware of something, I may discover a need to learn more about it. In the classroom, I worked to develop the students' awareness and used that with their readiness level, their ability to assimilate new cognition, to stimulate their learning activities, striving continually to expand their awareness and their cognitive skills.

While on the project, I was introduced to a new kind of time—the "here and now." This second. This second. Gestalt therapy uses this technique to establish a continuum of awareness. This continuum of awareness is very simple and, like most truly simple things, is difficult to grasp—just be aware from second to second of what is going on, of ongoing experiences, actual touching, seeing, moving, doing. Nothing exists except the here and now. Whether I remember or anticipate, I do it now. Having this new sense of time, an awareness of now, is like adding a third dimension of time. It is the difference between monaural and stereophonic sound. It is the feeling of space I get when flying in a light aircraft. Having a here and now in the classroom allows for a whole new time space, and that space is all life and living.

The specific aim of Gestalt therapy is for the patient to mature, to grow up, and that means to take responsibility for your life, to be on your own. That includes being in the here and now and simply being willing to say "I am I." Fritz Perls describes responsibility as *"response-ability:* the ability to respond, to have thoughts, reactions, emotions in a certain situation. Now, this responsibility, the ability to *be* what one *is*, is expressed through the word 'I.' "[2] Just as the concept of the here and now opened up a whole new range of time, so response-ability opened up a new set of alternative ways of being for me. To me the "i" in responsibility stood for "I should." I should teach Johnny to read, I should be creative, I should have a marvelous way to teach something I find boring, and on and on. This is a great way to trick myself out of here and now. It takes me out of the present moment into a world of fantasy. I spent a great deal of my time and energy attending to my so-called responsibilities, my shoulds. But by truly focusing on what I was responding to, my response-ability, I became more accepting of the here and now and also found that I was more open and available to meet my responsibilities.

These two Gestalt tenets were my major focus for the entire year of the Ford-Esalen project. They were not easy concepts for me. Over and over again I went to the meetings to seek advice and help from the group. Staying in the here and now was new for me. The new meaning of responsibility confused me profoundly. Until I had an exercise I could put myself through, I had to ask questions of others to know what was happening to me. Try this with me:

"At this moment I cannot be responsible for anything except myself, which includes . . ." My list goes like this: "At this moment I cannot be responsible for anything except myself, which includes sitting here, putting my ideas down on paper." (This also says, "At this moment I cannot be responsible for your reading this.")

This exercise, repeated over and over, helped me to develop an acceptance of the here and now, a willingness to be in the here and now, a faith in the productivity of the here and now. It gave me an entry into that third dimension of time. It also gave me a way to deal with my responsibilities, because at first I felt that accepting responsibility on Gestalt terms was too self-centered, too hedonistic. But gradually I discovered that it was not a negation of responsibility, not a negation of my yesterdays and expectations of tomorrow, but rather an efficient way for me to become aware of what I could and could not do. I cannot live yesterday or tomorrow today. I cannot live any life other than my own. The only moment of life I have is now. I was beginning to realize what Fritz Perls meant when he later wrote: "Authenticity, maturity, responsibility for one's actions and life, response-ability and living in the now, having the creativeness of the now available, is all one and the same thing. Only in the now are you in touch with what's going on."[3]

As a classroom teacher, one issue I faced was that I could not take responsibility for dull, meaningless materials that had to be covered in the year. What I was responsible for was the presentation of the content in those materials. This changed the focus of my energy from the ma-

[2] Frederick Perls, *Gestalt Therapy Verbatim* (LaFayett, California: Real People Press, 1969), p. 65.
[3] *Ibid.*, p. 52.

terials to the presentation of lessons dealing with that content in a variety of ways. First of all, I went to my administrator to determine exactly what content and which materials "had" to be presented. I found that many materials did not have to be presented at all. They were there for my use if I wanted them, but I could use other materials and resources for teaching the required content if I chose to do so. I listened to other teach-

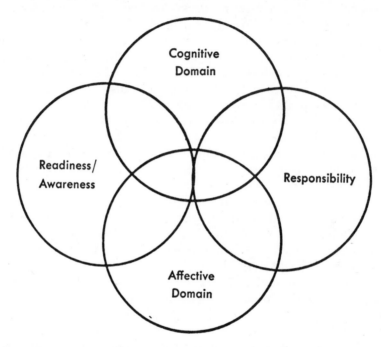

ers talk about materials that presented content in interesting or exciting ways. If someone had a good idea on how to present something, I either made arrangements for him or her to teach it to my class (while I taught something else to his or her class) or tried out the idea myself. Sometimes I gave the material to the students and let them present it in their own way. Finally, after much experimentation, I developed a strategy, a structure, or a model for my presentation of classroom materials.

I began by defining a space, setting the essence of what I had to teach and what I wanted to teach into some kind of framework that I could move around in, that I could handle with ease. This meant deciding what aspects of education were most important to me. Through this process, I devised a working model that looks like this:

Cognitive Domain: The subject content that is to be learned—intellectual endeavors, ideas, processes, skills, knowledge.
Affective Domain: The emotional content that is to be explored—

feelings, concerns, interests, desires, values, attitudes—development and expansion of fantasy and imagination.

Readiness/Awareness: Readiness to deal with cognitive demands—developing skills, ordering ideas and knowledge, building upon what is already known. Awareness of feelings, emotions, body—responding to the here and now.

Responsibility: Being able to carry out the tasks required of the learning situation. Being able to say "I am I." Being able to respond with new thoughts, actions, and emotions due to the learning process.

Confluent Education: The Gestalt, when cognition, affect, readiness/awareness, and responsibility are totally integrated.

This is just a model, a way to present curriculum in a meaningful, responsible way. In reality, when learning occurs, all these parts come together into one meaningful whole. There is no separation between cognitive and affective domains, between thought and affect, between readiness/awareness and responsibility. Although each part of the model will be described as it relates to the other parts, in reality they don't exist independently.

The cognitive domain represents intellectual content for the year: the what and how of my teaching responsibilities. What am I hired to teach? What are the cognitive goals of this grade level? What materials are available in the form of textbooks, teachers' guides, state frameworks? To begin with, I go over these materials thoroughly. In any unit, any subject, there are so many concepts, so many things to teach, that I have to make choices. From all that is available, I begin by choosing those items that stir some excitement in me. It may be that I disagree with the author's viewpoint, or it may be that I agree but want to add my own information, my experience, to the material, or it may be that I find the material exciting just the way it is. In any event, it is important that I choose to work with ideas that stimulate me. If I am not excited about learning, I certainly cannot get others excited about learning.

While still in the cognitive domain, I look to the rest of the model and ask some questions of myself. What affective experience can I provide to go along with the cognitive material? What readiness/awareness must the students have to be able to grasp the cognitive concepts that will be presented? What new knowledge will the students be responsible for acquiring? Many of these questions can be answered in behavioral-objective terms, and in the cognitive domain they can often be taken right out of the textbooks I am working from.

For example, while working on a math unit on geometric shapes, one of the goals is to have students name and identify a triangle and a circle.

An affective experience for primary students would be to have them "become" a triangle. I would ask, "How can you move? Where are your angles? Can you become a circle now? What do you have to do with your body to change it from a triangle to a circle? How can you move as a circle?"

I would provide many opportunities for the students to become aware of the angles of a triangle and the roundness of a circle. I would help them to identify other things in the environment that are like circles or triangles. "The clock is round like the circle. The legs of the chair and the floor make a triangle."

In considering the readiness/awareness aspects of the lesson, I might present only one shape at a time for very young students and more complicated shapes if triangles and circles seem too simple for the group. I might also have to allow the students opportunities to "become" objects before asking them to become shapes.

Once I have made my cognitive selection, I move my thinking to the affective domain. This represents the emotional content that will be explored. It is based on the interests and concerns of the students, on their readiness/awareness, on the level of responsibility they can assume, and on the interest and concern elicited directly by the cognitive content I have chosen to work with. It is the affective domain that gives meaning and relevancy to the rest of the program. It acts as the "supercharger," supplying life to the learning situation and energy for working in the other parts of the model.

In the affective domain, I must provide the students with some way to experience the cognitive concepts, or at least some of them. I do this primarily in two ways. One, I set up a situation so that students can "live out" the experience in the classroom setting. This allows them to bring their own here and now to the learning experience and provides opportunities for them to touch, see, hear, move. In math, for example, I once read the students a delightful story that illustrated the need for a standardized length when using the term "foot." Then, before issuing rulers, I had each student remove his or her shoes and socks, step into a pan of washable paint, and then step off six "feet." We compared the various "definitions" of six feet that resulted and discovered differences. We then discussed the mass confusion that would result if each of us used the same term but used a different "foot" to define it. We imagined how different things would look if each of several persons building one house used his or her own foot as the measure rather than a standard foot. Each student then measured out six standard feet and compared it to *his* or *her* "six feet." He or she then determined how many more of his or her feet would be needed in order to measure the same as the standard six feet. From there, I pointed out that a ruler is much easier to handle than a true representation of a foot and gives each of us the same definition of the world, at least in the mathematical sense. Later I discovered that this "lesson" had repercussions throughout the year. Often students would discover on their own that two or more of them might be using the same term but defining it differently, and that it was this difference that was causing difficulties between them, not a difference in beliefs, values, or judgments.

The second, and perhaps more difficult, way of working in the affective domain is to have the students imagine how living out an experience relates to their real world, their here and now. This is more difficult because it requires both dealing with the imaginary setting and bringing it back to the students' real world. There is an abundance of good materials available for getting students into imaginary settings. However, most of it stops short of adding the students' here and now to the experience. Take the classic "store in the classroom." Students may spend weeks moving about in a make-believe store. Certainly they have a wonderful time with it, and a great deal of mathematics gets reinforced by the selling and buying that goes on. But how much more valuable the store would become if it were brought back into the students' lives by providing them with a wide range of opportunities for discovery of self, particularly by asking them "now" and "how" questions: "Now what are you doing?" "Now what are you feeling?" "How do you experience that feeling?" "Who else is in the store with you now?" "How do you feel about his being there?" "How is the store like other places you know about?" "How would you like to change the store? Now change it." The possibilities are limited only by available time and possible limiting cognitive concepts. As before, there is so much that can be taught, it is necessary to make decisions.

Some of the questions I would explore are: What rules did you need to keep the store working? How did you know that? What happened when those rules weren't followed? How did you feel then? What do you need from a store? What do you need in order to buy things? What happens if you need or want something and you don't have money? How did you feel as owner of the store? How did you feel as a worker? Older students, in the fifth to eighth grade, can deal with issues that are current in stores today—rising food costs, the effects of strikes or boycotts, the creation of vacant downtown areas by movements of people, the problem of consumer information, truth in labeling, and so on.

It is necessary to find ways to relate the make-believe store to the student's own life; otherwise it remains at a simulation-game level. The modern supermarket is something that directly affects the life of the community it serves. Studying it affectively can help even a primary student begin to grasp what it means to live and grow up in a democracy with a capitalistic system. It can be another means for him or her to learn and discover how to cope with twentieth-century ways of life.

Take the specific cognitive goals presented in teaching materials and look for ways to express them in terms of values, concerns, feelings. For example, in reading, a typical objective in the teachers' manual is to evaluate a character in a story. Students can role-play the character and then go on to explore ways in which they themselves are like and unlike the character. They can answer all or some of the following questions: How did you feel being that character? What could you do as that character that you cannot do as yourself? What do you do that is like what the character did? What do you do that is different? What else might you be if you were that character? The affective dimension of the lesson consists of allowing for the students' exploration of the emotions available in them that are evoked by the cognitive experience of reading the story.

The affective domain is the heart and soul of the learning experience, just as the cognitive domain is the thinking, intellectual part. They are directly interrelated. The cognitive domain stimulates the affective domain, and, once students are involved in affective experiences, new cognition arises. In the affective domain, I look to the other parts of the model and again ask questions. What readiness experiences, if any, must I provide in order for the students to have the cognitive experience? What awareness must they have to experience the affective experience, the feeling, sensing, moving part of the lesson? What do I want students to become aware of while doing the experience? After the experience? What is it that I want them to take responsibility for and about as a result of the affective experience?

From these questions, I move the focus of my thoughts to the readiness/awareness space. This represents those lessons that will be required when introducing new cognitive or affective concepts. We have long been familiar with readiness concepts at the cognitive level. What level of readiness must the students have in order to be able to grasp the cognitive concepts? Is there vocabulary they must understand, clarify, or define? What must they be aware of at the cognitive level? From this, I plan a cognitive-learning program for them. Perhaps I will have to do a great deal of work in this area before moving on.

I then ask the same kinds of questions about the readiness/awareness of the affective domain. If I want students to experience something, what must they be able to do to be able to experience it? What do I want them to be aware of? Are there steps to be taken before they can come to that awareness? For example, if I should want students to respond physically to something that tastes "bitter," they must first know how bitter tastes in relation to other tastes. They must have the vocabulary to understand what I want them to do. They must have skills to represent bitter in a symbolic manner, and they must have enough imagination to represent that taste by moving their bodies in ways that symbolize bitter for them.

All too often I find that students have been educated out of their senses, and it is only at rare moments that they will have their emotions available for classroom use. This is what led to the development of the readiness/awareness space in the curriculum model. In the beginning it was a time of day specifically set aside from the rest of the school day for the development of awareness of the here and now, awareness of emotions, and of ways to express that awareness. It was a time when I explored new ways, words, and methods of getting and staying in touch with myself and the students and allowing them to do the same. It was a time for going through a learning process designed to free the affective domain—mine and the students'—for classroom use. After a while, this was no longer a set period in the day. It became an ongoing process, getting to know what was happening to each individual and what was happening in exchanges between individuals.

The readiness/awareness space is vital for confluent lessons—lessons that integrate cognitive and affective components of learning. Until now in my planning, all of this has gone on in my head, is in and of myself. When I begin to move my ideas into the classroom, it is paramount that I take a good look at where the students are. Initially, I must become aware of what the students are ready for, then take the necessary steps to allow them to be open to new experiences, both cognitively and affectively. Before having them paint with their feet, for example, it might be necessary to do some preliminary work to get them to feel comfortable about removing their shoes in the classroom or allow themselves to step into a pan of paint. This task might be handled by discussions of being and getting "messy," as well as by allowing them multiple opportunities to make a mess. In the cognitive domain, I might have to do more than this one activity in order to get students to understand and appreciate the need for uniform measurements, if that concept did not "take" in a single experience.

It is in this phase of developing my lessons that I need to use all my skill and ability to stay "tuned in" to the students and what is happening to them. This is the place where I choose either to follow my lesson plan fairly closely, because the students are where I thought they would be when I was planning it, or to abandon it and deal with a whole new set of ideas, because of the instant feedback I have coming to me from the class. It is here that I, as the teacher, make the most discoveries. The cognitive material is already planned for me by curriculum experts. Affective experiences will be influenced by what the cognitive concepts are. In both areas, I do a great deal of selecting. Of all that I *can* teach and do, what I actually teach and do for any one unit is my decision. But as soon as I begin to implement that decision, as soon as real students are added to the teaching and doing, a whole new experience begins to emerge. Until now I have been planning the learning experiences, I have been "the" teacher. Now enter the students—and there are as many teachers as there are people in the room. We all enter the lesson, which then begins to take unique shape and form because all of us are there. It is no longer the lesson I thought up. I give my knowledge, my experience, my planning to the lessons. But it is the students who give direction, movement, life to it.

For me, this is the true art of teaching. A machine can teach students factual information faster and perhaps at less cost than I can. But there is no way that a student can breathe life into that machine. When "learning" from a machine, he or she might just as well be a dog, an ape, a robot, or another machine, pushing the correct buttons. It is this readiness/awareness space that helps me to be an artistic and not a mechanistic teacher. The cognitive domain can be programed. It is also possible to program the affective domain, and more than one set of materials have been developed to do just that. There are programs available that deal with the affective domain from the standpoint of being a teacher or parent. They include manuals that have daily procedures to be followed. These programs do not take into account where any given student or group of students is at a particular point in time. They are concerned with presenting affective experiences in a step-by-step sequence. The adult, textbook in hand, is in control of the affective experience. Other programs are designed for use by the students. They, too, fail to take into account where the students in a given group might be. They present a wide range of human experiences—feelings of love and hate, acceptance and rejection, etc.—in a sequence that makes sense from an adult point of view but may be very inappropriate for specific students. I know of no way to program the readiness/awareness of a student. Certainly there are general guidelines in this area, but one must be there with the student in every sense—responding to him or her, learning from him or her—in order to be a part of the student's continuum of awareness.

It is in this area that I determine whether or not the structure of the learning environment is right for the students. If they do not do what I expect them to, I examine their readiness/awareness level in both the cognitive and the affective domains. Once, when teaching from the social sciences, I was having the class deal with the concept of the group. I had the students form groups and had planned various activities and tasks for them to perform while in those groups. Right away, as soon as they formed their groups, I discovered that they experienced a great deal of difficulty communicating when there were more than two of them in the group. Rather than continue with my plans, I began to give the students opportunities for self-awareness in a group, focusing primarily on their own experience: Choose two persons you feel comfortable with. Talk about the best day of your life. Now choose two persons you do not know very well and talk about a frightening experience. What did you experience in the first group that was different from what you experienced in the second group? Were you different? How? What was different? What was the same? What changes occurred while you were in the groups?

Once they became aware of themselves and what was happening to them, the students began to be aware that a group was a collection of "I's." There were comments like, "I just sat in our group." "I waited for someone else to take the lead." "I had some good ideas for this group, but someone else was always talking." They also learned to communicate with each other in more meaningful ways. They then went on to develop the group concepts that were presented in their social sciences material. As often happens, it was through the affective, experiential phase of the lesson that I was given the opportunity to observe and experience the readiness/awareness level of the group and make adjustments in my planning in order to be with the students. It was also in this area that I was able to observe how the students were, and were not taking responsibility, how they were, and were not, able to respond. They could handle the cognitive concepts of a group quite well. They "knew about" groups. However, they were having difficulty experiencing "being" a group.

A new question emerges from readiness and awareness: "What do I have available?" Asked in relation to the cognitive domain, that question means that I want to check my store of required skills and information. If I want to involve the class in a discussion, to use a simple example, do they and I have the skills we need to have a meaningful discussion, or will I do all the talking and they all the listening? Do they have enough information about the subject to engage in a discussion, or is the topic too strange to them? Do they share a vocabulary with which to communicate with each other? Do they know how to listen to each other? What cognitive skills do I have available in order to deal with my emotions and feelings?

When asking "What do I have available?" in relation to the affective domain, I want to check on my emotions, my fears, my expectations. What am I responding to, what need am I seeking to satisfy? It is not possible for me to know what any other person has available, and so this part of the question is addressed to myself alone. When the students enter the discussion, their responses provide me with some knowledge as to what they have available. Their responses give me further information, further ways of knowing how to extend what they have available to them in the learning situation.

Often when I ask teachers "What do you have available?" the answers are textbooks, resource personnel, books, other teachers, etc. All these things are "out there." They are important, too, but in order to have meaningful curriculum, it is vital to have self-involvement first. Involvement cannot come from, or be left to, others. The first thing a teacher must have available is one's self. This may seem an elementary statement, but meaningful teaching demands that each teacher be actively involved in *his or her own* development and learning. Each one must know how he or she responds to change, to the now, from second to second. Each must know how he or she responds to confusion, to love, anger, joy, and grief. Each one must be aware of how he or she responds when threatened.

Each must be aware of defense mechanisms and of when he or she is using them. It is necessary for one to become one's own critic, to know when one means "I won't" rather than "I can't."

Try this. On a piece of paper, make a list of the things that usually begin with "I can't. . . ." I can't teach this new math. I can't understand why Paul is so disruptive. I can't do a good job when I have too many students to teach. Now write them over again, beginning each with "I won't. . . ." Feel any difference?

A teacher must become aware of how he or she feels when students respond. Which responses are comforting, which ones cause alarm, distrust, uneasiness? What responses do those feelings elicit at that moment? Are any other responses available or possible? One must ask oneself endless what, when, where, and how questions. One must avoid asking the traditional "why" and thereby avoid rationalizing and explaining.

A critical aspect of readiness/awareness is the teacher's own readiness to accept the change that confluent lessons can produce. Each one must become aware of how he or she personally is as students respond. If he or she is fearful of letting students explore their own emotions or state their feelings in terms of "I," he or she must be content to let the students stay with cognitive content only. There may be many good reasons for responding that way, for not allowing students to be aware of what is happening to them, for not admitting what is happening at any deeper level. But the teacher must also be aware that this response does not allow students to mature, to grow up, to learn to stand on their own, to rely upon themselves rather than on the teacher.

A teacher may experience moments of great anxiety if he or she lets go of some old "shoulds" and explores the possibilities of the here and now, the creativity and productivity of the now. It may be reassuring to know that recent research shows that most people are more creative when they are slightly uncomfortable. Too much frustration seems to inhibit creativity, but a considerable amount of anxiety can be borne when the individual who experiences it feels an inner security.

It is necessary for a teacher to look inward to discover how secure he or she is, how he or she functions both in and out of the classroom. What kinds of expectations and goals are present when beginning a learning situation? How determined is he or she to actualize those goals and expectations? It has been my experience that with confluent lessons anything can and does happen. Sometimes I have chosen an activity that unexpectedly provoked so much laughter that I abandoned the goal of the lesson to explore laughter—what makes us laugh, what does laughter say, how can laughter help us to avoid our feelings, how does it show our feelings, etc. Sometimes even with the students' cooperation the lesson falls apart. It does not fit and so has no meaning at that moment. Sometimes everything works according to plan, and sometimes a whole new adventure emerges. How wide a range of experiences will the expectations of the teacher allow to exist in the classroom? How sensitive is he or she to criticism, especially if it comes from the class? In the lesson I have mentioned, if I had taken the student's laughter as criticism of the planned lesson, something very different would have emerged. As it was, attending to the here and now, listening to the message of the laughter, and directly dealing with that message allowed me and the students a unique learning experience.

In a confluent program, even more than in a strictly cognitive program, learning occurs at irregular intervals. There are bound to be emotional highs and lows. Lessons do not stop at the end of the period if they are meaningful. A tremendous amount of feeling may be generated and set loose in the classroom. What will the teacher do about all this? It is only in the here and now that these questions can be answered. How much control will he or she need? To try to change the learning environment can be a frustrating experience, and each teacher will have to decide individually if it is worth it or not.

Observation of the readiness/awareness level of a group leads to the entire area of responsibility. My responsibility is the year-long task of helping students take more and more responsibility for what happens to them during the year, to grow up, to stand on their own, both in and out of the classroom. This will necessarily be dependent upon the students' readiness/awareness levels, their abilities to tune in to their emotions, and the stages of their intellectual development.

In the cognitive domain, responsibility can be stated in terms of the goals and objectives of the textbook material. What is it that I want the students to know at the end of a unit? What factual information should they have acquired? What new knowledge should they master in the unit? At the affective level, responsibility means admitting and accepting at a personal level what does or does not happen to and for each individual. For example, "I am doing math." "I am fooling around." "I am drawing a picture." Let me illustrate this by the example of teaching about groups.

From the text, I learn the over-all cognitive concept of a unit. These are usually stated in very clear terms. In this example, these concepts included: the definition of a group, the structure of a group, the function of a group, the norms of a group, and the diversity of groups. In planning the presentation of the unit, I am careful to include opportunities for the students to master these cognitive concepts. It is usually fairly simple to determine whether a student has done so. The most common way of doing this is to give a test of some sort. In this domain the student's responsibility is to know about groups, and this can be stated in terms of behavioral objectives: I can give a definition of a group, I can describe what a group looks like, what different groups do, what group norms are; I can name different kinds of groups.

Looking at the affective domain, responsibility shifts from cognitive concepts to doing or experiencing, to being able to respond with new reactions and new awareness of emotions. It is a personal acceptance of behavior and feeling, both negative and positive. I feel I belong to this group; I do not feel I belong to that group. This feels like a group to me; that does not feel like a group to me. I want to belong to that group, so I act in this way. I feel good when I am in this group; I do not feel good when I am in this group. When I am in a group, I affect the group in this way. When I am in this group I am powerful; when I am in this group I do not feel powerful.

The responsibility space is where I as the teacher can see what the students are doing, what they are taking responsibility for, regardless of subject area. It is also the time and place to provide learning experiences that will allow for the continuing development of responsibility. Once students can experience themselves, and then groups within the classroom setting, I have them explore ways in which groups outside the classroom are the same and ways in which they are different. In this area, I return to the readiness/awareness space to continually broaden and expand the students' concepts of themselves and how they are in ever-expanding, changing situations. How am I when I am alone? How am I in this small group? How am I in the total group at school? My family group? My community group? My state? My country? How am I a human being? This brings me back to: How am I?

Attending to responsibility is vital in making learning confluent. It directly or indirectly provides for experiences that allow the students to assume responsibility for their learning. I generally start with lessons aimed at self-awareness, because only someone who knows what is happening to his or her self will be able to tune in to what is happening to others. In a classroom I expect a great deal of learning to occur as a result of the presence of other students, other adults, others' ideas as presented in books, films, etc. All this must move into the student's awareness for the development of responsibility. When each student assumes responsibility for what happens to him or her to full capacity, when he or she can choose that which will give the most satisfaction, when he or she can move from one appropriate response to the next, smoothly and easily, then teaching and learning are together in one meaningful whole, with the teacher and the student learning from and teaching each other equally.

Many teachers are alarmed when I speak of students having responsibility for themselves. But it is the students who do or do not learn, read, do math, cooperate, sit quietly, play vigorously, etc. I cannot be responsible for them in that final step. This does not mean that I can allow the students to do anything they want, whenever they like. Classroom learning excludes certain types of learning experiences. It also makes others readily available. The most obvious is the teacher-student relationship.

To teach is to show the students that more is possible. I feel that I have something to teach, and I want to teach it. And as I am engaged in teaching, I want the students to be engaged in what is happening to them. This will allow for a wide variety of responses. They may just go along with me, or they may become actively involved, or they may need additional information or help. I have a structure to work in, the confluent model, and I strive to provide a learning environment that will allow the students to define their own structure, but always within limits. I do not believe that students want or need license. They need to know that no matter what they do, they will be safe. No matter how confusing things may get, there will be a time of clearing. They need and want freedom, and with that comes responsibility.

Students, and adults as well, do not feel much responsibility for things over which they experience no control. Within the space of responsibility, therefore, I try to develop the concept "I control myself." This is achieved, in part, by asking over and over again, "What are you doing" and "Who is doing that?" It is also developed by enhancing the students' sense of their abilities to make themselves felt in their world. The classroom is a large part of the world for students, and so it is necessary to give them some of the responsibility involved in creating that world. Even kindergartners can be invited to share ideas on "What do you need a teacher to do for you?" There are real things that students need teachers to do for them, and at the same time there are many things they can be responsible for all on their own. People do not become responsible at a certain age. Responsibility involves lifelong learning. It is not a "subject" but an ongoing process.

It is possible to have many levels of awareness and responsibility in the same class at the same time. Even the youngest school-age child can be given a share of responsibility. Consider the following examples involving two boys in the same third grade class.

> My mother makes me dump the garbage.
> *How does she make you dump the garbage?*
> She tells me to.
> *Who dumps the garbage?*
> I do.
> *Well, could you not dump it?*
> No. I have to do it or I'll get in trouble. She makes me do it.
> *How does she make you do it? Does she take you over there and put your hands on it?*
> No. She makes me, and if I don't, I get in trouble.
>
> I have to be nice to my sister.
> *Who is nice to your sister?*
> I am.

Who makes you do that?
I do. I have to do that because if I don't, my father really gets
angry, and I don't like my father to get angry, so a long time
ago I decided that I would make myself be nice to my sister.

In the first example, the child seems to be very much aware of what his
mother does and as yet does not see what he does in that situation. He is
like a robot, with his mother the master controller. In the second example, the child realizes the rewards of doing what his father wants him to
do. He does not express the hopelessness, the powerlessness, of the first
child. He does something he has to do in order to get something he
wants. He has some control over the kind of relationships he has with his
sister and with his father, and he is aware of that control.

It is necessary to seek ways to permit students to have control in the
cognitive domain also. When students are permitted to be aware of what
is happening to them, when they take responsibility for what does and
does not happen to them, they can and will make the personal transla-
tions from the cognitive domain to their own beings. A fourth-grade girl
brought her math paper to me stating, "I can't do math." I asked her to
find *what* in math she couldn't do. It didn't take long for her to discover
that what she couldn't do was master a few multiplication facts. She could
add and subtract, borrow and carry. She put aside her paper and said, "I
need to work on these four multiplication facts." She left the assignment
until she was sure of those facts and then completed it in a very short
time. Later in the day she told me, "I like math now. I discovered what
I needed to learn, and I learned it."

In helping students take responsibility and be in control in the cognitive domain, it is necessary to tune into their readiness/awareness
levels. If the material is too far removed from the skills they now have,
if it is too foreign to their own readiness/awareness levels, they will not
be able to relate to it. It is important to identify what the students already
know that will help them master new materials. What else in the curriculum might be related to new cognitive experiences? What activities can
students engage in to test out new ideas? Students at any age can be re-
markably adept at designing methods for answering these and other questions that will emerge from cognitive materials. They satisfy their own
needs for learning while involving themselves naturally and easily in their
play and free-time activities. There is no reason they cannot be allowed
to do so within the limits of the classroom.

Giving control to students is not easy for most teachers to do. We
have been taught by teachers who were in control of us, and we have
been taught to be controllers. Experimentation with allowing students to
be in control and with various kinds and amounts of control by teacher
and class is a necessary part of confluent education.

Each teacher will have to deal with this issue in a personal way. No one can take that final step for another. All I can do is to share some of my experiences, some of my successes, some of my failures.

Once a group of teachers was working with this problem, meeting once a week to discuss what was happening. There were reports of everything from complete bedlam to great success. One teacher had nothing to say for more than a month. Then she came in all excited, proudly reporting, "My confluent program has begun. I kept in mind that the worst thing that could happen would be that the whole class would fall apart. I started a lesson and the whole class did fall apart. I got angry but shared my feelings with the class. They were frustrated with me, feeling that I assured their failure with my attitude. We had quite a discussion, and it was very hard for me to listen to what they had to say. We stayed with it and worked out new directions and now we are really moving along together."

Her decision was to face giving up control, to listen to what the students had to offer, and to allow herself to be uncomfortable for a while in order to "move along" with her class. There is a fine line between losing control and giving up control. In this case, the teacher actually gained control by giving up control, by sharing it with the class.

A teacher will have to find ways to discover what his or her children feel, what they think about when they are not made to think about school subjects, what they do with themselves when they are free. Continuing questions a teacher must ask the learners are: "How do you feel about this?" and "What do you already know that makes you feel that way?" Also, the questions that people always ask themselves, such as "Who am I?" "What can I do about things?" "Who am I really connected to?" "How do I fit into the scheme of things?" must be explored constantly. This may not be easy. Students have learned very well that the teacher is the source of power in the room and that they must somehow say what must be said in words that he or she will allow. For example, I had been doing morning lessons on taking responsibility for one's actions for about a week when suddenly one afternoon two boys began an all-out fist fight. Before I could stop them, one had a bloody nose and both were in tears, more of rage than pain. I asked what had happened. I got the usual, "He started it." Then, thinking back to our morning lessons, I asked, "What are you feeling now?" Since both boys were still obviously upset and quite angry, I was amazed and confused when one replied: "Sorry." I asked, "How do you know that you are sorry?" He answered: "My mother says to say I'm sorry." He had learned the words he was "supposed" to say after a fight, but he had no words of his own to express the enormous amount of feeling that went along with the act, or, if he had them, he knew that they were not to be used in this classroom.

Then I asked, "What *might* you feel when you are fighting?" This seemed less threatening than "What *do* you feel?" but still neither boy responded. Others in the class, however, were quite stimulated and very willing to share their ideas since they had not, at that moment, been involved in fighting.

This incident gave me a great deal of material to work on. I realized that these boys were not yet willing to go very far in stating their responsibility, assuming that they were aware of what they were doing. Only when the involvement was at a distance could they respond—they could answer such questions as "What might you feel?" instead of "What do you feel?" and "How does someone else feel?" Knowing this, I continued with readiness/awareness techniques. I found all kinds of opportunities to ask "What are you doing now?" and "Who is doing that?" We stopped during regular activities to finish the statement "Now I am . . ." or "Now I feel . . ." When students got into fights or quarrels, I had them talk to each other, not to me, about what was happening now, and not about what had happened earlier. When a student said "I can't," I asked him or her to say "I won't." In every way possible I helped, and at times even forced, the students to be aware of their own existence in the here and now.

About two weeks after the fight, one of the boys involved delighted me when he walked in from recess and proudly announced: "I had a fight with John. I gave him a bloody nose. I feel powerful. I feel good." By this I do not mean to say that I encourage fighting. But dealing with fights is part of being a teacher, and I do need to know what fighting does for the person so I can help him or her find more acceptable ways to get the same rewards he or she gets from fighting, whatever they may be. So it was necessary to allow this boy to experience his power in an acceptable manner. In every possible way, I helped him to become aware of his power to deal with curriculum (e.g., solving math problems), his power to influence others in the class, the multiple ways in which he affected us, and ultimately the power he used on himself to avoid solving his conflicts with his fists.

In the foregoing case, we had been exploring our feelings in general, allowing them to be present in the classroom, and we had been exploring ways of acknowledging those feelings verbally and nonverbally. It was not until weeks later that this boy was able to express those feelings as his own. One cannot just go through a set of lessons and come out responsible. But by listening, tuning in, going back to less threatening responses, leaving more risk and more involvement always available, applying skill, intuition, and knowledge, the teacher can direct lessons that allow for a continuing spiral of taking responsibility, having both more difficult and more easily reached levels equally available for himself or herself and the students. The doing becomes a trying, an experiment with the environment to find out what it is like. There is always something new to be learned, some new awareness, some new way of taking responsibility for one's life to be discovered.

In developing confluent curriculum, I often feel like a "herder," urging students to accept responsibility, checking a cognitive thrust that cuts off affective approaches, turning readiness and awareness into cognition, seeking to achieve a balance in the over-all curriculum, but still allowing myself to go "way out" in any one area if I sense a need or a desire in the students to do so. There is nothing new in confluent education. It is the discovery or rediscovery of the connectedness of things. Often, when I am doing a demonstration lesson or training workshop, teachers tell me, "I've done that before, but usually only in an incidental or accidental way." I readily agree. We have all had the experience of a "perfect" lesson. We know how to be human. It is just that sometimes we forget.

Teaching is a dynamic art that defies being put down and held down on paper. It is as if I have taken one frame from here and one frame from there out of a twelve-year-long motion picture to create a new picture, one that others can see. I have given it a name so that others may know what I am talking about when I speak of it: "A Confluent Education." Just as there is no "typical" child, no sixth-grader, no college student, even though we can speak of such things, so there is no one form of confluent education, no model. My "model" is a way of showing other teachers what I have done in order to help them develop what they can do on their own. It is a way of helping others to get started, something they can hang on to until they are free to let go. Each teacher will have to break down and destroy this model and develop something that is uniquely personal. Each one will have to develop his or her resources into a personal style, his or her own way of being "confluent," whatever that means individually. Individuality is what will make this teaching human and confluent, not merely another gimmick, another set of techniques to try out on students. This model and the lessons that follow are what I have to offer in the faith and trust that each person who uses them will continue to develop lessons which reflect the human dimensions of teaching and learning.

Lessons in
Affective Education

Twelve units are presented here, each with several lessons. Unit One, "Awareness of the Here and Now," is designed to develop readiness and awareness for the units that follow and should therefore be presented first. All of the other units are interrelated and can be presented in any order that looks interesting or exciting to the teacher. Some of the lessons within the units are presented in a recommended sequence, and this is indicated in the introduction to the unit.

Read a lesson in its entirety before presenting it to the students to determine how it fits the readiness/awareness level of your class. If the lesson seems too easy for the class, combine it with one or more other lessons. If it seems too difficult, find places where the lesson can be stopped before the end and still have some closure. Look at the vocabulary used in the lesson to see whether it is appropriate for the class.

There are timing directions in some lessons. These are only suggestions. You will need to be aware of the interest of your class while presenting a lesson to know whether you should pause for three or thirty seconds before going from one statement or direction to another. It will also be necessary for you to decide if an activity should be pursued for the suggested time allotted to it or if that time is too long or too short.

Feel free to make changes wherever and however you feel they are needed. It is not possible for anyone to know in advance the special needs, interests, and concerns of a particular class.

Not every lesson has specific suggestions for developing the cognitive domain. The intent of this part of the book is to focus attention and action on the affective dimensions of a lesson. Part Three will coordinate affective lessons with cognitive materials available to most teachers.

When it seems appropriate, age differences are noted in the lessons. In general "primary" refers to students in kindergarten or first grade, "intermediate" to students in grades 2, 3, and 4, and "advanced" to more mature students. Again, it is not possible to know the level of any one class without being with it, so the teacher will have to decide how those terms fit a particular class.

Awareness of
Here and Now

Attending to the here and now is not an easy thing for most of us to do. A great deal of the educational process as we know it emphasizes the past or the future, two aspects of the "then and there." We build on concepts developed in the past, and we develop new ones for use in the future.

This emphasis, of course, has a place in education. But the past is gone, and we remember only what we want or have been taught to remember about it. The future is yet to come, and we can only speculate about it on the basis of past experience. We learn only when we are really in tune, when everything comes together. Only the present, the here and now, is real, and it is almost completely ignored in school. It is usually only when a student cannot or will not deal with the then and there—what he or she already knows or what will have to be known for the future—that we make an effort to discover where the student is here and now. Even so, we do this only in order to make the student move once again from the here and now into the then or there, past or future. In a very real sense, we have been, and we continue to allow students to be, educated out of the awareness of the here and now.

Since we are so unfamiliar with the here and now, it is necessary to develop our awareness on a fairly simple level, one that does not involve too much risk. This means dealing with the here and now in its most recognizable form, taking inventory of our present external surroundings, the environment. For example: "Where am I—at school, at a store, in church, at home, on the street? What other people and what things are here with me in this environment? Who or what is available to me?"

When we ask, "What is available?" we ask for a check of the environment to look for what may have been overlooked before, for a response to the here and now. For example, if students at school are acting as if they're at home, they are responding to a "then and there." An only child may act as if he or she is an only child in a class of 35. A person with little responsibility at home may resist accepting responsibility for his or her life at school. In order to respond to the here and now, he or she will need to take in the school surroundings and see what is available in that environment.

In taking inventory of the here and now, ask yourself, "How much of this environment am I aware of? What do I see? What colors? What light and dark patterns? What people? What things? What sounds am I hearing? How much am I taking into my cognition? Is there more or something else available here, or have I adequately assessed what is available?" The answers to these questions can be discovered by repeatedly asking yourself, "What's available here and now?" and checking your answers with your surroundings.

The answers will change from moment to moment. Sometimes the changes will be minute and subtle. Sometimes they will be dramatic. For example, when I'm home alone during the day, what is available to me does not change very much. The light in the room changes, the telephone rings, sounds of birds come and go. But when the rest of my family enters that very same scene, what is available changes dramatically. I have their presence, their conversation, their responses available to me. At first it may be difficult to know if you are in the here and now or in the then and there, the past or the future. But by talking to, being with, and responding to who and what is in your immediate environment you will develop and expand your awareness of the here and now.

More complex and less visible, yet no less vital to an awareness of the here and now, are the internal responses to the external environment. For example: "How do I feel about this place? Am I responding to its distinctive features, or am I responding as if I were in another place? How do I feel about the people and things here? Am I responding to them, or am I responding as if they were other people and other things? In other words, what is happening to me at a personal level, here and now, in this environment?"

When we become aware of the here and now and all it has available, we can see, hear, and respond in ways appropriate to a given time and place. We are aware of our existence in our environment, and we are in control. We are no longer aimlessly molded, formed, pushed by people and things outside of us. Our actions are the result of a choice among the alternatives available to us, and we make such a choice knowingly.

When this happens, we stand on our own two feet, we take responsibility for our self. We do not need to blame the past, outside factors, or other people for our failures. We do not need to disavow our success. We can accept full responsibility for both.

Students also have a difficult time attending to the here and now. They too have been educated to consider only the "then" as important. They have not been expected to know what is important to them, what is happening to them. They too have to begin to develop an awareness of the here and now on a fairly simple level.

Although new experiences may be threatening, the lessons in this unit are presented in a step-by-step sequence. The first one introduces only one new idea, "Now." The last one deals with all the ideas in the unit. The lessons are arranged so as to build on what is already familiar to the students to ensure their success in becoming aware of the here and now.

The first three lessons deal with becoming aware of the external environment, with who and what is available. The fourth lesson focuses attention on the internal environment. Lessons 5 and 6 are designed to introduce the students to ways of taking control and responsibility for themselves. They are reinforcing mechanisms and are to be used throughout the school year.

Beyond self-awareness, the student should be able to explore the possibilities of extending awareness even farther—to the group, the family, the community. There should be many daily opportunities, in many forms, for the student to respond to "What am I doing now?" and "How do I feel?" This must be an ongoing process, something beyond the lessons contained here, for awareness does not come easily, and each new here and now brings new awareness. Lessons 7 through 10 focus on awareness of others. Lesson 11 concludes the unit by bringing the students back to themselves, with greater awareness of what they have available.

All of these lessons have been used with children from primary to advanced levels. Remember to read through them before presenting them to your class and make any changes you feel would be appropriate.

Objectives

To develop an awareness of the present, the here and now.
To discover new and fresh ideas about what is happening now.
To develop the ability to give a verbal answer to "What am I
    doing now?" and "How do I feel?"
To take responsibility for actions and feelings.
To identify certain peers as "friends."
To differentiate between reality and fantasy.
To increase response-ability to imaginative situations.

To develop an awareness of who and what are available in
different situations and settings.

Lesson 1. Now

Everyone sit in a circle with me. I'm going to share what I know
about me right now. I am sitting down. I see you looking at me. I
can hear my voice. I see Judy come in the room. I hear the heater
turn on. . . .

Continue with statements that are true at the moment you say them.
Give enough examples for the students to know what is expected, then
allow individual students to respond. Listen carefully, helping only if
and when it is necessary to remind a student to keep in the present tense.
This may be difficult at first.

Lesson 2. Looking

Sit in the circle again. What did you do in the last lesson? What
kinds of sentences did you use?

Their sentences had to be true as of the moment, had to be in the
here and now, and had to begin with "I," or with "Now I."

What do you see? Be sure you stay in the here and now and
begin each sentence with the words "Now I see . . ." Here is
what I see now. Now I see my shoes. Now I see the mole on my
hand. Now I see my ring. Now I see the window. Now I see
the door.

If students have difficulty recalling the experience of Lesson 1, review it briefly before going on. Again, begin the game yourself so you
can set the example. Listen and help each person keep the observations
in the here and now. Also help students, if necessary, to be specific. Have
them rephrase statements like "I see the shoes" as "Now I see my shoes,"
or "Now I see Ann's shoes."

Variation

Sit in small groups. Take turns going around the circle looking
at each person in your group. Don't look for anything special—

let images come to you. Begin each statement with "Now I
see . . ." Let new images emerge from moment to moment, with
each person you look at. Don't force anything.

Lesson 3. Touching Now

Sit in the circle again. Look around the room and see if you can
find something in the room that you did not see yesterday. What
can you find? Who can find something about themselves today
that they could not find yesterday? From where you are sitting,
show me what you can touch. Touch something of yours that is
hard. It could be your shoe, your elbow, your head. Touch
something warm. What on you is warm? Touch something on
you that is wet. It could be your eyes, your tongue, your lips.

   Now, one at a time, move about the room and touch many
things in the room. As you touch something, say, "Now I am
touching . . . It is . . ." Touch as many different kinds of things
as possible.

Examples: "Now I am touching the sink. It is cold." "Now I am
touching the window. It is smooth." "Now I am touching the rabbit. It
is soft and warm."

   If students make statements beginning with "Now I am touching
. . ." continue on. If not, review Lessons 1 and 2, reminding them to
make statements that begin with "Now I" and are true of that moment.
Then help them focus their awareness on touch rather than sight.

Lesson 4. My Feelings

At various times during the day, have the students stop what they
are doing and respond to "What are you feeling now? How do you experience it?"

   Help students state a complete sentence beginning with "Now I . . ."

   Help them become aware of how they are responding to their environments, how their responses change as their experiences change.

   Examples: *What are you feeling now?* "I am feeling tired." *"How
do you experience feeling tired?"* "I have a pain in my shoulders."

   "I am feeling hungry—my stomach hurts."

   "I am feeling happy—I am smiling and laughing."

   Students need opportunities to develop a vocabulary to express their
feelings in specific as well as in general terms. If a student says, "I am
feeling good," help him or her to express "good" in other words. What

does "good" feel like? Restate it, using other words to describe what is felt.

Lesson 5. I Am in Control of Myself

Sit in a group.
Who makes you do things?
How does that person make you do things?
What do I make you do?

The purpose of this lesson is to help the student see that he or she is actually the one who is in control, doing the action. He or she is the one who ultimately has to take responsibility for what is done even though others have expectations for his or her behavior. This lesson is difficult for a person who is used to having adults take responsibility for what happens. It may also be a difficult concept for you if you often feel overly responsible for what students do and do not do in the classroom.

When you first ask the students "Who makes you do things?" listen to the responses without interference, even if you know partial truths or views which differ from yours are being stated.

Examples: "My mother makes me practice the piano. My father makes me rake the leaves. My sister makes me clean up the mess we make playing house. My brother makes me do all of his work. Jimmy makes me get into trouble."

When you ask, "How do these people make you do things?" it is important, again, to listen to the student's reply without interfering. Use the responses to help each one see that he or she does what other people want done for a variety of personal reasons. Help the student begin to see that he or she alone makes the ultimate decision to do something or not.

Examples: "I practice the piano so I won't get a spanking. I rake the leaves so I can get my allowance. I clean up the mess because my sister helped me to have fun. I don't really do all my brother's work. Sometimes I get into trouble by myself."

When you ask, "What do I make you do?" listen again to the replies without interfering. If the student's responses still indicate a lack of perception that he or she is in control and has responsibility—for example, if one responds, "You make me do math"—play the following game:

Say, "David, it is time for math. Get your book and do page 34. Now say everything you are doing." It might go like this:

"I am getting my pencil. I am thinking, What is 7 plus 6? I am writing 13. I am doing my math."

Several repetitions of this lesson may be needed before you get clear statements from David that he is in control of himself. His responses reflect how much control he has had in the past and his awareness of it.

Games to Play with Lesson 5

"I AM A ROBOT"

Pretend that you are a robot. You can do nothing unless you are told to do it. I am the "Master Controller." Before you begin anything new, you must be told to stop the former action.

Walk forward. Stop. Walk backward. Stop. Wave your right arm. Stop. Walk forward. Sit down.

If any students do what you say on the last two commands, stop them and remind them that a robot cannot think for itself. Unless it is told to stop, it would have to walk forward and sit down at the same time. Even a robot cannot do that.

Give the students a few more clear directions, one at a time. Then choose one to be the "Master Controller." Help the rest of the class to do exactly what the "Master Controller" says, nothing more, nothing less.

Students can then write a story about being a robot. "How do I feel when I'm being controlled?" and "How do I feel being the 'Master Controller?'" are good topics.

"I AM IN CONTROL OF MYSELF: FOLLOW THE LEADER"

Stand in a circle. In a little while I am going to ask someone to go to the middle of the circle and be "It." The one who is "It" says, "I am in control of myself, I can (perform some action)." "It" then demonstrates the action. Then each one in the circle says and does the same thing. The one who is "It" then chooses another person to be "It." Each new person says and performs some action for the class to follow.

Discuss "How do I feel when I'm controlling the whole group? Would I rather be controlling the group or have someone control me?"

Advanced students can do more complex tasks, such as tumbling stunts.

Lesson 6. What Are You Doing Now?

The preceding lessons in a sense are preparations for this one. It is hoped that this "lesson" will continue throughout the day, week after week, through the year.

While the students are at regular activities, such as social studies, language arts, math, etc., ask one, "What are you doing?" At first the student may think that he or she has done something wrong and will stop all activity. Keep questioning the student until you get a complete sentence, beginning with "I." The following are examples of what might happen on the first try.

"Irene, what are you doing?"
"Nothing."
"Who is doing nothing?"
"Me."
"Now can you put that all together in one sentence beginning with the word 'I'?"
"I am doing nothing."

"David, what are you doing?"
"Working on my math."
"Who is working on math?"
"I am working on math."
"How are you working on your math?"
"Quietly, not bothering anyone."
"Who is working quietly, not bothering anyone?"
"I am working quietly, not bothering anyone."
"Now, what are you doing?"
(Quizzical look) "I don't know."
"I see you smiling at me."
"I am smiling at you."

The following are examples of responses students might give once they are used to responding in ways that reflect their presence in the here and now.

"I am hitting Philip."
"I am sitting here doing nothing."
"I am reading my book."
"I am scribbling on my book."

This lesson is a way of putting the student in touch with reality. It also helps the student to take responsibility for his or her actions.

Lesson 7. I Have Friends

Lie on the floor and close your eyes. Think of a special friend. If you cannot think of a real one, make one up. Look closely at your friend. Is your friend tall or short? Fat or thin? What color is your friend's hair? What color are your friend's eyes? Take a very close look at your friend. Try to know exactly what your friend looks like to you.

Now pretend that you and your friend are going to a special place. How do you get there? Do you run? Walk? Ride? Think of the place you are in now. What are you and your friend doing at your special place? Keep thinking about your friend and what you are doing. Do anything you want to do with your friend.

Now take your friend's hand and lead him or her home. When you get your friend home, leave him or her there and come back here and open your eyes. You don't have to hurry.

Look around and see if you have any friends here. What do your friends here look like? Would anyone like to tell us who his or her friend is? Try to say "I am (say your own name). (Name someone) is my friend."

With older students you may wish to expand this statement to include what the friend does for the speaker. Examples: "I am Chris. Robin is my friend. He helps me learn to play football." "I am Irene. Lonnie is my friend. She makes me laugh."

Lesson 8. I Am Aware of Someone Else

Sit in a circle. Now make statements about what another person is doing now. For example: "Chris is smiling." "Robin is holding his foot." "Lonnie is talking to Irene."

Listen to each statement, making sure that it is true. If the statement is something imagined or assumed, help the student rephrase it.

Examples: Rephrase "Lonnie is telling Irene a secret" to "Lonnie is whispering to Irene."
Rephrase "Sherry is sleepy" to "Sherry is leaning her head on her hand."
Rephrase "Bob is working hard" to "Bob has a red face."

Lesson 9. Choosing a Partner

Form a close circle. Lie down in the circle, feet to the inside. Be close enough to touch each other. Hold hands with the people on both sides of you. Close your eyes.

Now try to find a partner using just your hands. Let go of one person but hold onto the other. If the person you want

to hold on to keeps your hand, you are partners. If a person
lets go and will not keep your hand, that person has a partner
on the other side. Just lie quietly if you do not get a partner.

Open your eyes and, with your partner, move out to
form a larger circle so that each pair has its own space. Talk
to each other about how you feel about being chosen.

Now look around the room and see someone else you
want for a partner.

Say goodbye to the one you have now and find a different partner. Find a space together and spend some time
talking about how you feel about being partners. Is this the
partner you wanted? Talk about that and how you feel about
it. Say goodbye to each other.

Choose another partner. Find a space together and
spend some time talking about how you feel being partners.
Say goodbye to each other.

Sit all together. How do you feel about choosing a partner? How do you feel about being chosen? How do you feel
about not being chosen? How do you feel about getting the
partner you wanted? How do you feel about not getting the
partner you wanted?

Pair up the students who do not have partners. Let them spend time
talking about how they feel about not getting a partner on their own.

From this experience move into a discussion of other experiences
that involve choosing partners.

On what basis would you choose a partner if you wanted to
do a report? What would you look for?

On what basis would you choose a partner if you wanted
to win a ball game?

On what basis would you choose a partner if you wanted
help in creating a story?

Lesson 10. Making a Recipe for a Partner

Choose a partner and spend some time with one another. Ask a
series of questions to discover how each other is feeling today: What are you thinking about today? Is there something
you are looking forward to doing today? What would you
like to have for dinner tonight? If you were to go on a trip
right now, where would you go? How do you like the clothes
you are wearing today?

Write or talk about a "recipe" for the necessary ingredients to make your partner. For example:

To be Mike,

You need: Short blond hair

          2 green eyes

          1 smiling mouth

Add: 1 strong body

          1 pair of torn tennis shoes

Comb hair, part down the right side, then swish your hands through it. Place the eyes so that they see the sunshine and sparkle with it. To get the mouth to smile, tell a funny story. Be sure you add the torn tennis shoes, or you won't end up with Mike. Mix with 100,000 freckles. Laugh while mixing.

The age and development of the students determine the type of stories they write. A young student may describe physical characteristics only. A more mature student begins to recognize the personality characteristics as having more meaning. A primary student may only verbalize the recipe, while an advanced student can write it in true recipe form.

Lesson 11. I Have Available . . .

Sit in a circle.

Look around and see what you have available here and now. Be aware of the feelings you have available here and now.

Take turns sharing out loud what you have available, beginning each sentence with "I have available . . ."

For example, "I have available a chair to sit on. I have available a warm feeling about sitting next to Robbie. I have available ears to hear the sound of the jet overhead."

Variations

Have the entire group of students tell one particular person what they see or feel that person has available. "John, you have available very strong arms." "John, you have available a quick smile." "John, you have available a ten-speed bike."

With an older class, have students write what they have available in different categories, such as here and now, at home, on the playground, in peer groups, or in other nonschool activities.

Sensory Awareness

Education ideally is an active, interested exploration involving doing, gaining skills, coming to know. Too much of what passes for education is dulling and passive—memorization, compartmentalization, indoctrination. A student is a whole, but we often act as if he or she were compartmentalized. We teach only to one part of the living, functioning, interacting person, the brain. The student has more than just a brain though. He or she has feelings, senses, and a body as well.

A child by nature is sensitive, interested, and involved in sense play and exploration. Watch a two-year-old meet something new. He or she will touch it, look at it, taste it, smell it, get to know it. He or she is into sensory development. Formal education all too often stresses the cognitive functions of the student with little or no regard for sensory development. We teach non-sense. This subtle opposition to sensitivity creates an imbalance, a loss of feeling, sense-less-ness.

Every person, in order to mobilize full human potential, must get in touch with all parts of oneself and be able to bring those parts together into a meaningful whole. A student needs opportunities to remain, or learn to be, unified. One must be able to feel and think, to see and look, to hear and listen. Only then will one be willing to take risks, to be open, to be creative, to learn.

The lessons in this unit are in order of degree of risk-taking and development. The first eight lessons involve the individual student. Lesson

6, "Breathing in Touch," and Lesson 7, "Tension," are reinforcing mechanisms to be used as often as needed throughout the school year. Lessons 9 through 14 involve extending awareness in order to be with others.

There are no correct responses to these lessons except those that the body expresses. Between indulgence and inhibition is allowing—letting go, letting be, being free to permit or draw the line. Give yourself and the students the open possibility to move, act, or stay inactive in relationship to each ongoing experience, each here and now. Observe the students' movements to determine when they have had enough time to experience a given direction before going to the next one. Feel free to move quickly or slowly through these lessons. The point is not to judge but to be aware, to be in your senses, to do what feels good to you.

Objectives

To experience the body and the mind as an integrated unit.
To relax the body in order to move easily and freely.
To relax the body in order to study without excessive pressure.
To be able to relax and enjoy the company of others.
To develop vocabulary to describe parts of the body.
To develop vocabulary to express feelings.
To continue developing an awareness of the here and now.
To continue taking responsibility for actions and feelings.

Lesson 1. Self-Awareness and Physical Awareness

We have been learning to use our eyes and our hands to find out something about ourselves. Today I want to have you begin with something else. Close your eyes. Use your tongue to explore the inside of your mouth. Feel something soft. Feel something hard. Feel all of your teeth. What else can you feel? Feel your lips. How far can you feel with your tongue?

Now take just your fingertips and, still keeping your eyes closed, tap your head. Tap all over your hair. Feel your hair with your fingertips. Feel where your hair stops and your skin begins. Tap your forehead. Feel your eyebrows. Rub them one way, then the other. Feel your eyelids. Feel your cheeks. Feel your nose. Discover where it stops being hard, and where you can wiggle it. Feel your breath as it goes in and out of your nose. Feel your lips. Feel your ears,

inside, around, outside. Feel your jaw. Open and close it as
you feel it. Feel your neck. Now put your hands down and
feel your face with your mind. What does your face feel like?
Now, with your hands go back to any part of your face you
want to touch again and explore it on your own.

Encourage the students to close their eyes and keep them closed as
long as they can during the lesson. Assure them that if they open their
eyes they can close them again when they are ready to do so.

If students have difficulty closing their eyes, engage in some readiness activities such as: "Close your eyes while I count to three. Now
open them. Close your eyes until you hear me tap on the blackboard. Five
minutes before recess, close your eyes until the bell rings." In this way
you can build up their ability to be in the classroom with their eyes
closed.

Variation

Do this lesson again and then have the students draw self-portraits
of their faces only. Have mirrors available.

Lesson 2. Self-Awareness

Lie on your back in your own space on the floor. Close your
eyes. Now think of the floor and where you are touching it. I
am going to tell you to do some things and ask you some questions. Don't talk out loud, just think of the answers and do
what I tell you to do. You will be able to talk later and even
tell us other things to do.

Is your head touching the floor? Remember only to think
of the answer. How does your head feel? How do your
shoulders feel? Are they pressing down on the floor, or is the
floor pushing up on them? Feel your hips with your mind.
How do they feel? How does the floor feel there? Feel the
backs of your legs. How are they right now?

Now, still with your eyes closed, wave your hands in the
air. Let them slowly drop to the floor again. How do your
arms feel? How does the floor feel? Lift your head off the
floor. Hold it up. Slowly let it go back to the floor. How does
it feel now? Raise your legs from the floor. Hold them up
very high. Slowly let them back down again. How do they
feel now? How does your stomach feel now? Now think of

the floor again and where you are touching it. Does it feel
the way it did when we first began? If it is different, can you
feel how it is different? Now, who can think of something
we can all do while on the floor?

Again, students may open and close their eyes when they want. With
primary students, you might even assure them that you have your eyes
open and will see that nothing harms them while they have their eyes
closed.

Lesson 3. Right Hand, Left Hand

Make a bracelet out of red construction paper and put it on your
right wrist. I am going to ask you to do some of the things
you do quite often in this room. To begin, I want all of you
to do what I ask you to do using just your right hand. Even
if you are left-handed, use your right hand.
    Open a book. Turn the pages one by one. Watch and feel
your right hand as you do it.
    Take out a pencil and paper. Write your name with your
right hand on the paper. What is your right hand doing?
Where does it begin writing, where does it end? How do
you feel writing your name with your right hand?
    Use a pair of scissors. Cut something. What are your
right hand and arm doing? How do you feel now?
    Now use your left hand and do the same things.
    Open a book. Turn the pages one by one. Watch and feel
your left hand as you do it.
    Take out a pencil and paper. Write your name with your
left hand on the paper. What is your left hand doing? Where
does it begin writing, where does it end? How do you feel
writing your name with your left hand?
    Use a pair of scissors. Cut something. What are your left
hand and arm doing? How do you feel about what they are
doing?
    If you are right-handed, how did you feel when you did
those things with your left hand?
    If you are left-handed, how did you feel when you did
those things with your right hand?
    What things in our room are designed to be used by
hands? (Crayons, pencils, scissors, books, dials, knobs,
handles, etc.)
    Can you find things that are primarily designed to be

used by a right hand? (Pencil sharpeners, tuning dials on a
TV set, scissors, manual can openers.)

Can you find things that are primarily designed to be
used by a left hand?

Imagine how different this room would look if people
did not have hands. What might you see? (Doors would not
have knobs, pencils might be designed to fit into your
mouth, we would have different kinds of clothes on, etc.)

Imagine doing all school activities from a "left-handed"
point of view. What might that be like? (We would write
from right to left, books would read from back to front, some
handles and knobs would be on the opposite side, etc.)

As you go through the rest of the day, be aware of the
many things you do with your hands. Find some ways in
which our environment is adapted to using hands. You can
leave your red bracelets on to remind you to pay attention to
your hands.

If you are working with primary students, you may wish to do this
lesson in several parts over several days. Focus attention on just the right
hand one day, then on the left hand the next. Omit or change any part
you think too difficult. You might wish to have the students wear bracelets of a different color on their left hands.

You might also wish to take some extra time with the student who
is left-handed. That student does live in a right-handed environment,
and so it may take longer to do certain seemingly simple activities. (If
you are right-handed, try turning a few pages of this book with your left
hand. And remember, you have a great deal more motor skill than a five-
year-old does.) Be aware of "right-handed" activities at school and allow
"lefties" extra time to explore, experiment, and translate them to their
left-handedness.

Lesson 4. Right-Left Awareness

Lie on the floor again, finding your own space. Stretch out on
the floor, legs apart and arms out from your sides. Be sure
you are still in your own space. If you touch someone, move a
little. Today you are going to do some things with the right
and left sides of your body. Close your eyes.

Now raise your right hand. Have it wave hello to your
left hand, which is on the floor way over there. Have the left
hand wave back. Raise your right leg. Have it shake at the
left leg. Have the left leg shake back. Now have your right
hand touch your right eye. Blink your right eye only. Now

blink your left eye. Have your right foot wiggle. Have your
left foot wiggle. Have your left ear wiggle. Can you do
that? If not, just think about wiggling it. Have your right
hand tap your stomach. Have your left hand tap your head.

Continue in this way, keeping the directions fairly simple. Then bring
the students to a sitting position and have them talk about things they
do with either of their hands or feet. Examples: "I eat with my left
hand." "I brush my teeth with my right hand." "I kick a ball with my
right foot." "I wear out the toe on my right tennis shoe."

Lesson 5. Right-Left Split

Review some of the things experienced in Lesson 3. What things are
done with the right hand? What things are done with the left hand?

Lie on the floor again and close your eyes. Stretch out in your
own space again, being sure not to touch anyone else.
   Today you are going to do something that might be a
little difficult for you. I am going to ask you to pretend some
things about your own self. See if you can do it.
   Now I want you to pretend that your whole right side
is moving slowly away from your left side. Not too far away.
Just have the right side of your head, your right arm, your
right hip, your right leg, and your right foot move a little
way from your whole left side. Pretend there is a white line
down your middle, just the way roads have a white line down
the middle of them. Pretend that half of you is on one side.
Now have your right hand touch your nose. Have your left
hand touch your nose. Have your right hand touch your right
knee. Have your left hand touch your left knee.

You may wish to do more here, keeping right action on right side,
left action on left side, before moving into the "crossover," which follows.

Now have your right hand reach over the line and touch your
left knee. Have your left hand reach over and touch your right
knee. Have your right foot touch your left knee. Have your
left foot touch your right knee. Have your right hand touch
your left ear. Have your left hand touch your right ear.
   Now lie very still on the floor. Think about the parts of
your body that were touched. Think about the parts that did
the touching. Think about all of your right side. Think about

all of your left side. How do they feel now? Now, very
slowly, bring both parts back together again. Have them
come together slowly and have the white line down the
middle slowly disappear as your body becomes one whole
body again. Feel how it is to have one whole, complete body
instead of two halves. Does it feel different? How? How
does it feel the same? When you are ready, slowly open your
eyes and look at yourself. Do you see anything now that you
didn't see before?

With the student who is still having trouble with the terms *right* and
left, you might want to have the right hand touch only things on the
right side and the left hand touch only things on the left side at first.
With an advanced student you can give more complex directions such as,
"Have your right foot touch your left knee while your left hand touches
your right ear. Have your left elbow touch the floor and wiggle your right
foot, etc."

Lesson 6. Breathing in Touch

Lie on the floor in your own space and close your eyes. Take a
few moments to experience your body and how it feels on the
floor. Now, become aware of your breathing. Make no effort
to change it; just be aware and allow. After a while, place
both hands on your upper chest. See that your palms are flat
and that the fingers of one hand do not overlap or touch the
other hand. Experience the space between your chest and
your back. Now, slowly place your hands at your sides. Take
a few moments to feel the results of this touch. Next, place
your hands on your solar plexus, the area just above the
navel, and become aware of what, if any, movement you find
there. Again, after a while put your hands on your lower
belly, just inside your hip bones. As your hands rest there,
shift your attention to your nose and experience the air as it
moves in and out. Now bring your hands to your sides and
again become aware of how you feel.

With primary students you may want to change the vocabulary of
this lesson. The most important thing here is to get the students in touch
with their breathing as a way to relax.
This is an excellent quieting activity and is especially good after
coming in from rough playground activities. It is also good to use this
at the end of a long study session. You can also use it to reduce tension
after a test or a testing situation.

Lesson 7. Tension

Lie on the floor. Close your eyes.

Experience how you feel on the floor. Where do you feel the floor pushing against your body? Where do you feel your body pushing against the floor? What parts of you are not on the floor?

Now think about how the inside of your body feels. What parts of your body feel relaxed? What parts feel tense or tight?

Find a place in your body that feels tense. Concentrate on it. Make it feel even tenser. Now suddenly release that tension. Relax. Make it tense again. Suddenly release it again. Relax. Make it tense again. Release it again. Relax.

Now go back to that tense place, but this time do not increase the tension. Just let it be there. Keep thinking about that place, the tension, and how you are feeling. See if you can discover where the tension comes from. Is it just in that place, or does it come from other places, too? See if there is something you can do to release the tension.

Talk about what you experienced.

Tension does not come from outside you. It is something that you produce. Excessive tension can be a message from your body asking you to become more receptive and permissive, to let go and relax. It can also be a warning signal from your body. A headache may indicate excessive tension. It might also indicate dental or other physical problems that your body becomes aware of long before your mind.

This lesson provides another opportunity for expanding the students' vocabulary. They may be unfamiliar with the words "concentrate" and "tension." If that is so, you can give them the definitions or use synonyms that are familiar to them.

Lesson 8. Lifting

Lie on your back with your eyes closed. Slowly bring your knees up toward the ceiling, with your feet remaining on the floor. Experience how your back feels. Now, as if your hips were being pulled straight up by a string, raise your hips and buttocks off the floor. Ever so slowly, raise your entire spine off the floor as high as you can while your shoulders and shoulder blades remain on the floor. Hold yourself there, and then gradually, one vertebra at a time, lower yourself to the floor. Experience letting go to the floor. Feel yourself and the floor now. Repeat, this time raising only the lower half of your back off the floor. Hold, and then be aware of making contact with the floor as you come down. Feel yourself and the floor. Now, barely raise your hips and buttocks off the floor. Hold, and then take as long as you can to lower your back to the floor. Experience how the floor feels now—how you feel now. Slowly straighten your right leg. Slowly straighten your left leg. Feel how the floor is. Open your eyes and sit up.

Lesson 9. Hand Talk

Choose a partner. Lie on the floor, heads touching, feet pointing in opposite directions. Raise your arms over your head and touch hands with your partner.

Have your hands say hello to each other.

Have a conversation with just your hands. How do they feel today? Are they soft, rough, are there blisters or bumps? How else do they feel? Have your hands dance together. Run together. Walk. Jump. Whisper. Tell each other you are happy. Now be sad. Be warm. Be cold. Now just be together with your partner's hands. What do you want your hands to tell your partner? What are your partner's hands trying to say to your hands?

Have your hands say goodbye to each other.

Now sit up and talk to each other about what you did and how you feel about it.

Variation

Have the students do the same type of activity but this time restrict them to the use of thumbs only. Repeat, using other single parts of the body—for example, elbows, knees, feet.

Lesson 10. Tapping-Slapping a Partner

Choose a partner. One of you bend over from the waist, keeping your legs straight. Now the one who is standing begin to tap your partner all over your partner's back. Tap harder. Tap with a firm hand, so as not to sting his or her back. Be sure you tap every area of the back, taking about three minutes to do this. Now, starting up by the neck, begin tapping all over and down, down, over the buttocks, down the thighs, down the calves, down to the ankles, taking about three minutes to get there.

Change places.

Talk to each other about how it felt to be tapped and how it felt to do the tapping.

We usually think of slapping as a "bad" thing, as a punishment, as a way to hurt someone. However, a great deal of slapping goes on in classrooms that does not fit these categories. Slapping can also be a way of making contact, especially for students who are physically demonstrative.

Tapping and slapping stimulate nerves, increase blood flow, open every area of the body to be more alive. Use this lesson as an energizer whenever you sense vitality is low.

Variations

Encourage students to make sounds to accompany their movements and their feelings.

Have the partner who is being tapped kneel on the floor. This sometimes helps if a short person has a tall partner. It also allows a way for an adult to do this with a child.

Lesson 11. Mirrors

Sit in two rows, one behind the other, all facing the same direction. If you are in the front row, begin to move slowly from the waist up, including your arms and hands. Move slowly. If you are in the back row try to copy every move made by the person directly in front of you. You have about three minutes.

Turn and face in the opposite direction. Again, if you are in the front row, move; if you are in the back row, copy. You have about three minutes.

This is called "mirroring." What happens when we look into a real mirror?

Choose a partner. Stand and face each other. One be the "mirror," the one who copies exactly, and the other be the "doer," the one who controls the mirror's actions. Move slowly so that the "mirror" can follow. You have about three minutes. Change roles. You have about three minutes again.

Now move from your place and return again, with the "mirror" following the "doer." Imagine what it is like to be your partner. Discover what else you can do as "mirror" and "doer."

Lesson 12. Body Rhythms

What noises can you make using parts of your body other than your voice? Choose a sound that you would like to make and go to a space where you can make this sound and not be bothered by some other sound.

Now act like an orchestra, with the different types of "instruments" in different parts of the room. I will choose someone to be the "conductor" and lead the orchestra. One section starts, then the others join in—for example, playing slower, faster, louder, softer.

Some body sounds are: snapping fingers, clicking tongues, clicking teeth, breathing loudly, whistling, sputtering with lips, clapping hands, stamping feet, hitting stomachs for various sounds, slapping parts of the body. Allow the entire class to copy each demonstration.

List all the answers the students offer. You might wish to limit their sounds at first, having them all whistle, or all stamp their feet, or all sputter their lips until they get the idea. Then you can have them combine sounds. You might even tape-record the session.

Lesson 13. Body Building

Form small groups with not more than six students in each one. Now use all the hands you have available and make a house. You have about five minutes to experiment with many arrangements.

Now use all the hands you have to make a school.

This time, make a car. You can use more than just your hands. Use your arms, your legs, your feet, all of you. Be sure that everyone in the group is a part of the finished car. Can you make your car move?

Now change your group into an animal.

What else can your group become? I will allow enough time for exploration.

If the students have trouble realizing what you mean, demonstrate with one group. Have all the students in the group move their hands about in order somehow to represent the structure of a house. This might be done with many hands being the walls, some being the roof, some being the driveway, some being plants in front of the house, etc.

With primary students, it is usually necessary to come to an arrangement using both language and body. With an older class, it is more meaningful if the students are encouraged to do this without talking. It is then necessary to sense what the group is creating to know what each participant's role or addition to the group can be. Doing this nonverbally also reduces the possibility that one individual will take over and direct the entire group.

Lesson 14. A Group Fantasy

Close your eyes and let yourself go on an imaginary trip. You will go to four different places on this trip.

You go out for a walk. It is a warm, sunny day, and you can feel the sun shining on you. You walk to a big hill. It has green, grassy patches on it and places covered with rocks. You climb all over the hill. Even though it might be steep in places, you find you can climb it easily. Now you get to the top. You look out and see a beautiful blue lake.

Climb down from the hill. Run to the lake. Run right into the lake, splash the water all around you. Listen to the sounds it makes, feel how cool it is against your skin. Taste it. Spend some time at the lake. Have a good time with the water. You can swim in it, play in it, do anything you want.

Now come out of the lake and walk on. Again feel the warm sun on you. You are dry now and very comfortable. Now you see a high fence made of wood. Climb the fence. Feel the wood on your hands. Smell the wood. When you get to the top, you look out and see a junk yard. Climb down the other side of the fence and go into the junk yard. Look at all the things there. Over there is an old car. In another place there is some old furniture. There is a pile of bottles and cans in another place. Touch many different things. Listen to the sounds of the junk yard. Let yourself go and discover what else is in the junk yard.

Now you are beginning to get tired. Walk away from the junk yard. Not far away you find a patch of tall green grass. Lie down in the grass. Breathe deeply. Smell the grass. Look, there is a ladybird walking up a stalk of grass. Look at its bright red color and the spots on it. What other things can you see in the grass? Now close your eyes and rest.

When you are ready, come back to here and now.

When you first introduce students to a group fantasy, be sure to use sensory words and phrases to heighten their imaginations wherever possible. Feel free to expand this lesson. Change it as much as necessary to meet the needs, interests, and abilities of your class.

Variations

Start a group fantasy by setting the scene and then let the students direct it. One at a time, someone states out loud what comes next. Each person adds on to the fantasy. Everyone shares the fantasy.

Set a scene such as climbing the mountain and let the student develop the fantasy independently.

Imagination

Each of us has an imagination. Some of us are freer to use our imagination than others, and all of us find it more accessible under some conditions than others. It is an aspect of the learning process that is uniquely human and that most often goes uninstructed in our schools.

Emotions and fantasies can obstruct learning when they are uncontrolled; a feeling or image that cannot be shared is estranging; a feeling or image that cannot be controlled is frightening. Control of emotion and fantasy is essential for the attainment or discovery of knowledge and prerequiste for the formation or invention of knowledge. We need to provide relevant ways for students to develop, expand, and utilize their fantasies and imaginings as well as their cognitive realities.

Distinctions between reality and imagination are necessary, but it is important to teach the distinctions in ways that do not discourage the imagination.

In the process of learning there should be multiple opportunities for considering alternatives, expressing preferences, and arriving at conclusions independently. All too often we only involve students in other people's fantasies. The books they read, the stories they hear, the art they see are all expressions of someone else's fantasies. We teach them that others are creative, inventive, and knowledgeable. We need to teach them that the same is true of themselves.

Reality training as we use it now often puts exclusive emphasis on learning the rules and remembering the facts. It effectively discourages creative or inventive thinking and the exercise of judgment. The following lessons constitute a kind of reality training that does not discourage imagination. The student can learn that there are times for fantasy and times for realism, and that each is good in its own time and way. Just as education based on reality requires time and practice, so does fantasy and imagination development.

We can learn, and teach students to be intuitive and expressive, flexible and perceptive, and we can do it without giving up reason, communication, purpose, or emotional control. We can learn, and teach students to distinguish reality from fantasy and to discriminate the inner from the outer world without destroying either.

Objectives

To explore the domain of the imagination.
To compare real events with hypothetical events.
To stimulate thinking.
To make more creative use of imagination.
To provide a time and place for fun and laughter in the
    classroom.
To produce a large quantity of thinking with no "rightness" to
    it, such as the stories imagined and shared by the students.
To express oneself creatively and appreciate the creative ex-
    pression of others.
To develop a capacity to integrate fantasy from within with
    opportunities in the external environment.

Lesson 1. Body Parts

Lie on the floor in your own space. Explore every little detail of your ears with your fingertips. Feel the lobes. Feel the hard parts. Feel in back of the ears. Feel inside. Feel the curving lines. Plug one ear. What do you hear? Plug both ears and listen. What did you hear? Now plug your ears and whisper softly to yourself. What do you experience? Talk softly to yourself. What do you experience now? Put your hands at your sides and listen to the sounds of our room. When you are ready, quietly sit up. Share some of your experiences.

Now we are going to imagine some things about our ears. Imagine that somehow your ears moved down to your knees. What would happen if all of us had our ears on our knees?

Imagine that your ears are on top of your head. Now what would happen?

Imagine that your ears are on your wrist. What would that be like?

Where else could you imagine your ears? What would that be like?

When you ask, "What would happen if . . ." questions, accept the students' responses with an open mind. If they seem unreasonable to you, ask the students to explain further. It is amazing how many times students can make creative jumps between fantasy and reality. One first-grader told me that she could hear better if her ears were on her knees because her hair covered her ears. If her ears were on her knees nothing would stop sounds from reaching them. She imagined "many tiny sounds get caught in my hair."

This lesson can be expanded using other parts of the body.

Examples: What if your eyes were on top of your head? What if your hands were attached to your shoulders? What would it be like if your head and your stomach were to change places?

Lesson 2. Boys and Girls

The slashes (/) are used to indicate pauses. Do not read the next idea until the students have a chance to do what they want with the first one. It is important too that the students do this without answering questions aloud during the fantasy so that they do not interfere with another's imagination.

The name of this game is Boys and Girls.[1]

Let us imagine that there is a boy standing in the corner of this room./ Let us give him a hat. What color would you like the hat to be?/ Let us give him a jacket. What color jacket shall we give him?/ Let us give him some pants. What color do you want his pants to be?/ Let him have some shoes. What color will you let him have?/

Now change the color of his hat./ What color did you change it to?/ Change it again./ What color this time?/ Change it again./ What color?/ Change it to another color./ Change it again./ Change it again./ What color are his pants now?/ Change the color of his pants./ Change it again./ Change it again./ What color are his shoes now?/ Change

[1] Richard de Mille, *Put Your Mother on the Ceiling: Children's Imagination Games* (New York: Walker, 1967), Game One.

them to another color./ Change them again./ Change them
again./ What color are they now?/ Have him stand on one
foot and hold his other foot straight out in front of him./ Have
him stand on the other foot./ Have him walk over to another corner of the room./ Have him go to another corner./
Have him sing a song./ Have him go to another corner./
Have him lie down and roll across the floor./ Have him
run around on his hands and knees./ Have him stand on his
hands./ Have him sing a song while he is standing on his
hands./ Have him run around the room on his hands./

Have him stand on his feet./ Have him jump up into
the air./ Have him jump up higher./ Have him jump up and
touch the ceiling./ Have him sit in a chair./

Have the chair float up to the ceiling and stay there./
Have the boy sing something while he sits up there./ Have the
chair come down./ Have the boy float up to the ceiling without the chair./ Have him float to a corner of the room up
there./ Have him float to another corner./ Have him sing
"Three Blind Mice."/ Have him float to another corner./ Have
him float to still another corner./ Have him come down to the
floor./ Have him say "Goodbye" and go out the door to visit a
friend./ Look into one corner of the room and see that he is
not in that corner./ Look into another corner and see that
he is not there either./ Look into all the other corners, above
and below, and find that he is not in any of them./

Put a girl in one corner of the room./ Give her a red
hat./ Give her a blue sweater./ Give her a green skirt./ Give
her brown shoes./ Now make her hat blue./ Make her sweater
yellow./ Make her skirt purple./ Make her shoes black./
Change them to green./ Change them to yellow./ Change all
her clothes to white./ Change them to black./ Change them
to purple./ Change them to green./ Have her be in another
corner of the room./ Have her be in another corner./ Have
her sing a song./ Have her be in another corner./ Have her
float up to the ceiling./ Have her turn upside down and stand
on the ceiling./ Have her walk all around the ceiling looking
for the boy who was there before./ Have her look in all the
corners up there and find that he is not in any of them./ Bring
the boy back and put him on the ceiling with the girl./ Have
them standing on the ceiling playing ball./ Put another boy
and another girl on the ceiling with them, and have all four
playing ball./ Put some more boys and girls on the ceiling,
and have them all playing ball./ Turn them all right side up,
and put them on the roof of the house./ Put them in the play

yard at school./ Make twice as many of them, and have them all shouting./

Make a new crowd of boys and girls on the ceiling./ Put them on the roof./ Put them in the school yard./ Have all the children shouting and running around./ Look at the ceiling and see that there are no children there./ Put one boy there./ Put him in the school yard./ Put one girl on the ceiling./ Put her in the school yard./

Have no one on the ceiling./ Have it full of boys and girls./ Have it empty./ Have no one on the roof./ Have it covered with boys and girls./ Have it empty again./

Put one child in the school yard./ Is it a boy or girl?/ What color are his (her) clothes?/ What would you like to do with him (her)?/ All right, do it.

What is the name of the game we just played?

Allow students to complete the game in ways that satisfy them. If they wish to make up imagination games of their own, encourage them to go on as long as time permits and fun continues. Such spontaneous flights of fancy should take precedence over the game as written. You can always come back to the book, but the creative act of imagination must be caught when it happens.

Although this game is written for primary students, the style of writing is of great interest to intermediate and advanced students. They enjoy using it for writing their own imagination stories.

Lesson 3. Mixing the Senses

Allow students to explore imagination expansion through experiences involving the five senses. A normal, healthy, growing student responds to stimuli that activate all the sense organs. But sheer accuracy of perception may be emphasized in classrooms so forcefully that the student is unable to retain earlier abilities to transcend the limitations of adult vision, which typically does not allow for incongruity. The term "synaesthesia," used in normal psychology, means that a specific stimulus may rouse not only the specifically corresponding sensation but also a second sensation associated with the first. In color-tone synaesthesia, for example, the perceiving individual sees color while listening to tone. The chart that follows is designed to encourage experiences of synaesthesia by asking the student to look at the environment with a freshness that is not inhibited by accurate perception. It may well enhance one's feeling of potency to be able to ignore the contradictions inherent in describing a given sensory impact in terms that pertain to other sense modalities.

	Sight	Taste	Smell	Touch	Hearing
Sight		What does red taste like?	What does the sky smell like?	What do mountains feel like?	What does blue sound like?
Taste	How does sour look?		What does sweet smell like?	How does bitter feel?	What does ice cream sound like?
Smell	What does the smell of rain look like?	How does perfume taste?		What do the smells of dinner cooking feel like?	What does the smell of soap sound like?
Touch	How does soft look?	What does a rough rock taste like?	How does silky smell?		What does fur sound like?
Hearing	How does a whisper look?	What does laughing taste like?	What does barking smell like?	How does a siren feel?	

This experience will be enriched by having the objects on hand if possible. However, be careful to keep the experience one of mixed senses. That is, do not permit students to actually taste the perfume or the rock. If you have a soft object for them to touch and look at, be sure they describe what *soft* looks like and not the specific *object*.

Lesson 4. Situations

Look for curriculum content or personal concerns that are present in your classroom that can be adapted to a class participation story, in which a story is told and various parts are acted out by the students. This requires imagination and creativity on the part of both the storyteller and the actors. The story should center around something familiar to students and it should have multiple roles so that they can choose among many alternative ways of becoming involved in the story.

PRIMARY CLASS-PARTICIPATION STORY BASED ON A HOLIDAY:
THANKSGIVING

Tell a story about a pumpkin seed being planted by the farmer. It grows into a vine and produces a pumpkin. The pumpkin is picked and brought into the house, where the farmer's wife cuts it up and cooks it. She then adds the ingredients necessary to make it into pumpkin pie. The pie is baked in the oven. It is then carried out to the Thanksgiving table to join in the festivities and eventually be eaten.

Add as many details as you wish as you tell the story. Use many sensory words to describe colors, smells, sounds. It can take five or forty-five minutes to tell and act out this story. Let the students' interests and imaginative participation dictate the length of the story.

INTERMEDIATE CLASS-PARTICIPATION STORY BASED ON A CONCERN: INOCULATION DAY

Begin with the serum being in the needle. The needle enters the skin. The serum enters the body. The body responds to the injection. Different parts of the body have different responses. Eventually the reaction to the serum centers on the spot of the injection. The eyes of the body see the reaction, they communicate a message to the brain. The brain gets the body to react according to the message.

Again, let the students dictate the length of the story. They can even dictate the direction the story will take. If you sense that they have fears about what happens if the injection indicates the presence of disease, continue the story in a way that deals with what might happen next (e.g., being retested, getting further medical care).

ADVANCED CLASS-PARTICIPATION STORY BASED ON CURRICULUM: COTTON

Tell and act out a story about the cottonseed being planted in an area that allows for proper growing conditions. Continue the story from the fields through the processing in the mills to the final product.

There is a rich source of material in advanced curricula that can be developed into class participation stories. Many different stories can be developed during the year. Once a student has experienced a class participation story, he or she can create one to present to the class.

Lesson 5. A Secret Hiding Place

Close your eyes and find a place in your body where you can hide. Imagine that you are very small. How can you get inside your body? Look all around you once you are inside. What colors do you see? Do you hear any sounds? Find several different hiding places in your body. Where else can you hide? Where else? How do you get from one place in your body to another? Find the one place you like to hide in the most. Open your eyes and tell where you are. How does the room look to you from your hiding place? Close your eyes and look around your hiding place again. How do you feel in your hiding place? Slowly, slowly, come out of your hiding place, and join us back in this room.

Let those who want to do so share their stories. Encourage them to talk about how they moved about in their bodies and what the room looked like from their secret hiding place.

After the class completes this lesson and each student has a "secret" hiding place to go to, you can use this as a quieting activity. When the class gets "up in the air" about something, just ask each student to go to his or her secret hiding place, stay there for a while, and then come out and attend to the here and now.

Primary students would enjoy hearing the poem "Hiding" by Dorothy Aldis before finding their own secret hiding place.

Lesson 6. Your Name

Write your name. See how much space it takes up on the paper. Say your name. Listen to how long or short it is. Does your name fit you? Are you too big for it, are you too small for it, or is it just right?

Imagine you had a longer name. What would it be? How do you think it would fit you?

Imagine you had a shorter name. What would it be? How do you think it would fit you?

Write some long names. Try them on, one at a time. See how you feel wearing them.

Write some short names. Try them on, one at a time. See how you feel wearing them.

Write your own name again. Try it on again. How do you feel about it now?

Variations

Write other names you have been called—nicknames, pet names, variations of your name.

Say each one to yourself and let thoughts and images come to you.

Have the class form into groups of eight to ten. Have one person in each group be "it" and leave the room. Have the others in the group decide whom they will all talk about. It must be someone in their group. "It" returns to the group and asks questions to discover whom they are describing, but can only ask questions of this sort: What kind of house is he? What kind of tree is he? What kind of food is he? What kind of animal is he? What kind of bird is he?

Example—Possible answers for a tall, lean boy with curly black hair:
He is a two-story house.
He is a palm tree.
He is a celery stalk.
He is a giraffe.
He is a cormorant.

On the basis of this type of information, the one who is "it" tries to identify the person the group is talking about. After the identity of the person is discovered, that person has a chance to respond to the statements that were made—which responses did he or she agree with, which ones were a surprise, how does that person feel about the way the group sees him or her. There is no correct response. Each one answers with whatever seems appropriate at that moment. Do not allow anyone to ponder. Answers should be quick and spontaneous.

Lesson 7. Games with People

Think of a person you like. What kind of food would he or she be if he or she were something to eat?

Think of a person you dislike. What kind of food would he or she be?

Think of yourself. What kind of food are you?

What would you do with all of those different kinds of food together?

Think of a person you like. What kind of animal would he or she be?

Think of a person you dislike. What kind of an animal would he or she be?

What kind of animal would you be?

Close your eyes. Imagine a big green meadow. Imagine yourself as your animal. Be in the meadow. Have the animal of the person you like join you as your animal in the meadow.

Have the animal of the person you don't like join both of you in the meadow.

Imagine all three animals there in the meadow. Create your own story.

Talk about what happened in your fantasy. What did the animals do? How did your story end?

Lesson 8. You Remind Me . . .

Sit in a circle with four to six other students. Sit so you can see everyone and everyone can see you.

Look at the people in your group. Think about each one and who or what he or she reminds you of. It does not have to make sense. It can be that someone reminds you of another person, an animal, a color, or of anything in the world. Let images come to you.

Look around the circle and tell each person who or what you were reminded of, starting each statement with "You remind me of . . ." Some people may remind you of many things. Tell them as many as you wish.

Discuss what happened in your group.

Now all come together in one group. Are there times when you respond to someone as if that person were someone else because he or she reminds you of someone else?

When someone reminds you of something or someone else, does that help or hinder you in getting to know that person as he or she really is? How?

Lesson 9. Machines

One of you begin to be a part of a "machine" by making a mechanical movement and a sound to go with it. Continually make the same sound and movement. Others in the group, one by one, will attach themselves to you, each one adding another sound and movement to complete the "machine."

How does it feel to be the one to start the machine? How does it feel to add your own particular sound and movement to the machine? How do you work together to keep the machine going? What makes the machine stop?

Variation

Work in small groups. Each group make your own machine. Each machine move around the room and meet other machines.

Lesson 10. Paperclips

Sit in small groups with four or five students in each one. Here is a handful of paperclips for each group. Choose a recorder for your group. The recorder is to record each suggestion no matter what it is, while you and the members of your group come up with as many uses as possible for the paperclips.

Examples: "I can use the paperclip to clip my hair back." "I can use it to punch holes in this paper." "I can use it to wire my glasses together."

In five minutes the recorder is to draw a line under all your suggestions, and then continue recording. You have ten minutes to do this.

Now look at your list. Did any patterns emerge? Is there any difference between your answers in the first and the last five-minute period? When was the exercise most enjoyable? When was it least enjoyable? How did others in your group spark your imagination? What did you learn about the members of your group? What did you learn about yourself? If you were to do this again, what would you do the same? What would you change?

Lesson 11. Letter to a Baby

Write a letter to a newborn baby. What would you like to tell this child who has just come into the world? Since he or she is just a baby, he or she knows nothing yet. You know many things. What do you know that you would like to share with the baby? What do you know that is important for the baby to know? What do you know about this world that you would like to tell the baby? What is it like to live here and now? What do you imagine the baby's world will be like. Sign your name to your letter.

This lesson is done best when the student knows a family with a baby. It can be that one of the teachers has become a parent or a former teacher has a baby, or a student in the class has a new brother or sister. It also helps to make arrangements for a baby to be present in the classroom, if only for a few minutes.

Polarities

Education is a major preoccupation for many of our citizens. It seems that everyone is demanding the right to say what should and should not be happening in our schools; industry, government, universities, parents, and student groups are all voicing demands. Should the school be product- or process-oriented? Should it be more traditional or more innovative? Should the goal of education be survival or prestige? Should we strive to produce the world's greatest scientists or the highest literacy rate in the world? Should our goal be the greatest number of Pulitzer Prize winners or the development of a love of knowledge for its own sake—a passion for knowledge and a pleasure in learning; independence in seeking and using knowledge; an acceptance of learning as a lifelong process of self-development?

Today more than ever the issue is change. But what are we trying to change, and how are we to go about it? The computer-industrial revolution demands that what is technologically possible ought to be done and that humanity should strive for maximal efficiency and output. Unfortunately for the humanness of all of us caught in this revolution, maximal efficiency for the system often leads to minimal tolerance for individuality. Some critics insist that we need to humanize education by paying less attention to the process and more to the persons within it. And so the classroom teacher is caught in a dilemma, a polarity. How and what can we teach? In some ways we must prepare the student to cope with the "real" world, a world in which depersonalization and alienation are the rule rather than the exception. We "should" teach students to become cogs in the production machine. On the other hand, we "should" teach students to reach their full potential as unique individuals, and we "should" make the classroom environment full of meaning for them. This, of course, means making it the opposite of the "real" world.

There is no clear resolution to this polarity. There are times when we must prepare the student for the system. He or she will be subjected to a battery of standardized tests so that the system can judge if he or she is at grade level or working up to his or her abilities. We cannot ignore that aspect of the student's "education," even though personally we may disapprove of the principle. At the same time we do not have to, nor can we afford to, devote the whole teaching day to preparing the student to meet the demands of the system. A humanistic teaching approach discerns the needs and demands of the person as well as those of the system and provides opportunities for the expression of both.

Basic curriculum guides offer a wealth of materials for dealing with polarities in subject matter itself. To name just a few, in math there are addition and subtraction, multiplication and division. In English there are units on opposite words. In physical education there are many components that can be looked at as polarities—the desire to win and sportsmanship, skill and drill, personal ability and the ability to be a good team player. In the social sciences there are environment and heredity, physical and nonphysical characteristics, the commonality of all humankind and the uniqueness of each individual. There are many ways of looking at anything; attending to polarities can ensure that at least two views will be allowed and expressed. All too often, we, and the textbooks we use, tend toward a one-sided, simplistic view.

Offered here are lessons in what may be called universal polarities. They all have to do with human behavior, actions, and emotions. As such, they can be taught along with any subject matter, where and when it seems appropriate to do so.

The purpose of dealing directly with polarities is to become more aware of what each of us has available, and also to extend our boundaries. We all have characteristics unknown to ourselves, unexperienced parts, gaps in our self-awareness. We have all forgotten or disowned a great deal of what we know about ourselves, especially anything we might consider to be negative. The goal of an exercise on polarities is to become a more complete individual, containing fewer unknowns, fewer unexperienced parts of the self. There is nothing new in these exercises. They are concerned with rediscovery.

Objectives

To be able to think about a single part of the body and compare it with another single, particular part.

To be able to choose a word that describes you and a word opposite in meaning.

To be able to move in a way that others would describe as aggressive.

To be able to move in a way that others would describe as passive.

To develop the ability to look at yourself from two points of view.

To be able to state resentments and appreciations clearly.

To be able to role-play opposite roles and express how each one makes you feel.

To be aware of sending and receiving nonverbal messages.

Lesson 1. Polarities of Your Body

Lie on the floor. Relax, close your eyes.

Become aware of your breathing. Begin to increase your inhaling and exhaling until you are breathing as deeply and as slowly as possible. How does the rest of your body feel? Now shorten your breathing until you begin to pant. How does the rest of your body feel? Now come to a place in between and rest. How do you feel?

Now become aware of the weight of your body. What parts are heavy? Where is the heaviest part of all? What parts are light? What is the lightest part of all?

Become aware of the temperature of your body. What parts of your body are warm? Where is the warmest place? What parts are cool? What is the coolest place?

Become aware of the texture of your body. What parts are rough? Where is it roughest? What parts are smooth? Where is it smoothest?

Imagine dividing yourself exactly down the middle. Compare the right side of your body to the left side. Take each part in turn and compare it with its opposite, taking time for each part.

Imagine dividing yourself at your waist. Compare the top half of your body to the bottom half in weight, temperature, texture, and other characteristics that come to you.

Compare what you know about the inside of your body with what you know about the outside of your body.

See if you can discover other polarities in or on your body. Take your time. When you are ready, open your eyes, sit up and join the group.

Talk about any surprises, anything you discovered that you were not expecting.

Now begin to walk around, paying particular attention to

those parts of your body that surprised you, or the ones that are newly rediscovered. Be aware of your whole body.

Experiment with the parts you have rediscovered. Give them a voice, one at a time. What do they have to say to you and the rest of your body? Have each statement begin with "I."

"I am your left elbow. I am rough and hard and sharp."

"I am the base of your neck. I am tight and very warm."

"I am your bottom half. I give you support. I take you where you want to go. All you have to do is tell me and I will get you there."

"I am your top half. I make contact for you. I do all the thinking around here."

Throughout the day, continue to be aware of your whole body and all your separate parts. Pay particular attention to any messages you receive from any of the parts.

Lesson 2. Polarities of Your Voice

Speak in a soft, gentle, smooth voice. Say soft, gentle, smooth phrases. Examples: "I love you. Goodnight, dear. Are you happy? That's beautiful." Focus your attention on the muscles of your throat. Be aware of how your throat feels.

Speak in a harsh, grating, sharp voice. Say harsh, grating, sharp phrases. Examples: "Get out of here. Who invited you? Now what do you want? Get lost." Focus your attention on the muscles of your throat. Be aware of how your throat feels.

Gossip about someone you don't like, someone not in this room. Listen to your voice. Experience the muscles of your throat.

Gossip about someone you like. Listen to your voice. Experience the muscles of your throat.

How much range do you allow your voice? Is it quite different in different situations, or is it always the same? Experiment with your voice. See if you can exaggerate its polarities. As you go through the day, become aware of when and where you use the polarities and when you use a voice somewhere in the middle.

When do you use certain voices? Do you have a telephone voice? Do you have a teacher voice? Become aware of your special voices.

Lesson 3. Opposites I

Close your eyes and see how you are right now. Accentuate it. Sit that way, breathe that way, hold every muscle that way.

Choose a single word that best describes how you are.

Now imagine that your whole body is that word. If your word is "calm," let your whole body be calm. You might even want to lie down. If your word is "tense," tense every part of you—hands, fingers, spine, legs, feet, and toes. Let your whole body be whatever your word is. Let your word grow, completely filling your body. Now have it shrink until it is barely there. Now let your word and your body change however you want.

Now think of the opposite of your original word. Move your body in opposite ways to become that word. Be that word in every way you can. Let your entire body be the opposite of what it was. Sit that way, breathe that way, hold every muscle that way. Let your word grow until it completely fills your body. Now have it shrink until it is barely there. Now let it change in any way you want.

Be your original word again. Move your body to the original word.

Be your opposite word again. Move your body to the opposite word.

Now find a word in the middle, something between the two you have been using. Let your whole body be that way.

Talk about what you discovered. What were your words? How did your body express them? How did the words change? How did your body change?

Do not be concerned if the students do not use exact opposites for their words. You can take time for vocabulary development later. What is important is that students experiment with being opposite.

Lesson 4. Opposites II

Close your eyes and feel how you are right now. Accentuate it. Choose a word that best describes how you are now. Imagine that you can be just that one way; no other way is possible. Be just that word for the next ten minutes while you continue in regular classroom activities. If other moods, other ideas, other words come to you, reject them. Stay with that one word.

Now become the opposite of that word. Be just that word for the next ten minutes while you continue in regular classroom activities. If other moods, other ideas, other words come to you, reject them. Stay with that one word.

Now be a combination of all that you are, using your two words and whatever else you want.

What happened to you when you were your first word? What moods, ideas, and words did you have to reject?

What happened to you when you were the opposite of that word? What moods, ideas, and words did you have to reject?

Which way did you like to be most? What did you like about it?

Lesson 5. Passive-Aggressive

Each of us can have many different ways of being, depending on time, circumstances, and how we are feeling. Close your eyes and think of yourself and these two terms: passive, aggressive. Imagine yourself as passive. What are you doing? Who is around you? How do you feel?

Imagine yourself as aggressive. What are you doing? Who is near you? How do you feel?

Now decide if you are usually passive or usually aggressive, knowing that you are really both. Choose to be the one that you usually are, and accentuate it. Open your eyes aggressively or passively. Now begin to move around the room that way, accentuating how you are in every way possible. Breathe that way. Move that way. Begin to make sounds that way.

Freeze. In slow motion, and staying aware of how you do it, become the opposite. Continue to move.

Freeze. Again in slow motion and in full awareness, become your original word again.

Freeze. Now move in slow motion to how you want to be here and now.

Talk about what you discovered.

Which role was the most difficult for you? How did you feel changing from one to the other? Which role did you like most? What did you like about it? How did you feel when you change?

Have primary students respond to being "happy" and "mad" rather than "passive" or "aggressive."

Variation

Follow the same format using high and low energy levels; calm-frantic; busy-bored; any other opposites the students suggest.

Lesson 6. Superior-Inferior

There are times when each of us feels superior to those around us. There are also times when we feel inferior to those around us.

Imagine that you feel superior to all of us here and now. How do you move? Show us. How do you feel? Show us.

Now imagine that you are inferior. How do you move? Show us. How do you feel? Show us.

Choose a partner. One of you be superior, the other inferior. Find a way to stand with each other showing that one is superior and one is inferior. Now the one who is superior tell your partner what you have available by being superior. (Examples: I have a view of the ceiling, I have pride, I have a stiff spine, I have a loud voice.) What can you see from your position? What can you do in that position? How do you feel in relation to your partner in that position? How do you feel about your partner in that position?

Now, the one who is inferior, tell your partner what you have available by being inferior. (Examples: I can see no one, only the floor; I have fear; I have stooped shoulders; I have chewed fingernails.) What can you see from your position? What can you do in that position? How do you feel in relation to your partner in that position? How do you feel about your partner in that position?

Now find a way to be equals. Now what can you see? What can you do? How do you feel about yourself? What do you feel about your partner?

As you go through the day, become aware of when you feel superior or inferior. Ask yourself, "What does feeling superior do for me? What does feeling inferior do for me?"

Primary students may respond to the terms "better than anyone else" and "worse than anyone else." You can explain "superior" and "inferior" if it seems appropriate.

Variation

Follow the same format using leader-follower; boss-worker; parent-child; other polarities suggested by the students or by the curriculum.

Lesson 7. Love-Hate

Stand facing a partner. One will do the exercise, the other will observe.

Close your eyes and imagine a person you love. Begin to focus on that feeling of love. Let it grow, accentuate it. Where is it located in your body? Does it have a temperature? Does it have a color? Does it have texture? Continue to focus on your feeling of love. Put all your thinking, feeling, and imagining into it.

Open your eyes. Have your partner share what was observed. What did your partner see you do? What did your partner imagine you were thinking? Share what you discovered. Where in your body did you feel love? Did it have color, temperature, or texture?

Close your eyes and imagine a person you hate. Begin to focus on that feeling of hate. Let it grow, accentuate it. Where is it located in your body? Does it have a temperature? Does it have color? Does it have texture? Continue to focus on your feeling of hate. Put all your thinking, feelings, and imagining into it.

Open your eyes. Have your partner share what was observed. What was seen this time? What did your partner imagine you were thinking? Share what you discovered. Where in your body did you feel hate? Did it have color, temperature, or texture? How did it feel in contrast to love?

The one who worked will now become the observer, and the partner will do the exercises.

Repeat from "close your eyes and imagine . . ."

Lesson 8. Mixed Feelings

We all have times when we feel two ways at the same time about parents, teachers, brothers and sisters, and others.

Think about a person you have mixed feelings about. Imagine that person is sitting across from you. Tell that person what makes you angry or upset, what you resent about him or her. Begin each sentence with "I": "I get angry . . ." or, "I resent you . . ."

Now tell that person what he or she should do. Make demands. Begin each sentence with "You should . . ."

It may be necessary to help students begin sentences with "You should . . ." Beginning by saying "You should not . . ." somehow makes this part of the exercise less effective, less forceful.

Now tell that person what you like or appreciate about him or her. Again begin each sentence with "I."

Talk about what you discovered.

With primary and intermediate students, do not make a distinction between liking and appreciating. However, with advanced students, it is important to do just that. If you are to make sense out of your mixed-up feelings, it is important to know that you may dislike or resent *and* appreciate the very same thing. A student once told me that she resented me for holding her to an assigned task for a prolonged period of time, but that she appreciated my doing it because now she is quite good at that task and would never have stayed with it without my insistence. It is difficult to know when the appreciation is real and not resentment in disguise. The skill comes in seeing both the resentment and appreciation.

Lesson 9. Mixed Signals

We have all experienced a "double signal." There are times when people "tell" us two things at the same time. In some way, words and actions are the opposite of each other, or the tone of voice carries a different message from the words.

Choose a partner. Deliberately give mixed signals.

Talk to each other about anything you want. Whenever you say "Yes," shake your head "No."

Give your partner a compliment in words, and at the same time deny it by the tone of your voice, a hand gesture, facial expression, or anything else you can think of.

Say something negative to your partner, and at the same time deny it by the tone of your voice, a smile or other facial expression, a hand gesture, or anything else you can think of.

Share your discoveries and techniques with the entire group. What works best for you? What is your favorite way of giving a mixed signal? What mixed signals do you experience most often? How do you know they are mixed? Which signal do you choose to respond to? What would happen if you chose the other one?

Continue to become aware of mixed signals as you go through the day. Become aware of the ones you use as well as the ones that are used on you.

Lesson 10. To Do or Not to Do

Put your arm on your desk. Now try to lift your arm, only do not really lift it. Be aware of how the rest of your body feels. Now this time really lift your arm. Again, be aware of how the rest of your body feels.

Repeat.

Talk about what you experienced.

How is this exercise like other situations in your life? Have you ever experienced yourself exerting more energy *not* doing something than you would exert doing it? The next time you are faced with doing something you don't want to do, experience how much energy you exert in not doing it, and how much energy you exert when doing it.

With primary students, use "working hard" instead of "exerting energy." Ask them to relate this experience to one in which they have worked hard *not* to do a chore.

Lesson 11. Genius/Idiot

Choose a partner.

Roll up a single sheet of newspaper. Each one grab one end of it. You are to pull your partner over an imaginary line between you without tearing the newspaper. If you tear it, roll up another sheet and try again.

Choose another partner.

Imagine your *genius*, that part of you that knows all the answers, knows how to solve problems, can come up with a solution to any given problem. Be that genius as you work to pull your partner across the line without tearing the paper.

Discuss any difference between doing it now as the genius and doing it the first time.

Choose another partner.

Imagine your *idiot*, that part of you that never does anything right, makes mistakes every time, always needs help. Be that idiot and work to pull your partner across the line without tearing the paper.

Discuss the differences you experienced.

Choose another partner. Decide on one of those two roles, the genius or the idiot. Do not tell your partner which you are. Try to pull your partner across. Try to discover what he or she is as you are working.

Discuss how you experienced each other.

Continue to choose different partners, trying on one or the other role.

What happened when you were playing the genius?

What happened when you were playing the idiot?

When do you really play the genius? When do you act as if you know more than you really do?

When do you really play the idiot? When do you act as if you need more help than you really do?

When can the role of the genius be useful to you? When could it be harmful?

When can the role of idiot be harmful to you? When can it help you?

This is a particularly good exercise for students just before they take examinations. It gives them ways to act out their idiots and their geniuses. They can then enter the exam at ease, relaxed, and ready to do their best, leaving their idealized geniuses and their complete idiots aside.

Lesson 12. Paper Structures

Sit in a group with four to six students.

Without talking, each group is to build a structure, using newspaper as the building material. At the end of ten minutes your structure will be judged for height and stability.

Begin to work. Remember, you are not to talk to each other while you work. You can use gestures and sign language, but no words.

Wait five minutes.

Freeze. Think about how you have been working in your group. Choose a word that describes how you've been working, your role in the group. One by one, say your word out loud. (Examples: worker, helper, designer, goof-off, paper folder.)

Now imagine that you are the opposite of that word.

Continue working, again without talking, and in your opposite role.

Wait five minutes.

Stop working on your structure. Compare your structure with others in the room. Which is the highest? Which is the most stable? How can you decide?

What did you discover about yourself? What two roles did you play? How did you work with your group while you were in your first one? How did you work with your group while in your second role? Did you stay in your second role until the end, or did you switch roles again? If you switched, what did you switch to?

What did you discover about others in your group?

It is difficult for a group of students to work nonverbally at building a newspaper structure that is "high and stable." Yet amazing things happen when they do. Very often a group which gets going early in the lesson destroys their structure when told to be opposites, and then proceeds to build it up again just before the time is out. Conversely, a group that has not been able to get anything together builds a structure quite easily while being opposites. This exercise allows the students another way of being, another way to tackle a task.

The process of judging the structures can be a meaningful learning experience for the students. How can the height be measured? Who can be trusted to take accurate measurements? How can stability be measured? What will be the basis of judging stability?

Communication

Effective communication is essential in relating to others. Real communication involves sending and receiving messages, but most of us are primarily concerned only with sending messages. Very few of us can listen without talking, although most of us can talk without listening. The integration of talking and listening is a rare thing. Most of us don't listen and give an honest response but just put the other person off with a question. Instead of listening and answering, we immediately counterattack, ask a question, make a senseless remark, anything that diverts, deflects, dodges real communication. But without communication there can be no contact. We are only isolated and bored.

Communication concerned with receiving a message involves a willingness to understand another person's point of view or way of looking at the world, or perhaps even unspoken needs and goals. Communication associated with transmitting a message involves much more than organization of thoughts or clarity of speech. It requires sensitivity to the needs, level of comprehension, and receptivity of the receiver. If the other person hasn't received, we haven't communicated.

Most really significant communication between people involves feelings, not ideas, and is nonverbal. In most communication with people who are important to us, we listen as much to the unspoken messages as to the words. Even with people who are not important to us we have an inner ear tuned to nonverbal messages concerning sincerity, dependability, and frankness. We constantly rely on nonverbal feedback from others, but often we are not aware of the nonverbal message we transmit. We can and must increase our sensitivity to others' reactions, to their non-verbal communication, as well as to our own.

Typically we do not allow students at school to become actively involved in developing adequate communication skills. We often limit their receiving to hours and hours of listening only, ignoring that students have more available for receiving than their ears. They need multiple opportunities for sending messages too. They need opportunities to develop awareness of and skills in many ways of communication.

The following lessons deal with blocks in sending and receiving messages, in giving oneself, in making others aware of oneself, and in being willing to be open to other people.

In the first lesson students may discover that they do not listen very well or very often. But with practice they will improve their skills in listening to others, as well as be provided with instant feedback on their abilities to listen and to restate what they heard. By continuing through the other lessons, they can begin to develop an "inner ear" for listening. They will explore various ways to listen and various ways to interpret their listening abilities. They will be encouraged to use more of what is available to them in any listening situation.

Objectives

To communicate an interest in others.

To be perceptive regarding your effect on others and their effect on you.

To be open, receptive, and interested in the ideas, opinions, feelings, and reactions of others.

To be able to accept constructive feedback or criticism without reacting defensively, becoming hostile, or withdrawing.

To be able to provide constructive criticism, meaningful feedback, support, and encouragement to another person.

To develop the ability to listen to the totality of another person—his or her body as well as his or her words.

Lesson 1. Listen, Repeat

Sit in a group of four to six students.

Anyone in the group may say anything, but he or she must speak in a clear, simple sentence.

In order for someone else to speak, he or she must first repeat what the previous speaker said.

Example:

Speaker A: "I'm going to get some new shoes after school today."

Speaker B: "I'm going to get some new shoes after school today. I am going to help John build his fort."

Speaker C (may be Speaker A again): "I am going to help John . . ."

Strange things happen when you use this lesson. The student gets so intent on listening that he or she actually forgets what he or she was going to say—what was "rehearsed." It not only improves listening ability, but also aids in developing precise, clear English.

Lesson 2. Trite Conversation

Choose a partner. Talk to each other, but have a "trite" conversation. Talk of nothing that is of importance to you. Talk about what you ate for breakfast, how to clean your room, anything that seems trite to you.

Come up front in pairs and introduce your partner to the group. Check with each other to make sure that what you say is correct and is something you know about your partner because of your trite conversation, not from former information.

How did you feel having a trite conversation? How did you keep it trite? How did you feel introducing your partner? How did you feel being introduced?

When do other people have trite conversations? When do you usually have trite conversations? (Examples: When I don't know the person very well. When I feel the person isn't really interested in what I have to say.)

Lesson 3. More Conversation

Choose a partner, preferably the same one as in "Trite Conversation." One of you be "A," the other "B."

Alternate talking and listening for five-minute periods. Have "A" ask "B" the same question over and over for five minutes and "B" answer over and over, seeking new answers to the same question. Then "B" asks "A" the same question over and over for five minutes before going on to the next question.

Ask each other the following questions:

Who are you?

What do you pretend?
What makes you cry?
What makes you happy?
How did you feel answering the same question over and
over? Which question was easiest to answer? Which one was the
most difficult? Did you discover any answers that surprised you?
Did your partner say anything that surprised you?

Lesson 4. Kanga Talk

In this story Kanga and her baby Roo have come to live in the forest.
The other animals who live there decide to play a trick on Kanga by
taking her baby, Roo, and giving her Piglet instead. Kanga goes along
with the trick by taking Piglet to her home and pretending he is Roo.
Here is what happens:

"I am not all sure," said Kanga in a thoughtful voice, "that it
wouldn't be a good idea to have a *cold* bath this evening. Would
you like that, Roo, dear?"
　　Piglet, who had never really been fond of baths, shuddered
a long indignant shudder, and said in as brave a voice as he could:
　　"Kanga, I see the time has come to speak plainly."
　　"Funny little Roo," said Kanga, as she got the bath water
ready.
　　"I am *not* Roo," said Piglet loudly. "I am Piglet!"
　　"Yes, dear, yes," said Kanga soothingly. "And imitating Piglet's voice, too! So clever of him," she went on, as she took a large
bar of yellow soap out of the cupboard. "What *will* he be doing
next?"
　　"Can't you *see*?" shouted Piglet. "Haven't you got *eyes*? Look
at me!"
　　"I *am* looking, Roo, dear," said Kanga rather severely. "And
you know what I told you yesterday about making faces. If you
go on making faces like Piglet's, you will grow up to *look* like
Piglet—and *then* think how sorry you will be. Now then, into the
bath, and don't let me have to speak to you again."[1]

How can two people be talking "at" each other instead of "to"
each other? Can you think of another dialogue that fits the pattern? Share a similar conversation.
　　Can you recall any conversations like this between you and
someone here?

[1] A. A. Milne, *Winnie the Pooh* (New York: E. P. Dutton, n.d.), Chapter VII.

Can you recall any conversations like this between you and someone you live with?

Listen to how people talk to each other and try to discover the times when they talk "to" each other and the times they talk "at" each other.

Variations

Form small groups. Develop skits demonstrating how people talk "at" each other instead of "to" each other.

Examples: Classroom scene, teacher and student talking "at" each other. In the family car, parents and children talking "at" each other. Older child talking "at" younger child.

Write stories demonstrating examples. Here is one from an advanced student.

STRAWBERRY SHORTCAKE

It was a sunny afternoon in late June. Mrs. Green was preparing supper when Alice rushed in.

"I'm going to be in the spelling bee, Mother. First prize is a new television set," Alice burst out.

"What do you think we should have for dessert tonight, Alice?"

"I hope I win!" she said abruptly.

"What, the dessert?"

"NO—the spelling bee!"

"Maybe strawberry shortcake would be nice."

"I wonder if they have a color set," Alice said questioningly.

"Yes, of course, strawberries have color."

"Mother, you are not listening to me."

"Of course I am, dear."

Lesson 5. Build a Story

Begin telling a story that really sparks the students' imagination. It can be related to a holiday theme, a science or social-studies unit, or one just for fun. After a few minutes, stop and have a student continue the story. Let each student add at least one sentence.

Example: One dark and gloomy night I was in an old haunted house. The wind began to blow. Doors slammed shut, windows creaked. Suddenly I heard a loud crash in the kitchen. I ran in there to see what was happening and what did I see, but a . . .

Variations

PACK YOUR TRUNK

Speaker A: I am packing my trunk. I am taking a shirt.

Speaker B: I am packing my trunk. I am taking a shirt and a toothbrush.

Speaker C: I am packing my trunk. I am taking a shirt, a toothbrush, and a jacket.

Continue until all in the group get a turn to pack something. If time and interest allow, unpack the trunk.

DO WHAT I DO

One student stands in the group and begins a nonverbal activity. (Build a house, prepare a meal, put up a tent.) Others join in the activity once they imagine they know what the student is "saying." They can imitate the motion or join in doing the same task in their own way.

Lesson 6. Talking with Hands

Suppose you couldn't talk. How could you say "Hello"? Do it now, without talking. Say hello to a friend without talking. Say hello to another friend without talking.

Imagine you are angry. How could you show that using your hands and not your voice?

Now imagine you are shy or nervous. How could you show that with your hands?

Imagine you are happy. How could you show that with your hands?

Choose a partner. Say hello to each other using just your hands. Have a conversation with your partner using your hands. While your partner is "talking" try to listen with your hands. Stay together long enough to allow yourselves to have a hand conversation.

Lesson 7. Listening with Eyes

I am going to tell you some things, but I am not going to use words. I am going to use "body English." You are to listen to what I am saying, but you will have to listen with your eyes.

(Look and act very stern.) What am I saying?

(Look very pleased.) What am I saying?

(Act very proud and "stuck up.") What am I saying?

Now you do it.
Say you are a very old man.
Say you are a spoiled brat.
Say you are a very tired, sleepy child.
Say you are very anxious to get my attention.
Say you are angry.
Say you are happy and cheerful.
Say what you are really feeling now.
During the rest of the day discover what people say with their bodies and their voices.
Discover when they say two things at once.
Can you give examples of how a person might say two things at once? (Examples: Say "You can sit next to me," but act as though you don't want that person anywhere near you. Say "Stop it!" and smile.

Lesson 8. Nonverbal Statements

Choose a student to be "It."
Have other students in the group come up one at a time and make a nonverbal statement either to or about "It."

You can touch "It" if you wish, hug, hit without hurting, stroke, pat, etc.
You can imitate "Its" stance, facial expression, mannerism, way of moving.

Encourage the students to express their impressions in any way they can other than through the use of words.
Then have the student who was "It" respond, again nonverbally, to each one who made a statement of him or her. "It" can show each one agreement or disagreement, pleasure or scorn, in any way except that he or she cannot use words or cause pain or injury to the student. When he or she is through responding, he or she can choose another student to be "It." Help the students be aware of nonverbal messages received which influenced their choice of a new "It." Did he or she choose a student who smiled? Did he or she choose someone who seemed to be saying "Me! Me!" by some action? What nonverbal clues were available?

Lesson 9. Total Listening

Choose a partner. Face each other. One of you is to talk and the other is to listen. As you listen, imitate your partner's facial expression, how his or her hands move, his or her "body English."

If, when you are the one who is talking, you become speechless or embarrassed, tell your partner how speechless you are, how you feel about standing there face to face embarrassed.

Change roles. The one who was talking becomes the listener. The listener becomes the talker.

Choose another partner.

Repeat several times. Be talker and listener with different people.

Discuss: Who was difficult to talk to? Who was difficult to listen to? Who was easy to talk to? What do people do that make it easy for you to talk to them? Who was easy to listen to? What do people do that make it easy for you to listen to them?

Lesson 10. Imagining Sounds

Sit so that you are quiet and comfortable. Close your eyes. Think of a loud sound that is familiar to you. (A train going by, thunder, sirens, etc.) Concentrate on that sound. Where are you when you hear it? Is anyone else there? What time of day is it? How do you feel when you hear that sound? Where in your body do you experience that feeling? (Stomach, shoulders, back of knees, head, etc.)

Now think of a soft sound that is familiar to you. (Rain gently falling, whispering, leaves rustling, etc.) Concentrate on that sound. Where are you when you hear it? Is anyone else there? What time of day is it? How do you feel when you hear that sound? Where in your body do you experience that feeling? Is it the same or different from the place where you felt the loud sound?

Discuss what you discovered.

You might wish to make the students' responses to these questions into a math lesson by having them tabulate their answers. By doing this, the student discovers that even though one's answers are based on one's own experience, there are others in the class who share similar experiences.

Lesson 11. TV Commercials

Watch several commercials on TV. (This could be a homework assignment.)

Listen to how the announcers try to persuade you to buy their products.

List advertising sentences or phrases aimed at eliciting an emotional response.

Examples: "A little Accent's like a little love."
"You don't have to be expensive to be good."
"Your friends will agree."
"Score some points the easy way."

Make a list that includes the product being sold as well as the implicit by-product you will get when you buy the product. For example,

Product	By-product
Cosmetics	Romance
Hairspray	Long, curly, easy-to-manage blonde hair
Margarine	A jeweled crown, riches of a king
Hand lotion	A family enjoying each other, having fun

What effect do these commercials have on you? What do you imagine the people who make up the commercials see as being important to you? What is important to you?

Which commercials "turn you off"? What is there about them that you do not like? What makes you "turn off"?

With older students you can go on to explore the following.

Which commercials do you enjoy? What is there about them that pleases you? Have you ever bought a product because of watching a commercial? If so, did you like the product as much as you liked the commercial?

Be aware of how you are responding while you are listening to and watching commercials. Make notes. Share them with the class.

Lesson 12. Words, Words

Make a list of phrases that everyone uses frequently. For example: "How are you?" "Where have you been?" "Isn't it terrible?" "What's the matter?" "I'll see you later."

Now choose two or three students to work with you.

Divide a piece of paper into three columns. In the first column, list ten of the phrases on your list. In the next column, write what you think the speaker of those words really means to say. In the third column write what you imagine would happen if you were to respond to the phrase with complete honesty. For example: If asked "How are you?" what might happen if you took the time and effort to really tell how you are?

Since everyone uses these phrases frequently in meaningless ways, how do you know when someone uses them and means them? How do phrases like that teach you not to listen to one another?

Try to respond honestly to a meaningless phrase at least once today. Be aware of what happens to you and to the speaker when you do.

Primary students can respond to this orally. You might want them to consider only three or four phrases.

Lesson 13. Twenty Words

Take a piece of paper and a pencil to a place where you can be quiet and comfortable.

Of all the words you know, choose the four words you think are most important for you to be able to communicate.

Now get into a group of four to six people. Each of you use your four words, and only your four words, to communicate.

Now sit by yourself again. Look at your four words. Evaluate each one. If any of them did not help you communicate, cross them off your list and add more words so that you still have four words.

Now add four new words so that you have eight in all.

Get into a new group of four to six people and use your words. Use only your eight words, even as you form your groups.

Sit by yourself again. Look at your eight words. Again, cross off any words that you did not find useful. Add other words so that you still have eight.

Add four new words, so that you have twelve words in all. Now use your twelve words in a new group.

Evaluate your list of twelve words, making any changes you want.

Now add four new words, so that you have a list of sixteen in all.

Use your sixteen words in a new group.

Evaluate your list of sixteen, making any changes you want.

Add four new words to your list, making twenty in all.

Do not go into a group, but sit by yourself and look at your words. Read them through several times. Let thoughts and images come to you as you read them.

Use those twenty words to write a poem, make a statement,

or share an image about yourself. You do not need to use all
twenty words, and you can use any of them as often as you wish.

Bring the whole group together. Let anyone who likes read his or her
poem or statement to the entire group.
Here is one such poem written by a sixth-grade boy.

> Less aware I came,
> More aware I go.
> We share thought, trust, love and hope.
> What now is here
> I feel will be elsewhere.
> Less aware I came,
> More aware I go.

Building Trust

One of the most difficult things to do is to trust someone else, to give yourself to another person. We can all recall situations in which we have trusted someone only to be disappointed, betrayed, left "holding the bag." And yet very little is being taught in classrooms on how to discriminate between healthy and harmful contacts with people. We do not teach students how to avoid making the same mistakes over and over again in their interpersonal transactions. Instead we allow them to learn this very important aspect of becoming self-confident, self-actualizing persons on a purely trial-and-error basis. We do not teach them how to be careful, how to listen, see, think, and feel about the way in which contact with other persons affects them. We do not encourage students to ask questions such as "How do I feel now? What do I know that makes me feel this way?" If the contact is unpleasant, they are not helped to understand exactly what is unpleasant; thus overgeneralization, stereotyping, or withdrawal may occur. We leave the entire area of how to give and receive trust entirely to chance, and so we also leave students "holding the bag" when it comes to being able to build trusting relationships.

The lessons that follow are a beginning attempt to bring this important area into focus in the classroom. They are by no means exhaustive. This is one area about which little is supplied by traditional teacher materials. And yet how much trust must be developed in the average classroom for real learning to occur! If learning is, as one definition has it, discovering that something is possible, the bonds of trust must be well established and well developed. Without trust in one's peers and one's teacher, how can one be expected to venture out into unknown areas? If one cannot learn to trust others, how can one learn to trust oneself?

We teach students to compete with one another, to outperform others, to get better grades, and so on. But what does all this do to their ability to trust? I don't know, but I do know that using lessons designed expressly to establish bonds of trust between students has added a new dimension to my classroom. Competition has continued, but not on a devastating level. Students begin to appreciate one another more, begin to see worthwhile qualities even in those who cannot or will not compete in the usual way.

What are lessons designed to build trust like? Read *Black Beauty* to the students and explore the idea of the trust that exists between people and animals. Explore multiple answers to these questions: How do you know when an animal trusts you? How do animals act when they don't trust someone? How do you act when you don't trust someone? What do I need to do in order for you to trust me? What do you need to do in order for me to trust you?

Form small groups and have them stand in circles. Each person goes around to each of the others in the group and completes this statement: "In order for me to trust you, you should . . ." And then around again and finish this statement: "In order for me to trust you, I should . . ." And still again, "I trust you when . . . I do not trust you when . . ."

The following answers came from a fifth-grade class:

"In order for me to trust you, you should
    never make fun of me."
    speak to me in a soft voice."
    often smile at me."
"In order for me to trust you, I should
    spend time being with you."
    do something nice for you."
    be as good at baseball as you are."
"I trust you when
    you play fair."
    you do what I tell you to do."
    you are nice to me."
"I do not trust you when you
    are mean to me."
    are with Marcy."
    insist on having everything your way."

Have students talk about the people they live with and how they trust them. Have them write about the person they trust the most as well as the person they trust the least. They may discover that the one they trust the most is the same person they trust the least. Have them talk about that, too, and how sometimes life is very complex and perplexing.

Play trust games, such as "falling" (Lesson 3) or "trust circle" (Lesson 4). How close to you does the group have to be for you to trust them to catch you? Can you allow yourself to fall farther?

Another useful device is to take a trust walk or a blind walk. Have each student choose a partner, put on a blindfold, and let the partner take the student on a sensory trusting excursion. Have the students use that experience to explore the following questions: Whom did you choose for your partner? On what basis did you choose? Which did you like most—being blind or leading? What did you like about it? What did you discover about your partner on the walk? What did you discover about yourself? Imagine being on a blind walk with someone you don't trust. What might that be like? Are there real times in your life when you feel as if you're on a blind walk? (Some experiences related by children are visits to doctors or dentists and riding in a car with a reckless driver.) How do those experiences affect your ability to trust other people?

Deliberately establishing trust is a new area of consideration in the classroom, one that needs a great deal more study. A commonsense reminder before you continue: Don't force students to participate in any of the following activities. You must trust students to know what they can and cannot allow themselves to do. You can provide the opportunities for them to build trust, but they must know that they will be allowed to be where and what they are, that they will not be obliged to do anything. It is hoped that the following lessons will provide enough insight for you to continue the development of trust on your own.

Objectives

To learn to "give in," to let someone else take over.
To be able to work cooperatively with others.
To be responsive to personal needs and to be considerate of the
    needs of others as well as the requirements of a given situation.
To be able to trust others and to gain their trust.
To be aware of and express new appreciation for members of the
    group.

Lesson 1. Hand Painting

Materials: Fingerpaint paper (large, white, smooth sheets), dry tempera, starch.

On half of the desks, tape down one sheet of paper and place a container with enough liquid starch to cover the paper and another container holding dry tempera.

Choose a partner and sit down across the desk from each other, facing each other.

Clap your hands, shake your hands, rub your hands. Now clap hands with your partner. Shake hands with your partner. Rub hands with your partner.

First, without using starch or color, you and your partner move your hands over your paper together. Explore a rhythm of movement that is comfortable for both of you. Move in a variety of ways. Move slowly, quickly, in jerks, in slides, in taps and in slaps. Find a way that enables both of you to move as one.

Once you are able to move together easily, pour starch on your paper and spread it all around, still trying to move as one. Continue moving the starch around until it begins to get somewhat tacky or the paper begins to show signs of wear.

Now put your fingertips into the dry tempera and add color to your movements. Continue to concentrate on moving together rather than trying to paint something.

Do the movement you like to do the best while moving together. Make that movement all over the paper and leave it like that to dry. The paint will make patterns, and you will have a painting of your moving together.

Lesson 2. Feed Your Partner

Arrange it so that all the students can eat lunch in the classroom together. Have each student choose a partner and sit across from him or her. Each one is to feed his or her partner and not oneself.

This sounds simple, but actually it is quite difficult. We are all so used to "taking care of ourselves" that it is not easy to give in and let someone do something like feed us. If there is a student who is reluctant to experience this, allow the student to sit with the group and eat normally. He or she might take a bite or two from either you or a friend before the period is over.

Lesson 3. Falling

Have the students choose a partner. One be A, the other B. B stands behind A about ten inches away, facing in the same direction. A then falls back, letting B catch A. In order to really fall, A does nothing to assist B.

Change places so that A can then catch B. Repeat the process several times, discovering persons you trust to catch you and persons you feel will not be able to catch you.

With a student who is afraid of falling, decrease the distance. With a student who is not afraid, increase the distance to the limits of safety. Let the student define those limits by placing the partner at a comfortable distance.

Lesson 4. Trust Circle

Once the students are comfortable with falling, have them form small groups of six to eight. One person goes in the center, and the others form a close, tight circle to catch the center person as he or she falls. The one in the center has to keep both feet in one spot while keeping legs and backbone stiff so that the students in the circle can pass the person around by moving the upper part of the body from one to the other.

The circle must be small enough so that the person in the center has a short fall and is therefore not too heavy to be passed around. Be sure to stop the exercise before the students get too tired to continue to catch the person in the center.

Variation

Have the students sit in a tight circle on the ground using their feet to anchor the feet of the person in the center. The one in the center holds both feet still and his or her legs and back stiff. He or she then falls to the group. The group uses their arms and hands held up over their heads and slightly forward in order to pass the person from student to student. The one who "drops" the center person, or cannot pass him or her on, then becomes "it" and goes into the center.

This is a great experience. However, it is a strenuous activity and requires strong arms. It should be used with caution.

Lesson 5. Working Together

Take the students to a smooth floor surface. Give each pair of students a large piece of material to work on (double bed sheets are ideal).

Choose a partner. Both of you must stay completely on the sheet and must move from one side of the room to the other.

Choose a third student to join you on your sheet. All three of you must stay completely on the sheet and move from one side of the room to the other.

Have a contest with another group. See which can move in the most unusual way. Which can move fastest?

Have elimination races. Which group is the best team?

Increase the group to four and do the same.

Increase the group size until it gets too difficult to move in a determined direction.

Discuss what happens when you work in a group. What makes a group work? What do you do to make it work? How do you feel when you get the job done? What happens when your group doesn't work? What do you do when it doesn't work? How do you feel when your group is stuck, when it can't move in any direction? How is our classroom like the big group on the sheet? When in the classroom do you work well? When do you get stuck in the classroom?

Variation

Place two students on one sheet and tell them to move in opposite directions. Give them time to work out their conflict. (One solution is that they go first to one end and then the other.)

Lesson 6. "I've Got It and I Want to Give It to You"

Form a circle of ten to twelve people.

One student begins by saying "I've got it and I want to give it to . . ." (names a specific person). The first student then holds his or her hands as if holding something, goes to the named person, and hands it to him or her. The next student does the same thing, passing "it" from person to person.

Encourage the students to act out the properties of "it" without giving it a label.

Ask questions along the way, especially the first time through the game. For example: Is it heavy or light, big or small? Will it get away if you let go of it?

Lesson 7. Passing Invisible Objects

Sit in a circle. One student passes an invisible, unidentified object to the person next to him or her. Each one in turn passes "it" until "it" has gone all the way around the circle.

GAME 1. Hold your hands as if you had something in them. Pass the "object" to the person next to you, being sure you really give it away and the person really takes it. Be sure you pass the same object you received.

GAME 2. Begin passing an "object" as in game 1. When I say "change," the person who has the object is to change it in some way before passing it on. You can change its weight, its size, its temperature, or anything else you think of. Keep the object the same until I say "change" again. Change it several times around the circle.

GAME 3. You can say "change" when you pass the object to the next person or you can say nothing if you want it to stay the same.

GAME 4. Each one of you change the object when you take it so that each of you passes something different from the object you received. (Once while doing this game a mischievous fifth-grade boy "ate" the object as soon as he received it. The girl who passed it to him looked horrified and exclaimed, "How could you eat that? It was a leaf with a slug on it!")

GAME 5. Take the object passed to you. Decide if you want it or not. If you do, keep it and pass something else. If you don't want what you got, change it and pass that on.

If you have difficulty keeping the object in the group, you have an excellent opportunity to explore what happens to a game when someone refuses to play, what happens to a group when someone refuses to cooperate—how you feel about that person, what that person feels when he does that, and so on.

Lesson 8. I Can Make Contact

Sit in small groups.

Each person look at every other person in the group and think about how you can make contact with that person. Then, one at a time, each student in the group make a direct verbal statement to each of the others in the group, beginning each statement with "I can make contact with you by . . ." "Robert, I can make contact with you by playing football with you." "Sharon, I can make contact with you by smiling when you look at me." "Brad, I can make contact with you by hitting you."

As the teacher, it is important that you do not place value judgments on the statements, particularly if they are negative. Some students are limited to negative means of contact. If this is so, it is important that the student himself or herself, becomes aware of it. Until he or she is aware of it, nothing can be done about it.

Variation

I CAN AVOID CONTACT

Exactly the same as "I Can Make Contact," except that the direct statement is "I can *avoid* contact with you by . . ."

Some of the statements may be identical. "I can make contact with you by smiling at you" and "I can avoid making contact with you by smiling at you" may both be true statements, even addressed to the same person.

The purpose of these two exercises is for students to become aware of what they are doing when they make contact, and what they are doing when they are not making contact. Smiling may look the same in both cases but it does not feel the same. Confusion and mistrust of others occur when this distinction is not clear.

Lesson 9. I Seem to Be . . . but . . .

Complete this sentence. "I seem to be . . . but . . ." (Examples: "I seem to be bored, but I'm only waiting." "I seem to be real cool, but I'm only in a cold sweat." "I seem to be letting you have your own way, but underneath I'll never give in.")

Variation

Make statements about each other completing this sentence. "You seem to be . . . but . . ." "You seem to be rough but I know you to be soft too." "You seem to have lots of friends, but you can be lonely too." "You seem to know it all, but you still make mistakes." "You seem to be shy, but you are friendly."

Lesson 10. I See and
I Imagine

Sit in pairs or small groups. One at a time, look at a person and say something you see and then add what it is you imagine because of what you see. "I see you turning red. I imagine you are embarrassed." "I see you smiling. I imagine you are trying to reassure me."

Be sure that the statements that begin with "I see . . ." are actual observations. It may be necessary to restate some sentences. "I see you are nervous" should be changed to exactly what it is that is seen to cause the observer to imagine nervousness—"I see you wiggling around in your chair" or "I see you looking away from me," or whatever it is that can actually be seen. Then, "I imagine you are nervous."

Lesson 11. Giving of Gifts

Sit so that you can see each other. Today you are going to give gifts to each other. Pretend that you have the whole wide world available. The gift can be a real thing or an imaginary one. Look at each person here and see what it is you would like to give him or her. You may want to give something to everyone, or you may find you want to give to only a few. When you have decided what your gift will be, and whom you want to give it to, walk over to that person and tell him or her, one at a time. Begin each statement with the name of the person you are giving the gift to.
"George, I give you a big chocolate cake."
"Susie, I give you a kitten all your own."
"Bob, I give you a little green man to pick up after you wherever you go."
Discuss what you discovered while doing this lesson. How did you feel when giving a gift? How did you feel when receiving one? Which gifts did you like? Which ones would you rather not have? How did you deliver your gifts? Did you rush up, drop a gift off, and rush back, or did you do something else? Was it different for different people?

These questions are only suggestions, for when you involve your class in this game the kinds of questions you ask will be those that you feel should be brought to the awareness of the group. In a discussion of what happened, beware of judging it as good or bad. The purpose here is to deepen the students' awareness of themselves and others, not to place a value judgment on their activities.

It is important in this exercise that students use the name of the recipient of the gift and that they own the giving by saying "I give." If you hear the phrase "Here is . . ." have the student restate it.

Variation

Have small pieces of paper available on which the student either writes or draws the gift. When the person says, "_____, I give you _____," he or she hands the appropriate piece of paper to the receiver.

Aggression

"Teacher! Tell Susie to stop bothering me. She keeps pulling on my paper while I'm trying to work." The teacher looks up to see Tim grab a pencil from Bob and race around the room with it. Billy reaches over and socks the boy who sits next to him. When it's time for the class to go to recess, there are quarrels about who gets to take the ball out, with the strongest one imposing his or her will on the others. There is pushing and shoving to see who can be first in line. Eventually there are students in tears.

That scene is quite familiar to most teachers. Healthy, normal students are often aggressive. Aggression is not necessarily a negative force in the development of a thinking, caring, responsible person. Without it we would never question answers, never seek new ways to express life, never stand up for ourselves. Given rational objects, aggression is healthy. It provides us with initiative, drive, and energy to set out on a task and accomplish it. It is only when this energy is thwarted and directed toward destruction of self or others that neurotic derivations of aggression develop.

If students exhibit acts of aggression or become aggressive while in the classroom they are typically forced to suppress their aggression. Often they then divert that energy inward, using it to tear themselves down. This only adds to their feelings of frustration, impotence, and inadequacy.

This unit attempts to deal with aggressive attitudes and acts by giving the students acceptable releases for their aggression and by emphasizing rational, healthy forms of aggression rather than irrational and neurotic forms. These lessons help the students to become aware of their aggression and to gain control over what they do with it. Until they can become aware of what their aggressive impulses are and learn to put them to constructive uses, these impulses are certain to be misused.

Obviously students should not be given complete freedom to express their anger. The expression of aggression must be controlled in order to protect the students. The object of these lessons is to teach the students to feel their aggression, to be fully aware of it. How to express it is also taught within the context of reality. This here and now, this time and place, will necessarily temper how aggression can be expressed.

Suppose, for example, that a student becomes aware of a need to feel powerful through aggressive acts. Once it is recognized that power is being sought, the student can begin to experiment with acceptable ways to feel power. For example, power can be experienced by sawing a board in half rather than by punching someone in the nose. The development of this awareness will necessarily require a testing, a trial-and-error period. Even if trials are successful, aggression will still be aggression, but it will have been put to useful tasks and will not have been destructive to the student or others. It will have been expended as the situation demanded and allowed, and so it will not need to accumulate into an explosive volcano.

A teacher who cares about the total student will make a time and a place for aggression in the classroom. It does exist, and it does serve a purpose for the student who is using it. A student must have opportunities to become aware of all of his or her emotions. Dealing with aggression in the classroom gives students other ways of facing themselves honestly and openly. If they learn to identify and to accept their aggressive attitudes and acts, they can be in control of them. They can learn to use them for their growth and development, not just as forces for self—and other—destruction.

Objectives

To take part in a discussion of negative feelings and how they
   have effects on living with others.

To be able to experience anger where and when it occurs.

To know when and where anger can be expressed, and to express
   it at appropriate times and places.

To be able to describe negative feelings that emerge while playing games.

To be able to remain stable in the midst of stress and strain.

To develop a safe way to take on another student and engage in
   physical contact with him or her.

Lesson 1. Pushy Behavior

Each of you write a direction for what you consider to be a
"pushy" behavior on a sheet of paper. Write it so that someone
else can act it out. Examples: "Act tough. Show off. Be childishly
rude. Do something outrageous." Place your pushy behavior in a
box and draw out another one. Role-play it. Let the class guess
what role you are playing.

What pushy behavior do you see occurring in this room?
What do you see that makes you call it pushy? What is your favorite way of being pushy? Do you have a favorite way to be
pushed? Make a list of all the ways you are pushed about during
the day. Make a list of all the ways you push others during the
day.

Lesson 2. Pushing

Choose a partner. Face each other about two feet apart.
Raise your hands to shoulder level.
Reach out and place your palms on your partner's palms.
Keep your hands at shoulder level and push against each other's
hands. Push as hard as you can. See if you can push your partner
back.

Variations

Choose a partner and demand whatever you want from that person without thinking about what he or she may feel or want.
Change roles. Talk about how pushy the demands were and how
you felt about them.

Choose another partner. Repeat as before.

Now look around and find someone who really bothers you.
Push that person. See if you can push him or her back. Be sure
you stand face-to-face and begin with your palms together at
shoulder level.

What did you discover? Whom did you enjoy pushing? How
far did you want to push your partner? Were you strong or were
you a pushover?

Have the students stand with their right sides against their partners'
right sides. Push with the right sides together. Then push with left sides together. Discuss any differences discovered.

Have the students stand back-to-back and push with their shoulders. Have them stand back-to-back, bend over, and push with their buttocks. Have them experiment with other ways of pushing.

This lesson can be introduced in Physical Education or during a play period. However, it is hoped that once the students know what to do they will be allowed to use it often. For that to happen you must define safe limits. The limits will necessarily depend upon safety precautions appropriate to the area. When playing outside in an open or grassy area, for example, the limits might be between first base and home plate on a baseball diamond. In the classroom, only one pair of partners can push at a time in an aisle between rows of desks, and they can push only the length of the row.

This lesson is very effective with a class that pushes and shoves at every chance. By allowing a time and a place for the behavior, you can get a lot of it out in the open to be dealt with honestly, or to be over and done with. You might find it beneficial to allow the students opportunities to do this activity several times a day. Even a young person can offer tremendous resistance in this stance. You should join in this game too. There may be several students who would relish the chance to take on the teacher.

Lesson 3. Pulling

Sit in a double circle facing a partner. Join hands and lean back, pulling against your partner, but keeping in balance. How far back can you lean?

Stand on your knees. Lean back, still holding hands, keeping in balance. What do you have to do to keep from falling?

Stand up. Put your feet together close to your partner's feet. Hold hands and slowly lean back. How far can you let yourself go and still keep balanced?

Change partners. Repeat this sequence several times with different partners.

How well did your partners work with you? How well did you work with your partners? Did you have any difficulty working with anyone? If so, what made it difficult? What did you do about it?

Each student should have some success with this even if it is only at a sitting level. If you find a student who consistently pulls his or her partner over and if the partner complains about it, try to make the student aware of what pulling a partner over does for him or her. (For example, it proves one is strong, makes one fail early in the game on purpose so he or she doesn't have to fear failure while really trying, lets one's partner know that he or she does not want to work, demands control of one's partner, etc.)

This is also a good lesson for teacher involvement. Try to maintain a standing balance with a student you enjoy. Now try it with a student who irritates you. Do you feel any difference?

Lesson 4. Silent Scream

Close your eyes and imagine that you are going to some quiet, comfortable place by yourself.

Think of something that bothers you. Imagine that no one is near you, no one for miles around. Continue to think of the thing that bothers you. Let it bother you more. More. More.

Now, silently scream. Open your mouth and scream silently as loud as you can. You are alone, no one will hear you.

Now scream as loud as you can out loud. Loud. Louder.

Now think of the thing that bothers you again. See if you can imagine doing at least one thing about it that would stop it from bothering you. Imagine doing something real and possible to lessen the force of what bothers you or to stop it.

When you are ready, open your eyes. Discuss what happened.

Lesson 5. Living with Others

Sit in a circle. Close your eyes.

Imagine that you are talking to someone in your family, someone who has made you angry. Tell that person how he or she made you angry. You are doing this in your imagination so no one can hear you. Make your statements explicit. "I get mad when you tear my books." "I get angry when you leave a mess for me to clean up."

Now tell the imagined person what you like about him or her. Make your statements explicit. "I like you when you read to me." "I like you when you clean the bathroom after you use it."

Who in this room makes you angry? Again, in your imagination tell that person how he makes you angry.

Now in your imagination tell that person what you like about him or her.

Open your eyes and look around. Look at each one of us here. Share anything you wish to share.

If a student makes a negative comment about someone at home or at school, have the student go on to state something he or she likes about that person as well. Help the student keep the comments very specific, avoiding "it," "they," "he," and "she." Get the student to take responsibility for his or her anger. Change "It makes me mad . . ." to "I get mad . . ." Using "it" projects one's anger outward to some unidentified thing. By using "I," one can internalize one's anger and begin to integrate it with the rest of one's self. By using specific language, one will come to realize that one does not need to dislike the whole person but can dislike only certain parts of that person. In that way one's anger need not be overwhelming to oneself or others.

Lesson 6. You Should

Choose a partner, preferably someone you "boss around."

Partners take turns playing the following roles with each other.

Role A: "You should . . ." (Keep telling B all he should be and do.)

Role B replies: "You are right. I am so dumb I don't even know how to do that." (B finds many ways to agree with A.)

Change roles.

How did you feel when you were playing Role A? How did you feel playing Role B? Which role did you like better? Are there times when you really play one of those roles? If so, when and with whom? Are there times when you see people around you playing those roles? Who plays them? When do they play them? How and when might these roles be harmful to you? How and when might these roles be useful?

With primary students, have A be a parent and B a child.

Lesson 7. Let Off Steam

Sit in a circle.

Each one of you is to tell the others in the group what's bothering you. Direct your comments personally. "Laurie, you bug me when you chew your gum and snap it with your mouth open. Robert, I could kick you when you walk by my desk and knock my things off. Irene, you make me mad when you sit next to me and act silly."

Do not defend yourself when others address you. Just listen to what others have to say to you. You will have your turn to let off steam too.

Now, think about the things that were said to you. Sometimes you can change the things about yourself that bother others. Sometimes you cannot. Were some things said to you that you can and are willing to change? If so, state it to the person who said it to you. "I will try not to snap my gum when I am with you. If I forget, let me know before I start to bother you," says Laurie to the one who addressed her.

This is an excellent lesson when you sense that there is a great deal of nondirected bickering and arguing going on in the group. Having the opportunity to get everything out in the open allows students to air their resentments and to see what demands are being made of them and which of those they can attend to.

Variation

Have a "Mutter Time." Each student in the group sits in a circle and mutters about all the things that are bothering him or her. Nothing good can be said about anyone during that time. (Allow ten minutes.)

How do you feel when you are muttering? How do you feel when you know everyone else is muttering too? How do you feel after "Mutter Time" is over? Did you stop muttering?

Lesson 8. Gang Aggression

Divide the class into groups of eight to ten. In dividing the groups try to have aggressive students equally distributed.

Take time with your group to learn to operate as a single unit. Link yourselves together physically in some way. You can hold hands, link arms or fingers, but find some way to be together.

Develop a sound that belongs to your group. You can hum, grunt, moan, do anything you want to make a sound together. Now find a way to move together. Stay away from the other groups. Remain with your group long enough to really move and make a noise as one unit.

Now move out and encounter the other groups in the room staying in your group and making your sound. Be aware of what happens to you and your group.

Move back to your own group's space. Talk about what happened. Do you behave differently when you have the support of the group? How are you different in a group? How are you the same?

Now imagine this group (*indicate one*) has "it." All the other groups want "it." (*"It" is not defined or identified in the game.*) Experiment with how you and your group can get "it."

Allow time for a discussion of what happened with the game before leaving it. Depending on the group, you might explore situations that are real outside the realm of the game. What happens when two people gang up on one? What happens when one gang of people challenges another gang? What happens when one group outnumbers the other group? What feelings do you experience when you're in a big group (classrooms) that you don't feel in a small group (peer group)? When do we engage in ritualistic aggression (competitive games)? What does ritualistic aggression do for us? What happens in some .riots? How come the police don't simply shoot all the demonstrators? How come the demonstrators don't shoot all the policemen?

Variation

Indicate that one group has "it" and wants to give "it" to the others. Allow time to experiment with giving "it" to the others.

Is it easier to give or to receive? How do you feel giving, how do you feel receiving?

Lesson 9. Make Me

This is a lesson designed to help clarify the roles of responsibility within a classroom. If you have a drained, heavy feeling after being with the class for just an hour and feel as if you have been trying to push a huge boulder up a steep hill, try playing a game of "Make Me."

Ask, "What do I make you do?" List all the responses from the class on the blackboard so that everyone can see the list. Do not judge the responses or start justifying your behavior. Just receive all they have to say. Once the list is complete, and it may be enormous, sit with and be in the group and just look at the list.

For a while, nothing may seem to be happening. Wait. This is what could happen. One boy, Jeff, begins to chuckle. Others join in. Soon most of the group is laughing and shaking their heads. With such a list in front of them, everyone sees how absurd it is to expect one person to make them do all those things. Jeff then goes to the blackboard, takes the eraser, and says, "I said you make me do this but I can really do it for myself, so I'll take it off." He then erases his own statement and returns to his seat. Another student follows his example. In each case the student says, "I can take this." At the end there are still some things on the board. We then talk together about how we can help the student who still feels there are certain things he or she has to be "made" to do. Each of us then offers what we feel we can realistically do to help out in those situations. One girl leaves her statement "You make me do spelling." One student offers to give her advance notice that it is going to be time to work on spelling so she can be prepared. The boy who sits next to her says he will get the materials needed for both of them, and then continues by saying, "You'll just have to do the rest yourself!"

See if you and your class can invent or create your own game of "Make Me."

Lesson 10. Boys and Girls

All the boys in the class write, "Girls are . . ." and finish that sentence in a few words, with many sentences, or with a paragraph. Do not put any names on the paper.

All the girls in the class write, "Boys are . . ." and finish that sentence in a few words, with many sentences, or with a paragraph. Do not put any names on the paper.

When all are finished, have a boy collect the girls' papers. Have a girl collect the boys' papers. The boy reads aloud all the papers written by boys about girls. The girl reads aloud all the papers written by girls about boys. Allow time for discussion. Discuss male and female roles. How do we get them? How and when do they create problems? How do they offer solutions? What happens if we try on different roles? What would happen if you played the "wrong" role? How do you decide if a person is playing a "wrong" role?

Lesson 11. A Funny Story

Think of something funny. It can be something you said to someone, something that was said to you, or something funny that you did. It must be something funny that happened to you and not something that happened to someone else. Share your funny story with a friend as if it were happening now.

How many of you shared a story in which someone got hurt? (It could be someone that got hurt physically or got their feelings hurt.)

When do you use humor to hurt someone? When has someone used humor to hurt you? Is it possible to hide a cruel statement in a joke? How? How else do people get hurt with humor? Instead of hiding your anger in humor, how else might you express it?

Be aware of the times you experience humor during the day. Be aware of when you use it to hide anger. Be aware of when others use it to hide their anger.

With advanced students, you might want to discuss various categories of humor, such as farce, satire, slapstick, and irony.

Lesson 12. I Can't at School

Think of something in school you would like to change. State all the reasons you can't change it.

Now restate those sentences beginning with "I won't" instead of "I can't."

How many excuses did you discover? How many real barriers did you discover? (There *are* real barriers. Do not imply or let the student believe that anything can be changed simply by restating the problem.)

Lesson 13. I Can't at Home

Think of something in your life you would like to change.

State all the reasons you can't change it.

Now restate those sentences beginning with "I won't" instead of "I can't." Really listen to yourself as you say it this time.

Examples: I would like to make a new blouse. I can't because I don't have time. I can't because I do not have the materials. I can't because my mother won't help me.

Change to: I would like to make a new blouse. I won't because I don't have time. I won't because I do not have the materials. I won't because my mother won't help me.

Do you feel any difference? Which statements were really true statements? Which were merely statements of excuses?

Lesson 14. Frustrating Games

"THE KILLER" GAME

Pass out playing cards or numbered slips of paper equal to the number of people in the group. One student is identified as "the Killer" by a specific card (the ace of spades) or slip (number 3), determined beforehand. The Killer kills off people by winking at them. The object is for the Killer to eliminate as many people as possible without being identified. A person who is "killed" must wait a few seconds and then fall over dead. He or she is then out of the game. Anyone who is alive and suspects the identity of the killer can "accuse," but only after actually seeing the killer wink at someone. A false accusation eliminates the accuser.

If the group is larger than ten, have more than one game going at a time, have more than one Killer, or have the players mill around. When a player is "killed," he or she sits down. It adds to the excitement of the game if you play it in a dim light.

Discuss what happened with the game.
How did you feel when you were the Killer?
How did you feel when you knew a wink could "kill" you?
How did you feel about protecting the identity of the Killer after he or she killed you?

BLACK MAGIC

A and B both know the "magic" in "Black Magic."

B leaves the room while A and the rest of the group decide upon an object to be "it."

B returns to the room, and A asks him, "Is it . . . (names a specific object)?" B knows that A will at some time ask about a black object, and the next object named will be "it."

Example: B leaves the room. A and the group choose the teacher's desk to be "it." B is asked to return to the room.

A asks, "Is it the round table?" B replies, "No."

A goes on. "Is it that piece of chalk?" B says, "No."

"Is it the big hand of the clock?" (The big hand of the clock is black.) B replies, "No."

"Is it the teacher's desk?" B replies, "Yes."

When someone else in the group figures out the "magic," that person leaves the room. The group again decides upon an item. The person then comes back to demonstrate a knowledge of the magic. If successful, the person will have "Black Magic." If one has not correctly discerned the "magic," one simply rejoins the group and continues to figure out what makes "Black Magic."

How did you feel when you didn't know the magic? How did you feel when you finally discovered it? How did you feel about knowing it and not telling your friends?

GESTALT GAME

Materials: An assortment of pencils.

A and B know how to play the game.

A carefully and elaborately arranges all the pencils into some form. A then says, "Look at the whole thing and tell me the number I am making." B then tells what number it is.

A makes quite a fuss about arranging the pencils "just so." A also subtly but openly indicates the number the arrangement "represents" by placing his or her fingers on the table or floor so that B can read them. B tells the answer from A's fingers, not from what A has done with the pencils.

When someone in the group figures out what is happening, he or she calls out the numbers until someone else catches on.

How did you learn the game? How did you feel when you discovered the answer? How did you feel about those who still could not figure it out?

The answers to this game were easy once you knew how to get them. What other things do you know about that were easy once you knew how?

The next time you tell someone "it's easy," see if you should add, "once you know how." The next time someone tells you something is easy, see if they are leaving out "once you know how."

UNIT EIGHT

Nature

An important aspect of self-realization is the establishment of identity or unity with nature. Much of humankind's highest enjoyment is found in his experiences with and appreciation of the beauty of nature. Recently, we have begun to realize that an irresponsible disregard for nature, the depletion of natural resources, and the obliteration of natural beauty may result in the destruction of most, if not all, life on earth. Our relationship with nature now demands our attention. With the awareness that the natural world is shrinking and may be destroyed, a growing number of people are seeking ways of ensuring its preservation.

Increasing emphasis in education is being placed on developing this awareness and concern. It is recognized that transmission of facts alone will not solve the problems of our environment and ecology. Living in harmony with nature must become a personal value and objective of each individual. One's educational experiences should enable one to discover or rediscover one's place in nature and bring the realization that any separation is probably artificial and possibly destructive.

Unfortunately, it is very difficult to bring an identity with nature into the average classroom setting with any degree of reality. Older schools have been encroached upon by the ever widening cities. Newer schools are made of synthetic materials, on land that has been scraped bare by bulldozers. At both, what landscaping there is has been artificially constructed. There are few schools designed around natural settings, and in those that are, the settings are usually used in traditional ways: Students learn in the classroom, walk in the halls, play on the blacktop.

In such environments it is difficult for students to experience nature in ways that matter to them. They have no ways to develop values for living in harmony with nature when they live in an environment that locks it out. However, confluent education, in which discovering one's identity is a primary goal, affords some opportunities for dealing with nature in a real way in the classroom. The student who is engaged in self-assessment must assess the environment as well and must receive assessments from others in the environment.

Look for natural environments that are still available. (At the very least, films of nature are available for classroom use.) The students can make terrariums and observe the environment in them. Go on a field trip to a park and encourage students to experience it in a new way—blind-folded and/or barefoot, or imagine that it is vanishing. How would life be without plants, trees, and parks? Introduce the students to a tree or a patch of grass. Let students "become" that tree or patch of grass. Let them develop the roles as they go along. Let them move into it in their own ways, in as many different ways as possible—dance it, paint it, write a story entitled "I am a tree."

In any environment, urban or rural, and in any section of the country, students can become aware of how they respond to the weather around them. How do you usually feel on windy days? How do you act out those feelings? How do you feel on foggy or rainy days? How do you act out those feelings? How do you experience the colors around you in the morning hours as compared to noontime or dusk? Which time of the day feels best to you? What do you like about it? Give the students many opportunities to talk about nature and their experiences with it. The kinds of questions they ask and the things they discover on their own can change their experiences from "fun and games" to very meaningful affective-cognitive experiences.

The following lessons provide the student with opportunities to experience more, do more, discover more. They also deemphasize words as a way of knowing and stress various parts of the body. These lessons help the student to express and amplify the power that is within. It is in the vastness of nature that some of this power can be tapped. The student can learn to "tune in," to use his or her total being as a way of knowing. Many of the lessons require the student to be outdoors so that he or she can experience more of the environment than the limits of the classroom. To be outdoors provides more contact with nature and natural things and allows the student a oneness with nature that can lead to a more integrated, more aware self.

Be sure to read through these lessons to see how they apply to the particular setting of your school. Some can be done in any school anywhere. Others may have to be adapted. Still others may have to be omitted. See if they can serve to spark your imagination. For example, students in Santa Barbara, California, would rarely have an opportunity to make trails in the snow for others to follow. But they could do a similar activity by making trails in the sand at the beach while on a field trip.

Objectives

To be able to identify familiar sounds in the environment through listening.

To be able to utilize characteristics of a day for a learning experience.

To distinguish between human-made and natural changes.

To use listening as a way of knowing.

To be able to use one's entire body as a way of knowing.

Lesson 1. Sound Simile

Discuss the "sounds of nature." Talk about rain, wind, thunder, birds, water, leaves, etc.

Complete the sentence, "When I hear _____, I think of _____." Use a sound of nature in the first blank.

Lesson 2. A Sound Walk

Divide a piece of paper in half. On one side write "Human-Made Sounds," and on the other side write "Natural Sounds." Go for a walk on the school grounds for about fifteen minutes. Listen to the sounds around you. As you hear them, write them on your paper under "Human-Made Sounds" or "Natural Sounds."

Compare your list with someone else's list. What did both of you hear? What did you hear that the other one didn't hear? Were there any sounds that you heard that were difficult for you to decide which category they belonged in? If so, what?

The amount of time you allow for the sound walk will depend on the interest level of the students and the time you have available. It is important to allow enough time so that the students will have an opportunity to listen for quiet, subtle sounds as well as louder ones.

Variation

Go for a fifteen-minute walk on the school grounds. Come back
to the room and make a list of the sounds you heard. Go for another fifteen-minute walk. Make a list again, accounting for the
differences. (Example: I listened more. It was noisier. I went to
different places, I remembered more of what I heard.)

Lesson 3. A Feeling Walk

Go for a fifteen-minute walk on the school grounds, touching and
feeling everything possible along the way.
     Talk about the things you felt. What did you like to feel?
What didn't you like to feel? What was there about it that you
didn't like?

A familiar schoolground is an excellent place to do this. The student is
used to seeing all of the items there but will come to "see" them in a very
different way while on the feeling walk.

Lesson 4. Total Sense Walk

Go for a walk around a familiar area or somewhere new or special. For three minutes concentrate on the sounds around you. For
three minutes be aware of the smells around you. For three minutes touch everything you can in your environment. In the next
three minutes see everything around you as if for the first time.
Now sit down and close your eyes. Spend the next three minutes
on taste. Put something in your mouth—a leaf, a piece of grass.
Complete your walk, keeping sense activity in the foreground.
Allow yourself to experience whatever presents itself. See if you
can let sensations fuse and blend into a total experience.

Don't be concerned with exact timing. If students spend the entire
time on one or two senses, let them be. They can do the others at another
time.

Lesson 5. Acting Out Nature

This is a type of "class participation story" described earlier.
Choose an occurrence in nature that can be acted out by students.

There should be many parts for them to choose from. The one described here can be used after seeing a movie or reading a book describing seed dispersal. The parts are seeds, animals, wind, sun, water, and soil. Have each student choose a part to play before the story begins.

You are all seeds in a pod. (Just the seeds act out this part.) It is a tight pod. You cannot move. (Add details appropriate to the class needs.)

Next the water comes. (The students who are water come and water the pods.) Some pods grow larger. Some do not get enough water, and so do not begin to grow.

The water goes away. The sun comes out to warm the seed pods. The pods break open. The pods are now many seeds.

The wind comes and tumbles and rolls the seeds in all directions.

The animals come and run around in the seeds. Some seeds get stuck in the animals' fur and some of the animals take the seeds for food.

Now all the seeds find a place to settle. Stay there, since seeds cannot move on their own.

The wind blows soil over some of the seeds.

The water comes and washes soil over some of the seeds.

The sun comes out to make the soil warm so that the seeds begin to grow.

The water comes to give the seeds moisture to help them grow into a plant.

The wind comes and gently blows the plant.

Animals run and play in and around the plant.

Soon the plant begins to grow new seed pods. These pods fall to the ground and the whole story begins all over again.

The themes on acting out nature are limited only by your own imagination and ability to transpose written or seen material into stories that can be acted out.

Some other suggested themes:

A storm and its effects on the rivers, animals, homes, and people.

Changes of weather, from sun to rain.

The cycle of a drop of water.

The life cycle of any plant or animal.

A food chain, either in the ocean or on the land.

An advanced class took the basic idea of this lesson and developed a play at the end of a health unit on the digestive system. They had their own narrator. The teacher was just an observer. The class "became" the digestive system, with students taking the various parts of the system.

They gave each part a voice and an action, based on their own knowledge and awareness of the part.

Be sure you allow adequate space for these activities. It may be necessary to push all furniture out of the way or go to a multipurpose room or, even better, go outside.

The lesson described above might be followed by these questions:

How did you feel when you were in the seed pod at the beginning? (Let "pods" answer.)

How did the water help the pods? What might happen if too much water falls at one time? What might happen to seeds if there isn't enough rain?

How did the wind help the seeds? Could it be harmful too? How?

What did the animals do with the seed pods? What might happen if the animals didn't take some seeds? (Animals died. Plants died because of lack of space, resources.)

How did you feel when you were a growing plant? Did you like the sun, wind, and water? What did you like about them? What did you not like about them? When did they help? When did they cause harm?

How did you feel about growing more seeds? Why did you grow so many of them? What might happen if you grew only two or three seeds? What would happen to animals who need to eat the seeds? (Let animals answer.)

If you were to do this over again, what part would you like to play?

Although you would not necessarily use all of these questions, it is important to allow the students to express the feelings evoked by playing the various parts. This is also an excellent opportunity for discussing negative feelings and provides experiences in answering "what if" or "what might happen" questions.

Lesson 6. Changes

Set out at least three items that will begin to change. Examples: A dish containing metal objects and water. A pot of dirt with seeds buried in it. A goldfish in a bowl. A dish containing an egg with no shell.

Look at each of these items. What do you see? Draw or write a description of each one. Compare your description with someone else's to be sure you did not leave anything out.

(Wait three days.) Look carefully at each item again. What

do you see? Compare what you see now with what you saw three days ago. What things have changed? Are there other things in our room that have changed in the last three days? What other changes do you know about that have occurred in the last three days?

Which items seem not to have changed at all? What in our room is the same today as it was three days ago? What other things do you know that have stayed the same over the last three days?

When do you like things to change quickly? How do you think you would feel if every day everything were changed in this room? What if you had different places to sit, different books to read, a different teacher, different students to be with you?

When do you like things to change slowly? How do you think you would feel if nothing ever changed in here? What if you had the same places to sit all the time, the same books all the time, the same teacher all the time, the same students with you all the time?

Be aware of the changes around you during the day. Be aware of the times you feel there is too much change, occurring too quickly, and the times you feel there is not enough change, or it's occurring too slowly to satisfy you.

Variation

If possible, bring a picture of your school that was taken some years ago.

Discuss all the changes around the school since the picture was taken. Visit some place that has changed. For example, walk through a tract of homes where an orchard once stood. Look for remains of the orchard.

Imagine changes around the school that will occur in the future. What might a picture of the school look like if it were taken twenty years from now?

Lesson 7. Natural Collage

Go for a walk around the school and find one natural thing that in some way symbolizes you. You might choose a rock to symbolize your strength. You might choose a leaf to symbolize your love of being with a large group of people. You might choose a weed to symbolize your rebellious self. Let your imagination go.

Look at many things. Try them on. How does a rock fit me? What part of me fits a rock? You can choose the same item as someone else, for entirely different reasons.

Bring the item that fits you best back to the classroom. Each one in the class is to put the item into a collage. Discover where you want to put your item in relation to the total collage, in relation to where others have put their items. Experiment with several different placements before leaving it there.

Now talk about yourself as your item in relation to where you are in the collage. Talk in the present tense and use "I." Example: "I am an orange flower. I am soft and tender. I am on the very edge of the collage. I am there so I will not get bruised or broken by the rocks and sticks." "I am a weed. I am long and rangy. I am in the center of the collage. I will eventually spread out and completely cover the collage."

Lesson 8. Rainy-Day Activities

Take any day that has an accentuated weather feature and look for some way to take advantage of it. Usually teachers face rainy, hot, or windy days with something akin to dread. See if there is something special you can do with the students because of the weather. Here are some starters.

Sprinkle different colors of powered tempera on a piece of paper. Place it in the rain where it can be observed. Watch the rain paint a picture. Bring it in when you feel it is finished.

Concentrate on the sound of rain for a set period of time. Graph it, draw it, dance it.

Read "Chapter IX, in which Piglet is entirely surrounded by water," from *Winnie the Pooh,* by A. A. Milne.

Place a stick upright in a puddle. Observe it several times during the day. Watch the water rise or fall.

Watch a puddle grow. Measure around it with a piece of string. Measure it every fifteen minutes. Compare the length of string each time. (Each time a different student bundles up and "braves the storm" in order to measure it.)

When the rain stops, but while water is still running, have a contest floating paper boats down street gutters, rain drains, free-form ditches. Time the paper boats. Measure the distance they travel. Compute the speed at which they travel.

Watch raindrops sliding down the windowpanes. Time them with a stopwatch. Graph them. Imagine you are a raindrop. Write a story about your journey. Begin with "I am a raindrop."

Learn to read weather maps. Where else is it raining? What might students be doing there?

Learn to read rain tables. Make your own and keep it up to date. Compare it with last year's data (available in local newspapers in your nearby library). Make predictions for next year.

Write words that describe the sound of rain. Write words that describe how you feel about rain. Use as many of those words as possible to make a poem or story about rain.

Work in groups to make a list of things that go up in the rain (e.g., rivers, umbrellas, earthworms, etc.). Be as creative as possible. Explain your list to another group.

Work in groups to make a list of things that go down in the rain (hairdos, flags, hillsides, etc.). Be as creative as possible. Explain your list to another group.

Lesson 9. Snowy-Day Activities

Go outside and catch a snowflake in your mouth, on your eyelid, on your elbow, on your knee. Talk about how it felt to you and what happened to it.

When it is not snowing, but snow is on the ground, one student is to go out and make a snow trail. Another student is to find the trail and go on it. Pretend you are the person who made the trail. How do you feel when walking in those footsteps? What might it be like to be that person?

Make snowmen, snow women, and snow sculptures.

Have a relay race getting dressed and undressed in snow togs from head to foot.

Imagine you get snowed in here at school. What then? Where could you sleep? What could you eat? How would you manage? What would you like about getting snowed in? What wouldn't you like?

Go for a walk in the snow. If a park or a woods is nearby look for animal tracks and other signs of life. In a city, observe traffic patterns in the snow. What patterns do cars make? What patterns do people make? Can you see other kinds of patterns in the snow? What do you imagine from what you see?

Go sledding. Use inner tubes, plastic disks, sleds. Measure distance, compare results.

Choose a certain thing, tree, a fence, or a building, that you can observe from the classroom. Record, in pictures or writing, how it responds to the snow, how it changes in appearance.

Build a snow fort. Engage another class in a snowball fight.

Lesson 10. Cold-Day Activities

Put out a pan of water and see if it will freeze. How long will it take? Make predictions. Who came closest?

Be aware of feeling cold on various parts of your body. How do your hands feel cold? How do your feet feel cold? Your nose? Your cheeks? How do they feel when they change from cold to warm?

How do you feel when you are bundled up for the cold? How do you move? What don't you like about being bundled up? What do you like?

Bake bread in the class. Watch the changes, enjoy the smells, savor the taste. (You can make it from scratch, or bring in frozen dough ready to defrost, rise, and bake.)

Draw pictures on frosty windows. Watch them change.

Discuss "How cold is cold?" Look at temperatures in other places, particularly cold places. Would someone at the North Pole think our temperature is cold?

Go outside and send smoke signals to one another with your breath. Did you send a message? Did you receive a message? How well can you communicate with smoke signals?

Pop popcorn. Eat it while it's hot.

Make sugar cookies in the shape of your initials.

Make a class stew. Everyone bring something to make the stew.

Lesson 11. Hot-Day Activities

Bob for apples. Feel the cool water on your face, in your hair. Do not wipe the water off, but let it evaporate. Be aware of your face and how it feels.

Go out in the sun and engage in a vigorous activity. Play a game, have a relay race, or run a lap. Come into the classroom. Turn off the lights. Sit or lie down. Read a story, listen to a record, or play a quiet game. Be aware of your body as it adjusts to a cooler temperature and a quiet activity.

Record the temperature every thirty minutes. Write one word that describes how you feel at that temperature. Make a graph to show the temperatures. Make a graph to show your feelings.

Think "cool." Go to the coolest place in your body and work from there. See if it makes a difference in the temperature of the room.

Work out the details for a class swim in a public or private pool. How will we get there, what will we need to take, what time will we leave and return? Do it.

Have a water-balloon throwing contest. Choose a partner. How far away from each other can you stand and still toss the balloon back and forth?

Observe changes of color of your skin in the sun. Wrap a piece of adhesive tape around a finger. Leave it there for one week. When you take it off, compare the difference.

Go swing. Feel the heat when you work. Feel the air as it passes over and around you.

Lesson 12. Windy-Day Activities

Go to an open space with a crepe-paper streamer. Let the wind take the streamer. Measure how far your streamer went with the wind. Whose goes the farthest?

Crumple a piece of paper. Throw it into the wind. Follow it around. Move when it moves, move where it moves.

Listen to the sounds of the wind in the room. What sounds are strange because of the wind? How does your home sound in the wind? What do windy sounds remind you of?

Run into the wind. Run away from the wind. Feel the difference. Time a run into the wind. Time a run away from the wind. Compare the difference.

Make pinwheels. Pin them to your pencil. Go into the wind. Which directions does the wind come from? Feel the wind push the pinwheel, the pencil, and your hand. Talk about the way people use the wind with windmills, sailboats, clotheslines, etc.

Make kites. Go fly them.

Lie on the ground. Feel the wind on your body. Stand up. Feel the wind now. Now build or find a shelter from the wind.

Lie on your back and watch the wind move the clouds. Find as many different things as you can in the clouds.

UNIT NINE
Space

One way to experiment with and develop confluent education is to choose something old and familiar and look at it in a new way in order to derive new meanings in terms of its effects on us.

To do this in a classroom setting, look at the "space" in and around a classroom. In every way we deal with that space, we should be able to derive new meanings in terms of boundaries and territories, rules and regulations, and how interpersonal relationships are affected by space.

Imagine entering a classroom. How is that space used? How does that use reflect the life that is being experienced in the classroom? What pleasurable sights do we see? In what way does the use of space in this room reflect life for the students as we would like to see it? How does the space include the students? What signs of their lives do we see? Is the space organized so that the students can move about in it on their own, or do their actions have to be dependent on an adult? What is unpleasant? In what way does the use of space seem to make life more difficult for the students, less rewarding than it might be? Is this the students' room, or are they visitors here? Are they in control of this room, or are they controlled by the room?

Now imagine experimenting with making some changes in that classroom. The easiest changes to make are those of organization. Imagine that we have seen some ways in which the organization of materials does not allow the students to use them to their advantage: Perhaps the art materials are too far away from the working area, the arrangement of the science materials discourages students from taking them out and experimenting with them, the area for noisy activities is too close to the area for quiet activities. Even a simple organizational change can have multiple effects. When art and science materials are easily available, students may demand time to be able to use them. A student engrossed in a science investigation he or she has set up resents leaving it to join the group for a teacher-directed activity. A change in organization may necessitate some time-schedule changes as well as the formulation of new rules and regulations for how and when equipment can be used. It may also require a teacher to abandon his or her plans and go with what the students develop as a plan for using their space, at least for certain time periods.

Developing an awareness of the space of the classroom can bring out conflicts over the use of space and the use of things in that space. These conflicts are present in every classroom, but they are not usually dealt with directly. When there is space for only one and three want it, what happens? Who makes the decision? How is it decided who will get the space? By playing that out in a lesson, the students become aware of the many times they are faced with decisions on how they use their space and the many ways it must be shared.

Conflict between group and individual needs for space must also be explored. The student involved in a group activity has to share the available space, and still be aware of personal needs for space. New boundaries may have to be established. Sometimes it is possible to change boundaries, to expand the available space by moving to another place or going outside. Sometimes it is necessary to learn ways to live with that conflict.

At first, even simple changes in the use of space may seem to have overwhelming effects for the teacher. Many decisions may have to be made on the basis of the effects of the change—rearranging time schedules, making new rules and regulations, deciding how and when space can be used in new ways. But gradually students can make these decisions as they begin to have an awareness of themselves in their space. They experiment with ways to share their space with others. They become aware of how their space is influenced by the things and people in their space. They become aware of how they invade the space of others in physical ways—and in other ways too, as when one individual reprimands them for having disturbed one's "imaginary" space by talking out loud in a fantasy game. They begin to experiment on their own with making changes in the space of the room and watching how those changes affect the group. Others express how such changes affect them. They learn to express their feelings about how the changes others make affect them. They experiment with changing rules and regulations, and so learn to appreciate those that aid them and others in sharing and using a space.

They learn to accept rules made by others with greater understanding. Gradually, they gain control of the use of their space and further develop their responsibility.

These lessons begin with the teacher looking at the classroom. You are asked to look at the space of your classroom in a new way. Then the students are asked to focus on their personal space in the room. From there, other students are introduced to that personal space. Finally, we look at the space beyond the classroom, at home and in the school. Each lesson is concerned with helping students to be aware of their space, both how they affect it and how it affects them.

Objectives

To be able to observe the physical space available.
To be able to share the available space with others in the group.
To experiment with making changes in a space.
To be able to verbalize the effects of changes on yourself and
    others in the group.
To be able to verbalize how other people and things influence the
    rules and regulations for the use of space.

Lesson 1. Teacher's Room

Walk into your room. Imagine that you are a foreign visitor, here to observe and to learn about the teacher and students who live in that room. Here are some questions that might help you to "see." How is the room organized? How do you think that organization aids or hinders learning activities? How much "student space" can you observe? How do you know it is "student space"? How much space is shared? How do you know?

Observe the students using the space of the classroom. What invisible boundaries do they observe? What signs do you see that tell you a student lives in the room? What signs do you see that tell you an adult lives in the room? Who put the furniture in its current arrangement? How do you know? Is there a dominant feature in the room? Who is responsible for its being there?

If you were a student entering the room, would you feel it belonged to you or to the teacher? How do you know?

If you were the student, what would you like about the room? What wouldn't you like?

These questions do not have correct responses. They are asked in order to help you become aware of the space of your room and how it is being used. How it is being used necessarily reflects what living and learning occur there.

Lesson 2. My Space

Sit in your normal place in the room. Close your eyes. Take a few breaths. Relax. Listen to the sounds around you. Listen to the sounds going on inside of you.

Slowly, slowly reach out with your hands and explore the space in front of you. Reach up and explore the space over your head. Explore the space behind you. Reach down and explore the space underneath you. Explore the space all around you, even the student sitting next to you if he or she is in your space. Now use your feet and legs to explore some more space around you. Slowly open your eyes.

The space around you can be defined as "your space." It is the space you are in, the amount of space you are taking up at any given time.

Where is there a lot of space around you? (Above their heads.) Where is there very little space for you? When you had your eyes closed, which spaces seemed to go on and on? Which spaces seemed very small? How much space do you usually like to have around you? When can you have that amount of space in this room? When do you have a smaller space than you like to have? What do you do then? Are there times when you have a larger space than you like to have? What do you do then? As you go through the day, be aware of the different amounts of space you have available for your use. Be aware of when you wish you had more space, when you wish you had less space, and when the space feels just right.

Lesson 3. More Space

Walk around the space of our room. Imagine it is the very first time you have been here. Take your time as you walk around. Touch, smell, taste, listen to as much as possible.

Now find a space you experience as a public space—a space that is open and shared by everyone. Find a space you experience as a private space—a space that is closed and for you only. Find a space just big enough for you. Find a space big enough for every-one. Join everyone in that space.

Talk about what you discovered about the different spaces you visited.

Do not be concerned with exact definitions of terms in this lesson. Let the students show you how they experience different spaces. For example, some students might experience closed space as a small physical space, such as a cupboard, or they might experience it as pulling themselves into a tight ball and closing their eyes out in the middle of the room. If terms seem to confuse them, or if they do not know how to respond, let them experiment with developing a definition and a response.

Lesson 4. Physical Space

Stand in a space of your own so that you are not touching anyone and you have enough room to move about somewhat without touching anyone.

Imagine that you are beginning to grow larger. Use your arms, your feet, your neck, your entire body to take up more space. Stand on tiptoes, stretch your back, hold your head as high as possible. Take up as much space with your body as you possibly can.

Now slowly, slowly, begin to shrink and shrivel. Become as small as you possibly can. Tuck all of yourself into a small ball. Become smaller, smaller. Take up as little space with your body as you possibly can.

Slowly begin to unfold yourself and stretch again. Do it in slow motion. Feel your body stretch and expand. See if you can become bigger this time than you were last time. Take more space.

Shrink again, very slowly. Make yourself as small as possible again. Do it in slow motion. Feel how you make yourself take up less space.

Now unfold, and take up your usual amount of space. How did you feel when you stretched as large as possible? How did you feel when you were as small as possible? When is it possible for you to stretch out and take a lot of space in our room? (Perhaps when using puzzles or Cuisenaire rods, or playing games.) How do you feel when you take up a lot of space? Are there times when you have to make yourself as small as possible in our room? (Perhaps when lining up, sitting with the entire group, crowding to be able to see something.) How do you feel then? What other places do you know about that allow you to stretch out and take a lot of space? (On the playground, at home.) What other places do you know about that require you to take as little space as possible?

Lesson 5. A Tight Space

Sit on the floor by yourself. Close your eyes. Imagine that you are sitting inside a big cardboard box. Feel the cardboard underneath you. See the four sides of the box all around you.

Now shut the lid of the box, with you inside. Imagine the box is getting smaller and smaller. Pull yourself closer together or else the box will push against you. Don't push the lid up. Don't move, you're pushing the lid up! Make yourself even smaller, as small as possible. Feel how it is in that tiny box. It is getting hot and stuffy in there. Hotter and hotter. As it gets hotter and hotter, you feel you must have air, but you are going to have to push your way out of your box. The box wants to hold you in, but you must get out so you can breathe. Push the box. Come out!!

Take a deep breath. Feel the air as it goes through your nose, and into your lungs. Feel the hot, used air as it leaves your body.

Are there times in our classroom when you feel as if you are in a tight, stuffy place? (Sometimes when coming in from the playground, sometimes when taking a test or working on something difficult, sometimes when everything is closed to show a movie.)

Are there times when you get into tight spaces in other places? (Riding a crowded bus, being in an elevator, sharing any small place with many people.)

How does your body respond to tight spaces? What do you usually do when you get into a tight space? What happens to you when you cannot get out of a tight space as soon as you want to? How do you feel when you finally get out?

Remember, a tight space can be psychological as well as physical.

Lesson 6. 100 Inches of String

Measure out a piece of string 100 inches long. Use that string to mark the boundaries of a space. Put yourself into the space of your 100 inches. How well do you fit in there? See how many different kinds of spaces you can make with your 100 inches of string. Make a small space with it. Make as large a space as you can. Make a space with wavy boundaries. Make a space with straight boundaries.

Go outside and find spaces that will fit into your 100 inches of string. Can you put a tree into your string? How would you do that? (Wrap the string around the base of the tree.) Can you put a bicycle into your string? Can you put a chair into your string? Experiment with your string on your own.

Talk about what could and could not be encompassed with the 100 inches of string.

Now put your string around a space you like. Write about the things in your space.

How did you feel about the spaces you could make? If you were to do this again, what would you do over again? What would you change?

Lesson 7. A Full Box

Bring a large cardboard box into the room.

Look at the box. How many books do you imagine we could put in the box? How many desks do you imagine would fit in there? How many of you would fit into that box?

One of you get into the box. Do you have enough room for yourself in there? Do you have room for someone else? If so, choose someone to join you.

Continue adding one student at a time until the children state the box is full.

But here is another student. (Choose one.) This person, too, wants to be in the box. There is nowhere else to be. Somehow all of you in the box will just have to find room for this person, even though you have already said the box was full.

Allow the students time to make room for the new person.

How did you make room for one more person in the full box? (Possible solutions: Each person takes up even less space than before, they stretch the boundaries of the box by pushing the sides out, they find a new arrangement of their bodies in order to allow for one more.)

How is the full box like other things you know about? (Making room for a new baby in a home that already seems full, making room in a home for company, density of population and overpopulation concerns.)

Lesson 8. Sharing Space

Walk around the room and find the space you like best. Take your time. Experiment with several spaces. When you have made your choice, sit down and experience how it feels to be there. What thoughts come to your mind while you sit there? Do not think about anything, just let thoughts come to you. Look around you. Where are you in relation to other people in the class? Is that important? If so, how?

Now that you have been in your own space for a few minutes, find four other people to join, and together choose a common meeting space, a space that all of you agree is comfortable. Talk to each other and share ideas on your favorite spaces, both inside and outside the classroom. Talk about how you share your favorite spaces at home and other places out of the classroom, and with whom you like to share them.

Lesson 9. Dividing Space

Divide the class into groups. Give each group a large sheet of butcher paper.

Imagine this piece of paper is all the space your group has available. Work together to find a way for each person in your group to share that space. You can divide it up or share it any way you want, but you have to come to a group decision on how to use it.

Allow them time to work to some conclusion.

Different groups of students may solve this in various ways. Some may quickly divide the paper into equal parts, measuring out one share per person. Others may take into account the size of the individuals as a way of dividing the space, giving a large share to a large person and a small share to a small person. Others may not divide it all but may leave all of it available for each to use, as needs for space occur. Encourage multiple and diverse solutions. There is no "right" solution.

Discuss how their solutions are similar to or different from the way space at school is shared. Are there unassigned spaces that are shared according to need (e.g., multipurpose room, gymnasium, library)? Which spaces are of equal size and measured out one-to-one (classrooms, lockers, desks)? Are there some spaces that are assigned according to the size of the students who use them? Do the "big kids" have a greater or lesser share of the playground? Are there bigger classrooms for bigger students?

Lesson 10. Room for One

Place one chair in the middle of the room.
Choose four students to "want" the chair.

Each one of you tell us why you want the chair, what you intend
to use it for, why you and not any of the others should have it.

We will listen to your presentations, and then decide who
will get the chair.

Discuss: How did you decide who should get the chair? Did
you listen to what they said, or did you base your opinion on
something else? If so, what else (e.g., "body English," friend-
ship)? How did you feel about denying the others the chair?

(*To the one who got the chair:*) How did you feel about getting the chair, knowing that three others could not have it? Do
you feel you had the best reasons for getting it, or did you get it
because of something else? If so, what?

(*To the other three:*) How do you feel about not getting the
chair? What do you feel allowed _____ to get it? If you were to do
this again, what would you do differently? How is this like other
things you know about?

Variations

Allow the students opportunities to role-play some of the ideas they
suggest at the end of the lesson. Other situations for role-playing follow:

There is one ball available. Four students want to take it out to recess. Who will get it? How will it be decided?

There is one piece of cake left at home. Everyone in the family wants
it. Who will get it? How will it be decided?

Six hundred students want to use the playground. How can it be
shared? Who will decide? How?

All people living in the city demand to be able to use the city in their
own way. Who uses what? How is it decided?

Lesson 11. Space Invaders

How do people invade your space? How do other students in
this class invade your space?

The students should have many examples of times when they were all
set to do something, and another student upset their plans and their
space.

When do you usually resent others invading your space?

When is it usually all right for others to invade your space? (When I am bored in my space, when I really don't want it anyway, etc.)

When do you invade the space of others? How do you know you have invaded their space? How do you know if you are welcome in that space? How do you know if you are not welcome?

What things besides people invade your space?

Do bells invade your space? How? When?

Do telephones invade your space? How? When?

Does television ever invade your space? How? When?

For one day, keep a list of people and things that invade your space. Put an X by the ones that pleased you, and an O by the ones that irritated you.

Compare your list with someone else's.

Lesson 12. Making Changes

Find something you want to change in this room. Change it. (Move your desk, rearrange something, change a bulletin board.)

What effect does that change have on others here? How does it affect the space of the room? How does affecting the space affect activities?

Find something you want to change in this room but cannot change by yourself (e.g., new seating arrangements for all, change in schedule). Find someone to help you change it.

What effect does that change have on others here? How does that change affect the space of the room? How does it affect the activities?

Let's live with your changes for a while. Let's see how they work out. If at any time you want to change it back to the way it was, or change it again, do so. Tell someone what made you want to change it again.

Let the students have many opportunities to experiment with making changes in the room. Let them live with some of their "bad choices," as long as they are not harmful to them or others in the room. Let the students decide if their changes help them, hinder them, or are simply made for the sake of change. Let them experiment with as much change as possible, for the only certain thing in their future is that they will be faced with making many changes. In order for them to make responsible changes, they will need to know what effect those changes have on them and their space as well as the effect those changes will have on others and their space.

Variation

Discuss in realistic terms:

> Things I can and cannot change by myself.
> Things in our class we can and cannot change.
> Things our class can and cannot change at school.

Help the student realize what is involved in making changes and the difference between working to make change happen and wishing it would happen.

Lesson 13. Rules for Using Space

Have the students play a regular game of basketball or some other game that has defined boundaries.

Have them play the game again, only this time change the dimensions to a very small space. This can be done either by making the space long and narrow, using the entire length of the court and having it only 6 feet wide, or by confining the game to a small rectangle around one basket.

Play the game again, but this time change the dimensions to a space approximately twice the regular area.

Have the student talk about what happened in the three spaces.

> How is the game affected by the amount of space you had available? Which rules of the game made sense when we changed the space? Which ones would you want to change if you were always going to change the space? Which way did you like to play the game the best? (Primary students might prefer the smaller space.) What did you like about playing it that way? What other games do you know about that have space requirements or are played in a specific space? What might happen to each game if you played it in a different amount of space? What new rules might you need to play with a new space?
>
> In what other ways does available space determine its use and its rules? (Compare a four-lane highway to a two-lane road, sharing a bedroom with one person as compared to sharing a

classroom with thirty, rules on the playground with rules for using hallways, etc.)

Lesson 14. X Marks the Spot

Make a map of our room. Put an X in the middle of the room. Put an X where you are right now. Put your name by it. Put an X where your best friend is. Put his or her name by it. Put X's where two more friends are. Put their names by them. If there is some other place in the room where you would rather be, put an X there and circle it.

Now read your map. Make at least three statements based on that information. Share your map and statements with a friend. See if your friend can add another statement to your list based on the information on your map.

You can use this lesson with one on mapping skills. Help primary students draw the room in relation to north, south, east, and west, placing at least one feature in each direction (e.g., the windows on the north wall, the door on the south wall, etc.). Advanced students might be able to draw the room and everything in it to scale. With either class, once the mapping of the room is complete, let the students place the X's on their own. Don't be concerned if they don't put them exactly where they belong. Accurate mapping is not important at this point of the lesson. What is important is that the students have some visual representation of where they see themselves in relation to the space of the room.

Lesson 15. Space at Home

Draw a map of your house. Mark the spaces you use the most at home. Mark the spaces you use the least. Use different colors to define the different spaces.

Do you have a very special, favorite space at home? Mark that space with an X. Describe it. What do you usually do when you are there? How do you usually feel when you are in that space?

Do other people in your home have favorite spaces? Mark those spaces with an O on your map. Describe someone else's favorite space. How do they usually act and what do they usually do when they are in their favorite space?

What spaces in your home are shared spaces? How does your family share the space of your home?

Listen to their answers, and choose a few to extend into role-playing.

Role-play sharing space in the kitchen.
How is that different from the way we share the space where we eat at school? How is it the same?
Role-play sharing space in the living room. Have company come. How does sharing space change when company comes? How is sharing living room space like sharing our room? How is it different? What happens in our room when visitors come?
What might our homes look like if we did not share spaces with each other at home? Draw a home for a family like yours, with each person having the most possible private space, and the least possible shared space. Write a story about what it might be like to live in that kind of house.

Lesson 16. School Space

Imagine that you do not know about your school and how it is used. Imagine that the entire scene is strange and foreign to you. Let's go outside and look at the space of the school. We will walk the geographic boundaries of our school and look into it. From what you see, imagine multiple uses of the spaces you find. What could be done in the grassy areas? In planted areas? Are there walls that could be utilized? How? Are there blacktop areas with and without lines? What could be done with them? What equipment do you see? How might it be used? Are there fences? What could be their purpose or function? Do you see any spaces you have not seen before? How might they be used? Is there a space that is unique to our school (e.g., a hill, gravel area, grove of trees, dirt area)? How could it be used?
Make a map of this school. Mark "student only" spaces on your map. Mark "adult only" spaces. (If there are spaces the students can use only with an adult in attendance, mark it as "adult only" space.) Mark "shared" space, space the students and adults use with equal freedom. Use a different color crayon to mark each kind of space.
Read your map. What does it tell you about space at this school? How do you feel about the use of space at this school? What would you like to see changed? What would you like to see remain the same?

Do only the first paragraph of this lesson with primary and intermediate students. Older, advanced students can go on to the second paragraph if appropriate. Every teacher should do the whole lesson.

UNIT TEN
Art

The idea that students can create something in art is not new. What confluent education has to offer that *is* new is the idea that the students themselves are already works of art. By isolating certain parts of their bodies
and reproducing them in classic artistic forms, in a painting or a print,
they will gain not only an appreciation for art but also a new appreciation
of themselves and the beauty that is already and always with them.

None of the following art lessons can exist without the students.
Each lesson demands something from them. Each one is offered with the
intention of creating continuing experiences in self-discovery, self-appre-
ciation, and self-awareness.

In most schools a portion of the student's time is spent in art, dance,
drama, or music classes. Unfortunately, however, these classes most often
are intended to serve only cathartic functions and therefore remain set
off in the students' minds from their heavier academic duties—their "real"
lessons. Not so here. These art lessons continue to deal with students'
feelings and concerns. They are not truly concerned with art in the sense
of "works of art." They are concerned with multiple ways to allow the
students to express themselves. They provide another way for them to
work, discover, imagine, and create a continuing awareness of themselves.

Like the other units presented so far, the lessons here have the students as the main focus. They are introduced to ways of viewing themselves as objects of art, as a collection of objects of art. A most familiar

thing to a student is his or her name, so that is where we start. The students are then literally taken from head to toe—from an art project dealing with their heads to another one dealing with their feet—finding ways to represent themselves through art. If a class shows a need for more work dealing with body awareness, the lessons here will show the teacher how various parts of the body can be the central point of an art lesson so that he or she can provide the class with experiences using other body parts. For example, do "Footprinting" (p. 186), then make hand prints, knee prints, and elbow prints, then draw a picture with your toes holding a crayon, then paint a picture holding a brush in your mouth. Above all, experience yourself as you do so.

From self-awareness we move the students into their environment to explore ways of relating to it in an artistic form. There are lessons in and out of the classroom—helping to reinforce the students' awareness of their environment and their place in nature and blending it with ways that allow them to express their experiences nonverbally, in an artistic form. Again, the particular needs of any given group should dictate how much these lessons are expanded and developed. A class could go beyond the lessons contained here to experience a tree—its leaves, bark, shade, its shelter for birds, its place in ecology, its aesthetic contribution to man— before setting out to express it in artistic form. The objects in a still life can be brought to the student's awareness in the same way. Experience all the qualities of the objects—smell the flowers, taste the fruit, listen to the musical instruments—then express them in an artistic form.

Finally we introduce another person into the artistic scene. These lessons reinforce the students' relationships with those who are around them. Once again, nonverbal communication is stressed. The essential part of these lessons is what the students experience, not what they produce out of their experiences. They should never have to justify or explain their work. It is important that the teacher and the other students respond to the experience with the student, not to the artistic representation done by the student.

In all these lessons, the main concern is that they be pleasurable experiences for the students. Give them the necessary materials, a basic idea, and let them go. Often what they will do under these circumstances will be very different from any preconceived idea—and much better, both as an "art object" and as a learning experience.

Objectives

To represent various body parts in artistic form.
To reproduce a quality of a familiar object artistically.
To interpret familiar words artistically.
To interpret something in nature artistically.

To be able to work with another person to produce an artistic
  form.
To do what one can artistically without self-consciousness.

Lesson 1. My Name

Materials: Graph paper, colored crayons, construction paper, scissors, paste.

Print your name on graph paper in large letters, about three inches
high. Trace over your name with a dark crayon. Then outline it
with another color. Do this over and over until the letters of your
name are full and fat. You might even build them up so that they
overlap. Use a variety of colors.
    Cut out the shape of your name and mount it on a piece of
bright-colored construction paper.
    How do you feel about your name now?
    Did you discover anything new about your name?
    Is there something you particularly don't like about it?
    Is there something you particularly like about it?

With primary students, you might have to do the first printing of their
names for them. With advanced students, have them do the same thing
with words more suited to their interests or concerns: Love, Peace, War,
Sex, Hate, etc.

Variation

Fold a sheet of construction paper in half lengthwise. Write your
name on the fold. Draw around the letters of your name, making
them about ¼″ wide. Cut your name out without disturbing the
fold. Cut out the spaces inside any loops, such as in l's, a's, o's, etc.
Mount your cut-out name onto a contrasting piece of construction
paper.

Talk about the design of your name. What does it remind you of? If you were to do this again, how would you write your name differently? If so, how?

This lesson can be done with names in manuscript print too. Just be sure to keep the fold uncut and make the letters wide enough to touch each other.

Lesson 2. Thumbprint Paintings

Materials: Stamp pads, white construction paper, fine-line felt-tip pens.

Press your thumb onto the stamp pad and then make a print on white construction paper. Repeat until your paper has many thumbprints scattered over it. Now add fine lines to your thumbprints to turn them into drawings, for example, flowers, animals, machines, faces.
What did you discover about your thumb?
What else could you do with your thumb?
How could we do thumbprints again in a different way?
What other body parts might you use?

Advanced students can do this on a large sheet of lightweight paper (colored newsprint) and use it for wrapping paper, or on heavy brown paper (paper bag) before turning it into a book cover.

Lesson 3. What's on My Mind?

Materials: Construction paper, crayons, magazines, paste, scissors.

Draw a silhouette of a head in profile on a piece of construction paper. Make it large. Cut it out. While doing this, talk about what's on your mind. What are you thinking about? What thoughts run through your head?

Now paste the profile on a piece of construction paper. Fill the profile with the things that are on your mind. You can cut out pictures from magazines, or you can draw your own pictures.

What did you discover about your mind?

How do you decide what's on your mind?

What was easy or difficult about that lesson?

Variations

Draw a line across the top part of the profile. Put drawings or cut-outs above the line. Draw in your face below the line.

Have a student stand with his or her profile in the beam of a flashlight while another student traces the outline of his or her profile onto the construction paper and then proceed as in the lesson.

Lesson 4. Footprinting

Materials: Large sheets of butcher paper, pan of tempera paints, washcloths.

Remove your shoes and socks. Step into a pan of tempera paint and then onto a piece of paper, making footprints all over it. Use different parts of your feet. Tiptoe for a while. Walk on your heels, walk on the sides of your feet. When you are through making your footprint, wipe the paint off your feet with a washcloth before putting your shoes and socks back on.

What can you do with your footprints now? Here are some ideas.

When the paintings are dry, create a story to go with it.

Cut up your footprints and rearrange them into paintings.

Take two types of footprints, a tiptoe and a full foot, cut them out, paste them onto separate sheets of paper, and make up sayings to go under them.

Cut out a footprint and use crayons or pens to make it into something else.

What else can you think of to do with your feet?

What might the picture be like if we each had three feet?

Caution: This is a messy lesson. Cleaning twenty-eight pairs of feet can be a lesson in itself!

Variation

Materials: Recordings of music that has a variety of tempos, themes, and rhythms (Walt Disney's *Fantasia* is excellent for this lesson), pans of tempera paints, large sheets of paper, washcloths.

Listen to the record. Be aware of what you are feeling as you
listen to the music.
What movements would you make to go with the music?
What color would you use to go with your feelings and the
music?
Step into a color that best shows how you feel.
Step onto your paper and move the way the music makes you
want to move. Dance a painting.

Lesson 5. Body Outlines

Materials: Pencils, large sheets of butcher paper, scissors, paints, crayons.

Choose a partner. One of you lie down on your piece of paper.
Your partner will trace around your outline, being careful to get
the fingers, neck, hair, and shoes on the paper. Then you do the
same for your partner.
Cut out your outline. Now fill it in with details. Paint the
clothing to match the clothing you are wearing now. Now you
have a paper doll of yourself.
Tell a friend something new about you.
How does your paper doll of yourself make you feel?
What would you like to do with your paper doll? If possible,
do it. (Hang it up on the wall. Put it in your chair.)

If the student holds the pencil straight up and down and keeps it gently touching the partner, it is possible to get an accurate outline. Allow the students to make corrections before cutting out their outlines if necessary.

Lesson 6. Castles in the Air

This is excellent "warm-up" activity as well as a good way to deal with the statement "I can't draw."

Stand so that there is some room around you. Use your finger as if it were a magic pencil, and use the space around you as a drawing board.

Now let's all draw an imaginary castle. Begin at the bottom and draw the base of your castle. (Stoop down and begin to draw.) Draw your castle as you see it. Is the base made of large stones or small ones? Is it rough or smooth? What color are you painting with?

When you have the base finished, draw the doorway. What is your castle doorway like? What else does your castle need?

As you work drawing your own castle, ask the students questions about what they are doing. Encourage their own ideas and contributions to the game. Stimulate their imaginations. Get them to move their entire body while drawing. Try to get them to take over the conversation, while you continue to be busy on your own castle, following the leads and ideas suggested by the students.

Variation

You can encourage the students to draw anything with this technique. In springtime you may hear, "I can't draw a rabbit. Will you do it for me?" This is a good time to draw rabbits in the air. You may not improve the students' drawing abilities with this activity, but you will help them use the skills they do have unselfconsciously.

Lesson 7. Animated Words

Think of an action word. Write the word, drawing the letters to look like what the word does.

jump, BREAK, BANG

Think of a word that describes how something feels. Write the word, drawing the letters to show how the word feels.

Think of a word that describes an emotion. Write the word, drawing the letters and adding lines in a way that expresses that emotion.

Lesson 8. Familiar Objects

Find a small object to hold. Look at it from every angle. See it as if you were seeing it for the first time. Throw it into the air and catch it. Roll it on the floor. Close your eyes and feel your object with the back of your hands, with your elbow, with your knee, with your cheek. Put your object on top of your head. Walk it around the room.

Place it on your desk. Find something that you can draw with but do not usually use for drawing. Find something to draw on that you usually do not draw on (paper towels, tissue paper, wrapping paper, newspaper).

Now do not draw your object but draw something *about* it. Draw how it felt to the back of your hand. Draw its texture. Draw a feeling you got holding it. Draw the sound it made while rolling on the floor.

Lesson 9. Nature Collage

Materials: Wax paper (two 8″ x 10″ sheets per person), wax crayons, an iron, scissors, staples, construction paper.

Go for a walk and collect several natural things from the school grounds (leaves, grass, stems, small stones).

Place your items in some arrangement that is pleasing to you on one of your wax paper sheets. Use your scissors to scrape off bits of different colored crayon. Sprinkle the bits of color over your arrangement in a pattern that is pleasing to you.

Place the second sheet of wax paper over the entire arrangement. With a warm iron, press all of it together. The wax of the paper and the crayons will melt and hold the arrangement together.

Staple strips of construction paper along all four sides for added support. Hang it in a window so that the light can shine through it.

Variation

When the class is on a field trip to a park, a zoo, a beach, etc., have the students collect natural items in that environment to make a group collage. Each person arranges his or her items in relation to what others have to contribute. They can use a table, a bench, or some other defined area to hold their items. They have to work together to get the items in an arrangement that is pleasing to all.

Lesson 10. Shape and Color Walk

Go for a walk, paying particular attention to shapes and colors. Look for things that stand out in sharp contrast to each other—the smooth glass window in the rough stone wall, the rough bark of the tree and its smooth shiny leaves, a tiny black ant on white cement, bright sunlight, dark shadows.

Talk about shapes or colors seen that surprised you. Begin each sentence with "I." "I was surprised to see round drops of water still hanging on to thin blades of grass." "I saw three blackbirds in the blue sky." "I saw a cat come out of the shadows. At first I thought it was a black cat, but when it got in the sun, I saw it had many different colors on it."

Lesson 11. Texture Walk

Go for a walk, paying particular attention to the various textures that surround you.

Feel and handle as many different textures as you can.

Feel different textures while closing your eyes.

Be aware of how you feel as you touch and handle each

item. Take time to feel it in different ways; stroke it, rub it, tap it.

As you change items be aware of how you feel about the new texture compared to the one just handled.

Be aware of your hands and how you feel when you are not touching anything.

Talk about what you felt that surprised you. Did something feel smoother or rougher than you expected? Softer or harder?

Variation

Take a sheet of paper and a soft crayon with you on your walk and do a texture rubbing picture.

Be aware of seeing the texture, feeling it, and then rubbing over it.

It is better to take the texture walk before doing this. Many textures may be overlooked when viewed with the task of rubbing them in mind. You can see many textures that you cannot feel or would not want to feel— the rough texture of a shingle roof, the silky slime left by a snail. There are textures that you might like to feel but cannot get in a rubbing: the soft fur of a rabbit, the bumps of a cyclone fence as you walk by it, the smooth surface of a puddle.

Lesson 12. Draw Your Partner

Materials: Pen or pencil and several sheets of paper.

Choose a partner.

Look at your partner. Put your pen down on your sheet of paper and begin to draw your partner. Do not lift your pen from the paper at any time until you are finished, and do not look at your paper. When both you and your partner are finished drawing, tell each other what happened. Talk about yourself and what happened to you, not about your drawing.

Take a new sheet of paper and do it again. Talk about anything new you discovered about yourself or your partner.

Look at the drawings you have done. Decide if they are mostly straight or mostly curved lines. This time do it again, using the opposite type of line as much as you can. Talk about what happened.

Now use either only straight or only curved lines and

draw your partner again. This time you can lift your pen whenever you want to. Talk about what happened.

Begin again with a clean sheet of paper. Close your eyes. Draw yourself without lifting your pen from the paper. Be aware of what you are experiencing as you do the drawing. When you are finished drawing, talk about what happened.

If the class has difficulty getting started in a discussion, ask some leading questions: How do you feel about the size of your drawings? What were the surprises? What did you leave out? How do you feel about what you left out? This type of question can be asked after any or all of the drawings.

Variation

Repeat the entire sequence having the students use the opposite hand. Focus the discussion on differences between the hands.

What did you see when using the opposite hand that you had not seen before? What were the discoveries, the surprises? Again, talk about what happened to you, and not the "outcome" of the drawing.

Lesson 13. Painting Poem

Choose a partner. Spend some free time together, just talking and being together. (Allow five to ten minutes.)

Now take a sheet of paper and, without paying attention to what your partner is doing, draw your partner as you see him.

Now share your drawings with each other.

Turn your drawings over, and on the back write the following:

Your partner's name.

Two words that describe him or her.

Three words to give action to him or her.

Four words to tell how you feel about him or her.

Your partner's name again.

Read your poem out loud to your partner, one at a time so the entire group can hear.

Share anything else you want to with your partner.

Discuss the entire exercise with the whole group.

Lesson 14. Group Pictures

Materials: A large sheet of paper (18″ x 24″), brushes of various sizes, paints, jars of water.

Close your eyes and think of a time when you were very happy. Think about how you were then, and how you felt.

Add as many details as you feel are needed to get them into a "happy" fantasy.

Now open your eyes and pick a color you feel represents that happy feeling. Start drawing with a brush that seems to be the right size and shape for that happiness. Let the memory of being happy direct the movement of the lines. Don't think about drawing anything, just think about being happy. Be aware of your lines and how you feel as you make them.

At my signal, go to another picture. Look at the new picture and be aware of how it makes you feel. Do not judge it, just look at it and be aware of your own feelings. Now begin to put those feelings on the paper. Again choose a color and a brush that represent your feelings now. Work on the paper in front of you as if it were your own. Add to it and change it as your feelings direct. Do not think of drawing something, just express what you are feeling now.

At my signal, go to another person's painting. Look at the new painting. Be aware of what you feel. Again, choose a color and a brush to represent that, and begin to work on that painting as if it were your own.

Now get the paper that was yours in the beginning. Look at your paper, keeping in touch with how you are feeling. Do not judge the work as good or bad. Just look at it and be aware of your feelings. Be aware of how you feel about what others have added to your work. How do you feel about having changed someone else's work?

Share any surprises.

Be careful to avoid making judgments in terms of an "art project" during this lesson. It is the experience and what the students discover about their feelings while doing this that are important, not the final product. Help the students talk about how they *feel* about the experience and not the product.

UNIT ELEVEN
Blindfolds

Babies freely and enthusiastically use all their senses in order to learn about the world around them. Give one an object and he or she will get to know it thoroughly. He or she will feel it, taste it, shake it to discover if it makes any sounds. But by the time a child reaches school age, the child has learned otherwise. "Don't touch." "Don't put that in your mouth." By the time students are in school, they have become heavily dependent on their eyes for learning about their world. They have learned to ignore their other senses almost completely as sources of information. Traditional curricula tend to reinforce this restriction by emphasizing reading, writing, and arithmetic—primarily visual experiences.

In order to reintroduce students to their other senses, it is necessary to reduce their dependency on their eyes. This may not be easy to do. When you first ask students to close their eyes, you may encounter a great deal of resistance, related to their dependency on their eyes as their only way of knowing. Students who use all senses easily will not have much difficulty closing their eyes since they know how to receive information from their other senses.

One way to allow students to reduce dependency on their eyes is to provide opportunities for them to experience their world while blindfolded. (You can either have the students bring scarves to tie over their eyes or make blindfolds for the class by cutting a piece of fabric-backed vinyl like a sleep mask and sewing elastic to the sides.)

Students are enthralled by wearing a blindfold at school. Students

140

who may be afraid to keep their eyes closed for very long without peeking will keep wearing the blindfold and so increase the time they feel safe while blindfolded. They will develop a willingness to wear it for longer times than they could manage to keep their eyes closed. By really removing their sight on their own terms, and for only as long as they are comfortable, the students become aware of seeing and bring new life and excitement to whatever work they do following wearing a blindfold.

Once the students can wear blindfolds comfortably for at least five minutes, they return to old materials in the classroom with renewed interests. Blindfolds delight students who learn best through tactile experiences. If they are blindfolded, they do not get questioned by other students for going back to materials that have been mastered visually, since they all know how difficult it is to do even familiar things when blindfolded. Many of the students will return to old puzzles and learn to do them again blindfolded. They will experiment with Cuisenaire rods in new ways. They will experience art materials—particularly clay—anew. Even dancing feels different when blindfolded. All lessons concerned with any of the five senses are intensified. By removing the use of their eyes, the students can concentrate more on touching, smelling, listening, or tasting. Even vision can be more intense if it has not been experienced for a while.

Objectives

To identify objects through senses other than sight.
To identify sounds without sight.
To identify odors without sight.
To experience taste sensations without sight.
To develop a new awareness of old familiar scenes by being
    in them without sight.
To develop the ability to receive information from all five
    senses.

Lesson 1. Free Exploration

Here is a blindfold for each one of you. What can you do
with it?

Allow the students time to play with the blindfolds. Besides wearing it on their eyes, what else can they do with it? It can be worn as a hair band. It can be a sling for a "broken" arm. It can be worn around the neck as a decoration. After they have had some free time, bring the group together again.

Who can put a blindfold on correctly? When is it on correctly? (When you cannot see.) Who can walk from here
to the other side of the room and back again? (Allow one
student at a time to do so.) How do you walk when you are
wearing a blindfold? How do you know where to go? What
would you like to do with your blindfolds now? If possible,
do it.

Don't be concerned if at first some students peek while wearing their
blindfolds. However, praise and encourage those who allow themselves
to move about without seeing. Allow time for free exploration. It may
take some students a long time even to try on the blindfolds. At the end
of this game, leave the blindfolds out and available for the students to
play with during their free time, activity time, or recess.

Lesson 2. Passing Familiar Objects

Sit in a circle. Put your blindfold on. I am going to give each
of you a familiar object from our classroom. You will have
time to feel the object. When I make a sound, you are to pass
it on to the person on your right and receive a new one from
the person on your left.

Give each person an object from the room—scissors, paint brush, ball,
pencil, etc. If there are several objects of the same kind—several pairs of
scissors, for example—pass them out so that they are not all together, allowing the student to feel other objects before receiving scissors again.
Use a sound, such as snapping your fingers, to signal them to pass their
objects to the person on the right and receive a new one from the person
on the left. Stand in the center of the circle to retrieve dropped and lost
items. Don't wait so long that the students become discouraged and remove their blindfolds.
Encourage the students to go beyond just identifying the objects.
Expand "This is a spoon" to "This is a spoon. It is hard and smooth. One
end feels narrow and flat. The other end feels round and curved." Or
"This is a stapler" to "This is a stapler. It can move. It feels rough here
and smooth here."

Lesson 3. Passing Strange Objects

Repeat as in Lesson 2, except this time give the students items that
have a special olfactory or tactile quality, such as whole cloves, fruits,
flowers, scented candles, or bits of fabric, sandpaper, fur, and metal.

Encourage the students to keep their blindfolds on throughout the experience. This may be difficult for some. Assure them that it is all right not to know, not to be able to label what they have. Urge them to use their fingers, noses, mouths to know—at least for a while.

Leave all the objects out for the students to see and handle when the lesson is over.

Variation

Place the items to be passed in open boxes. This removes the sense of touch as well as the sense of sight. See how many items the student recognizes by the smell or the sound the item makes in the box.

Lesson 4. Eating

Prepare a bag with small bits of foods of different textures and tastes for each student. Select foods that are hard, soft, sweet, sour, crunchy, and mushy. For example: peanuts, raisins, chocolate chips, lemon drops, potato chips, prunes. It is important that all the items be dry; otherwise the tastes and textures will get mixed up.

Put your blindfold on. Eat the items in this bag, one at a time.
Feel the item with your fingers before you chew it. Be aware
of your tongue, your teeth, and your throat as you chew and
swallow it. Pause a while before putting another item in your
mouth.
What did you discover? Which things did you like to eat?
What did you like about them? Which taste did you like most?
Which texture did you like most?

You might wish to have extra amounts of all the foods so that the students can have more of the ones they liked best.

Lesson 5. Feel a Familiar Place

Take the class to a familiar place—it may be the school playground or a nearby park. Have each student wear a blindfold for as long as possible while attempting familiar activities. Do not insist that the students keep the blindfold on. Let each one decide when one's eyes as well as ears and hands must be used to be able to be comfortable in the environment.

Encourage students to experience a variety of activities: swing while blindfolded, go across traveling bars, run in an open space, feel sand or grass, go down a slide. For safety's sake, have one student do this blindfolded while another student watches in order to warn of any danger.

Try to get each student to wear the blindfold long enough to experience a newness of seeing when the blindfold is removed.

Lesson 6. Blind Walk

When the students can wear a blindfold comfortably for at least five minutes, have them choose partners. One puts on a blindfold, the other does the seeing for both of them. The seeing partner takes the blind partner for a walk, providing as many experiences along the way as possible.

The partners can do this anywhere, even in the classroom. However, the space and variety available outdoors obviously make it desirable to move outside if possible.

When they are ready, have the students change places. The one who was blind becomes the seeing partner, taking the other on a blind walk.

Allow time for a discussion at the end.

Which role did you prefer? Taking your partner, or being taken for a walk? Did anything special happen to you along the way? If you were to do it again, is there anything you would do differently?

Lesson 7. Blindfold Games

"SAYS WHO?"

Tap one student, who begins talking, saying anything but his or her name. The others guess who is talking.

STRANGE TASTES

Give each student something small enough to put directly into his or her mouth—a peanut, a piece of popcorn, candy, a piece of carrot, celery, apple. Have the student tell what was eaten without naming the item by describing its taste, sound feel, etc. Have the others guess what was eaten from the description.

"WHAT'S THAT?"

Make a noise. The student who identifies it then makes a noise for the others to guess.

BLINDMAN'S BUFF

Blindfold one student and have him or her move around in the group of students, identifying individuals through touch.

STILL POND

Form groups of six to eight students. Each group forms a circle.

One person stands in the middle, wearing a blindfold.

The students on the outside of the circle move around until the center person calls "Still Pond."

The student in the middle finds a person and tries to identify the person through touch.

The person who was thus chosen then goes into the middle, and the game continues.

UNIT TWELVE
Sheets

In order to work with sheets in your classroom you need a double bed sheet for each student, a large space in which to work, and a great deal of stamina and courage.

The advantage of using sheets is that each student can have a place inside the class that is private. The sheet can become a protective shield between oneself and the eyes of peers. A very shy, quiet student may let loose while under the sheet—yelling and pushing—only to become placid once again upon removing the sheet. Other interesting things may also develop. A very aggressive, boisterous boy may refuse to leave the group to go under a sheet by himself. Or a boy whom you had observed in many awkward movements may go through the life cycle of a plant with surprising grace and beauty, using his sheet to shield him from the eyes of others. In his own private world he can move in more fluid ways. A fearful little girl may crawl under her sheet, stay very still during an entire lesson, and then resist coming out and returning to the group. Two students who would not even look at each other in regular class periods end up being partners while under their sheets. From that they begin to see each other when sheets come off. Each student begins to let the other into his or her awareness, into his or her life.

The lessons in this book have been divided into units for the sake of convenience. In reality, many of them overlap each other, and the decision to put them into one unit or another was completely arbitrary. Each

146

one adds something to and enriches the others. Sheet lessons can be done as a unit, or they can be used in conjunction with the preceding units. Any of the preceding lessons will enrich these lessons with sheets—and sheet work will enrich the other lessons.

The effectiveness of sheet work depends on a great deal of imagination, self-awareness, other-awareness, and responding to nature. If the teacher and the student have shared experiences and have learned to relate to each other in other lessons in other units, and to bring to the classroom other life experiences, this will not be difficult.

If you do not force students into doing a lesson, into going beyond their own inner limits, if you give them the right to be responsible for what they can and cannot do, the sheet lessons may be the most exciting of all to the students. You cannot know what is happening to them when they are covered with a sheet. It is not necessary for you to know in order to be their teacher.

The greatest times of all with the sheets come when the students are allowed to experiment and create with them on their own—at Halloween when they make up costumes, using the sheets as "rugs" in a make-believe bakery so that spilled flour will not show up, using a pile of sheets as a nest to lie on while reading. There is no way to predict how the students will use the sheets next if they are available to them.

Objectives

To provide the student with another way to relate to the here and now.
To expand the student's imagination.
To provide alternative ways of dealing with aggression.
To provide alternative ways to act out roles in nature.
To experience a new kind of space.
To provide alternative ways to create an artistic expression.
To review other experiences in this book in a new way.

Lesson 1. Then and There . . . (Here and Now)

Spread your sheet out flat. Lie on top of it. Do not talk while you are lying there.

Look at all the other students here. When you feel like it, get under your sheet. Completely cover yourself.

Once you are covered, go somewhere in your imagination. Go wherever you want to go.

When you are ready, come back here, take your sheet off, and look around.

Then go under your sheet again.

Go away and come back when you feel like it.

Allow time for the students to establish their own rhythm of withdrawal and contact. Let them go away and come back several times.

When all, or nearly all, are back, ask them all to come back and stay here now.

Where did you go? How did you feel when you were there? How did you feel when you came back here? What are the differences between here and there?

Ask the students how things looked when they opened their eyes here. Were things in sharp focus, or were they fuzzy? Generally, if vision is sharp, they are in the here and now; if vision here is fuzzy, they are still in the then and there. There may be nothing you can do to make the student want to be in the here and now, but with this lesson at least you can know, and help the student to know, that he or she is in the then and there.

Lesson 2. Being Alone
(Here and Now)

Sit in a circle, not touching anyone.

Put your sheet over your head.

Now try to think of how you feel when no one wants you.

You know you are in a circle. When you feel like it, move away from the circle in slow motion.

Find a place to stop.

You are all alone. No one is near. Only you, the sheet, and the floor. Be completely alone for a while. (Allow no more than three minutes.)

Now lie down on the floor—still covered with your sheet.

Roll yourself up in your sheet as tightly as you can. Be very still. Feel the sheet all around you.

Now begin to roll around. If you roll into someone you may still wish to be alone. If so, move away. If you want to be close to someone, stay near whomever you touch.

Return to the circle.

Discuss what happened. How do you feel when you are alone? Did this remind you of a time when you were really alone? How did it feel to have other people touch you after you had been alone for a while?

Lesson 3. Dancing
(Sensory Awareness)

Find a private space in the room.

Crawl under your sheet.

Listen to quiet music. Do not think of anything, but let thoughts and images come to you. Let your mind drift with the music. Let it go anywhere it wants. (Allow about fifteen minutes.)

Gradually come out from under your sheet. Take your time. Don't talk. Meet one person at a time with only your eyes.

Slowly move to someone.

Join others until the whole group is together.

Play lively music.

Dance.

How did your mind and body respond to the music at first? (The quiet music.) What images came to you, what sensations did you have? What did you do with those sensations? How did your mind and body respond to the music that was played later? What images came to you, what sensations did you have? What did you do with those sensations?

Lesson 4. Orange and Blue
(Imagination)

Crawl under your sheet in a space of your own.

Imagine you are a ball.

Imagine you are either an orange or a blue ball.

Move around as an orange or a blue ball.

Make an orange or a blue ball sound to go with your movement.

If you are orange, try to find a blue ball. Dance with the blue ball.

If you are blue, find an orange ball and dance with an orange ball.

Find another ball to be with. See if you can discover what color the ball is by the sound and movement.

Find another one. Dance with that ball.

Join with other balls. Keep joining until you are all together, dancing.

Remove your sheets if and when you want to.

Lesson 5. Making Contact (Polarities)

Completely cover yourself with your sheet. You cannot stand up. You can be on your hands and knees. You cannot talk.

Now imagine that you are either very large or very small.

Begin to move around that way. If you are large, move as if you are large. If you are small, move as if you are small. (Allow at least three minutes for movement.)

Now make a sound to go with your size.

Now, if you are large, try to find someone who is small who will stay with you and be your partner.

Once you find a partner, find a way that large and small can move together. Move to a space of your own. Continue to make your own individual sound.

Discover if the two of you can now make a sound together—make one sound instead of two separate sounds.

When you can move together and make a sound together, take your sheets off. See if you can continue to move together and make sounds together.

Now talk to each other about what you did.

If the group has a great deal of difficulty making contact, have them repeat the process several times before they take the sheets off and encounter one another face to face.

Lesson 6. Aggression

Get under your sheet. Remember the time when you were a baby, or think about a baby you know. Begin to move about on your hands and knees like a baby. Make sounds like a baby. Still staying under your sheet, meet other babies. Talk to them with your baby sounds. You do not have words yet, but you do have sounds. Now find a space of your own.

Slowly take your sheet off, but still be a baby. Crawl around and meet other babies. Remember, you don't have any words, just sounds.

Now you learn your first word. It is "No." Keep crawling, meeting other babies. Talk to them using your one and only word. See how many different meanings you can give to the word by using it with different sounds, and by using it with different voice inflections.

Go to a space of your own again. Now imagine you are as old as you really are. Take some time to "grow up" and then come together as a group.

What did you discover? Was it easier to be a baby under your sheet or out of your sheet? How many different ways did you find to use the one word you had? How did you feel being a baby? What did you like about it, what didn't you like? How do you feel about being your own age now?

Lesson 7. More Aggression

Get under your sheet. Imagine you are a baby again. It can be you as a baby or a baby you know. Begin to crawl around and meet other babies. Today you are in a grumpy mood. You feel like pushing everything and everyone around. Push other babies around as you come into contact with them. Remember, you are a baby, and you can only push in ways a baby can push.

Now go to a space of your own. Be alone for a while. Remember how it felt to push others around as a baby. Now imagine you are about three years old. Get up on your knees to show that you have grown up somewhat. Move around on your knees. You are still in a grumpy mood though, so as you meet others, you want to push them around. Push them as a three-year-old would push. Now you become a tired three-year-old. Go to a space of your own and curl up in your sheet. Take a little rest. Since you are only three, you may even want to suck your thumb as you take a rest.

Now imagine you are still in a grumpy mood, but now you are as old as you really are. Walk around and meet other children who are in a grumpy mood. Do whatever you usually do when you are in a grumpy mood.

Now go to a space of your own again. Think about yourself now. How are you really feeling? Take your sheet off, and join the group.

Discuss what happened. How was your behavior now like your behavior when you were a baby? How was it different? Is it easier for you to be grumpy under a sheet than it is when you don't have a sheet on? In what other ways do you and other people hide grumpy behavior?

Lesson 8. Nature

Use the sheets to act out a variety of scenes taken from nature.

Be a seed, with the sheet being the seed covering. "Grow" out of it. Use the sheet as a part of the growing plant—waving in the wind, blossoming, drying up, falling to the ground as the plant begins to die. Create a new seed. Then be the seed again, ready to grow next season.

Be a caterpillar egg inside the sheet. Grow out of it and become a tiny caterpillar by wrapping yourself in the sheet.

Be the caterpillar. Grow out of your skin several times.

Go into your sheet to be like the caterpillar in the chrysalis. Come out as a butterfly, using the sheet as your wings. Be the butterfly.

Be a bird's egg.

Hatch. Be a baby bird.

Grow.

Designate areas for migration, north and south. Have the birds migrate.

Make a nest with the sheet.

Be the egg again.

Lesson 9. Space

Get under your sheet. Close your eyes. Clear your mind of all thoughts, ideas, words. Take a few deep breaths. Just relax. Let yourself relax so that you seem to sink into the floor.

Now, still with your eyes closed, imagine that where you are now is your total space, your environment. Listen to the sounds around you. Smell the air as you breathe in. Feel it leave your body as you exhale. Feel the floor underneath you. Feel the sheet on top of you.

Now, slowly open your eyes. Begin to look around your space under the sheet. See where the sheet meets the floor. See it on parts of your body. Slowly you discover you can move your fingers, your hands, your arms. You can move your toes, ankles, legs. Slowly bring all their movements together so you can get up on your hands and knees. Watch how your movements affect the movements of your sheet, how they affect your space.

Slowly crawl around. Be aware of your space as you crawl. See how it changes. See what new things come into it as you move. Encounter other beings. Watch their effect on your space. Where do they push into your space? Where do you push into theirs?

Move into a space of your own. Slowly bring yourself to a standing position. Be aware of your entire body as you do so. What changes occur in your space as you stand up? Once you are standing, look again at the space you have created. Look at the sheet. Feel it on your body. Be aware of your breathing. Slowly begin to move about, being aware of the changes as you do so. You may meet others. Be aware of their effect on your space. Imagine your effect on their space.

Move to a space of your own. Slowly, slowly, remove your sheet. Be aware of the space around you now. Be aware of what you see and how you see it. Be aware of the smells. Be aware of how the air feels on your skin. Be aware of the sounds around you.

When you are ready, join the group.

This may be an intense experience for the students. If you experience them as being very quiet and withdrawn, don't be concerned. Let them go to a quiet activity. Give them some time and space. It may also be that they are excited after this experience. If so, let them talk about what they discovered. What were the surprises? What did they like about the lesson? What didn't they like?

Lesson 10. Art

Get under your sheet. Be by yourself for a while. Imagine that you are a work of art, but you are a part of a larger sculpture or picture. You need others to make you into a complete sculpture or picture. Experience different settings, different people. Experiment with different forms. Then settle on one. With another person or persons, form your sculpture or painting. When you think you have completed it, remove your sheet and look at your creation.

Talk about what you experienced.

If possible, have a Polaroid camera available for this lesson. Take pictures of the students before they remove their sheets.

Lesson 11. Paint Your Sheet

This should be done after the students have used the sheets many times, and only with sheets that are ready to be discarded.

> Think about the times you have used these sheets. Think about the lessons you did with them. Think about the things you discovered about yourself and others while using the sheets.

You might wish to review the things they have experienced with their sheets.

> Lay your sheet out flat and, using crayons or paint, draw pictures on your sheet to show what you experienced with it. You can draw a picture of something that happened, or you can make a design to symbolize what happened to you while using the sheet. If possible, use all of the sheet to show what happened to you.

If some students do not have sheets, let them work with someone who does.

> Describe your drawing and your sheet experiences to someone in this group. Take your sheet home and describe it to someone at home.

A Confluent
Learning Experience

It is possible to develop confluent learning by integrating affective experience with the cognitive dimensions of learning. It is also possible to do it the other way around: by bringing cognitive dimensions into an affective experience. Up to now, the lessons in this book have all but ignored the cognitive domain. Here is a lesson to illustrate how much cognitive material can be elicited from one affective lesson, and how even one affective experience can become a total curriculum by integrating the cognitive dimensions available from various subject areas.

THE ANGRY SOCK

Materials: One sock per student and material for stuffing the socks, e.g., beans, rice, sand, small pebbles.

Take your sock and, using the things you find here, stuff it. As you do so, think about all the times you get angry. Each time you put something into your sock, really stuff it in there, saying, "I get angry when . . ." Fill the sock with your anger. Stuff all your anger into the angry sock. Leave room enough at the top of your sock, the cuff part, to be able to tie a knot in it.

Double-check to be sure all socks are securely tied before going on.

Throw your angry sock in the air and catch it. Feel the weight of
your anger. Throw your angry sock against the floor. Listen to the
sound. Throw it against the wall. Listen to it again. Hit it with
your hand. Feel your anger. What else would you like to do with
your angry sock? If possible, do it.

Wait to see what the students do with their socks. It may or may not be
necessary for you to set limits for the sake of safety. If you see the students engage in hazardous activities, stop them and make a few explicit
rules: Don't hit anyone with a sock full of pebbles because it might hurt
them. Don't throw your sock at the windows or lights because they might
break.

It is best to do this lesson when you experience the class as needing
a release for anger, at a time when they are difficult to live with and
seem about to explode, when every little thing sets them off.

Here is how "The Angry Sock" lesson may be integrated into normal
classroom subject areas.

Language Arts: The students can write about their experiences. They
can read their stories to other students. They can listen to other stories.
They can use their stories to work on spelling, diction, and grammar
appropriate to their grade level. Advanced students can write stories from
the sock's point of view. "I am an angry sock . . ." Vocabulary can be
developed. One class coined the word "hardfast" while working with
their angry socks. When someone hit another so as to cause pain, that was
called a "hardfast." This led to further investigations into the origin of
words.

Math: Primary students can throw their socks and see which goes the
farthest, which is the closest to a mark, which is the heaviest, which is the
lightest, etc. Intermediate students can throw the socks and accurately
measure the distances they traveled. Which sock went the farthest? What
could account for that? Advanced students can estimate the number of
beans it will take to fill their socks and check out their guesses.

Fill a small container with beans. Count the number of beans in it.
Count the number of times the small container must be filled in order to
fill the sock. Multiply the number in the small container by the number
of times it is used to fill the sock, and that gives a close estimate of the
number of beans in the sock.

Science: The students can be introduced to problems concerning
weight, mass, and energy by throwing socks stuffed with different materials. They might also learn about the origin of the material of the sock as
well as the material used to stuff it.

Art: The students can turn their angry socks into angry puppets.
They can draw on them, paste facial features on them, and add yarn or
string hair. They can then create a puppet theater and puppet plays to
act out angry scenes.

They can draw pictures of angry faces, angry animals, angry skies, etc.

Social Studies: The socks can help to develop responsible citizens. "Who is angry?" "I am." "Who is hitting Johnny?" "I am." "What else can you hit?" "My angry sock." It can be used to help develop an awareness of others who share the same space and needs. "Don't hit me, I'm not your sock." Primary students can carry their socks around as if they were pets when studying animals or as babies if they are studying families. They can hold them close to them during times of stress or fatigue. Advanced students can turn the socks into voodoo dolls upon reading about witchcraft in another culture.

Here is just a partial list of behavioral goals and objectives available from experiencing "The Angry Sock."

Language Arts: Talk about an experience using sentences beginning with "I."

Be able to listen to what others experience.

Write about an experience.

Read what others wrote about an experience.

Math: Be able to make comparisons of distances and weights.

Be able to record accurate measurements.

Be able to estimate a large number and check it out with counting and multiplication skills.

Science: Be able to define weight, mass, and energy in scientific terms.

Be able to translate experiments with weight, mass, and energy into a scientific formula.

Be able to describe things in terms of their weight, mass, and energy.

Be able to describe the origin of a material.

Art: Be able to represent anger in an artistic form, either through drawing or through making a puppet.

Become involved in creating a play.

Social Studies: Be able to express anger in a socially acceptable way.

Be able to express fatigue in a socially acceptable way.

Be able to role-play something from another culture.

Going from Cognitive to Affective Experiences

Confluent education is not just a set of lesson plans around a theme or a subject area. It is a way of being, a process, an experience. I can share all the lessons I have developed, give multiple examples of things I have experienced, and describe processes I have seen evolve in classrooms. And still, I am not able to teach anyone to be a confluent teacher any more than I am able to teach a student to read. As a student told me years ago, that last step in the process must be taken alone. At first it can seem to be a frightening step. Life itself is sometimes frightening. Confluent education *is* life, and so it challenges the mind, deepens feelings, opens communications and utilizes energy. Although it can be frightening, it is always exciting, always alive.

In this section, confluent ideas are presented around four subject areas: language, science, reading, and mathematics. The lessons are designed to bring emotions, actions, ideas, and new awarenesses into the classroom.

There is so much cognitive material available in each one of these subjects, it would be impossible to deal with all the concepts in even one of them in any depth. It is not the purpose of this section to "cover" the subject. These ideas are offered instead as starters. They are meant to stimulate thinking on that subject, to provide a starting point, and to help teachers develop their own style of "left handed" teaching, their own confluent learning program.

Begin slowly! If you or the students have had no experience using a confluent approach, you can learn together. Begin by using this approach once a week in your favorite subject until you and your students become accustomed to it. Then gradually, use the approach more frequently and in various subject areas until you reach the level appropriate for you and your students in each subject.

Be selective in the cognitive materials you choose to work with. The concepts at each level must be limited to those that can be investigated using processes within the capacity of the students in your class. Use texts and teachers' guides as indicators of what your students are expected to learn. If your knowledge and your experiences with your students indicate that the text is not well suited to their capacity, edit and revise the material, or choose other materials which are more appropriate for their stage of development. Many teachers' guides offer excellent conceptual frameworks, indicating the progression of concepts. Make use of those to determine not just what your students should know at a particular grade level, but also to know what they are assumed to know before reaching that level and what will come after. Allow students multiple opportunities through discussions and class activities to let you know what they know and what they need to learn next. Let them tell and show you what they already know and then plan the next step of their development with and for them. Do not waste their time going over and over materials they have already mastered. Do not stifle their enthusiasm for learning by constantly presenting concepts beyond their abilities. Reviewing known materials or exploring something beyond the reach of the students should be practiced in the classroom, but the materials covered should be used selectively, knowingly, and carefully.

The following illustrates one example of how to selectively choose cognitive materials in order to meet the varying concept levels of a class.

A second grade teacher asked if I would teach a lesson to determine what she should teach her class about telling time. The curriculum required knowing time on the hour and half hour. While I presented a lesson from their standard text to the entire class, the teacher became one of the group. By observing the activities of the students and listening and contributing to the informal discussions which were going on all through the lesson, she realized that four students already knew how to tell time beyond that required for their level. In fact, they could read the clock as well as she could. About a third of the class could already read the hour and half hours correctly. Another third were able to respond correctly to the time on the hour, but often didn't know how to call the half-past mark. They would say half-past two, instead of half-past one. The rest of the class ranged from knowing the hour if they really thought about it to not having any idea of how to produce a correct response to questions about time.

To make students who already know how to tell time go through pages and pages of work indicating the correct hour and half hour is to waste their time. It can also make them impatient and intolerant of students who still do not understand the concept. To expect those who do not understand anything at all about telling time to do pages of seat work is to encourage them to either copy down any answer and hope it is correct, or just simply to give up. In this case, the classroom teacher had those who knew how to tell time work with the school librarian and develop a report, which was later presented to the entire class, on the history of clocks. The middle group was given multiple opportunities to read the clock on the hour and half hour, as well as given limited practice on work sheets designed to quicken their responses at reading time. The teacher spent her time with those who needed the most guidance in order to master this skill. She went back to materials which may, or may not, have been presented at previous levels and worked through them once again, one step at a time, until the students reached the level appropriate to their stage of development.

Students must be allowed to work together, not competing with each other, but cooperating with one another. They should be taught to work together *in* a group, but not *as* a group. All students can be on the same topic, but working as individuals, doing their own manipulating, thinking, and writing. As the teacher works first with one group and then with another, he or she may notice that a particular assignment causes more trouble than anticipated. This, of course, is an indication that special attention should be given to the readiness/awareness level of the class, a group, or individuals. It may be that a totally new assignment or several assignments have to be developed and worked through to successfully return to the original assignment. Or, as with the four students described above, it may be that the entire assignment is inappropriate and some other learning experience needs to be developed for the students.

Another way to develop confluent lessons is to extend the student's response-ability by developing as many opportunities as possible to live or act out, to experience, the cognitive concepts which they are working to develop. Students usually learn more readily through direct experiences than in any other way. If direct experiences are not built into the curriculum materials being used, it is necessary and vital for the teacher to take this next step. For example, a mathematical concept is operations and sentences. The first step of that is set formation, next comes sharing, and then division. In a primary class, allow students to form multiple sets of their own by physically directing their peers into sets. Find all the students with brown hair. Now find all the students with brown eyes. How do those two sets intersect? How do you know? Name the students in the intersecting set.

On higher levels, have the students develop the concept of sharing and division, both as a math activity and as a way to teach cooperation. Bring a bag of multicolored candies into the class. Have the students make sets of the candies, discovering how many ways they can form the candies into sets: by color, by shape, by size, by the way they are wrapped, etc. Based on the set formation, have them discuss all the ways they could share the candy. Then have them divide it equally. Have the students eat the candy and describe how it tastes, what other things taste like it, what does it feel like as it melts in the mouth. From there on, a math lesson becomes a language lesson. It may cost a bit to buy a bag of candy now and then, but when one realizes all the lessons that can be learned, and all the fun and enjoyment that can be had in the process, it is well worth the price.

Modify usual procedures to place more responsibility on the students and less emphasis on "sit still and listen to me." Rather than present large amounts of information through a lecture, pose problems dealing with the information and let students seek solutions on their own or in small groups. Then discuss how they reached their solution as well as its accuracy. What did they learn about themselves while seeking that solution? Who contributed to their solution? What resources were consulted? Who might agree with their solution? Who might disagree? Do not offer your own ideas right away. Then, do it only as part of the group, and not as the final authority. Whenever possible, leave evaluation to the student. The students' communication of ideas and their own evaluation of the results of their inquiries increase their depth of concept formation and their sense of personal worth and identity as well. In every way possible, use curriculum to liberate rather than to enslave the students. Use it to help them to think, to question, to test possible solutions. Allow them to push beyond accepted customs into serious and creative analysis of all types of situations. If they are reading a story, have them consider how they would have ended it had they written it. If they are working through a science problem, how did they come to their solution? Offer them ideas and suggestions from "experts" but never lose sight of the fact that each student is a unique human being and that each one is *the* expert on his or her own need and ability to learn.

Confluent education is an exchange between students and teachers, teachers and students, and students and students. Learning occurs for everyone. Teaching is someone showing someone else that something is possible—students showing students, teachers showing students, and students showing teachers. It is an opportunity for everyone in the classroom to be involved in the creative art of teaching, to be developing their humanness, to be creating life and living.

Language

What the young become, they become in part because of their use of language. To use language as a means of sharing experiences, is to foster personal growth through the discoveries in thought and feeling that come from trying to comprehend that experience. If language is simply a tool for sending messages, the effect is to diminish a person to an impersonal data passer. The value of language then lies in the help it can give a person in knowing him/herself and in developing a sense of sharing that understanding with others through words. A sense of communion requires words. Language gives experience meaning and allows us to share that meaning. Thought is possible without words, but not to an advanced level. By means of words, we develop concepts which enable us to organize our experiences, and in that sense, create and give meaning to the world we live in.

I began to develop confluent lessons through language lessons. I felt confident in that area, and I felt it was a subject which allowed me a great deal of freedom for exploration. Through developing speaking and listening skills, I was able to learn much about my students. As they talked, I listened and learned much about matching my teaching with their learning. Language gave me the opportunity to share much of myself with them. Through language and the mastery of language skills, the students and I were able to deepen our own self-awareness as well as develop more positive relationships with each other.

Another reason I began developing confluent lessons in language was that I could combine language development with other subjects I was teaching, such as reading, social studies, math, music, and art. One learns language by being in a situation that calls language forth. Language activities provide students multiple opportunities to express a single experience or idea across a wide range of subjects. This, in turn, leads to a more integrated approach to teaching and learning.

A language objective might be to correctly use personal subject pronouns (I, you, she, he, we, they) and possessive pronouns (my, your, his, her, our). That could very easily enrich social studies objectives by having the students use those words to explore the concept that people are alike and people are unique, e.g., have them mill around the room and meet other students; have them find others who are like them and state the likeness in sentences using personal subject pronouns, beginning the first sentence with "I" and a second sentence with the word "you": "I have brown hair, you have brown hair." "I have freckles, you have freckles." Have the students use possessive pronouns to state differences: "My hair is black, your hair is blonde." "My hands are big, your hands are small." Have them form into several types of small groups and use the plural forms: "We are boys, they are girls." "We are short, they are tall." Have them form as many different types of groups as necessary to experiment with all the kinds of pronouns they are expected to use correctly.

To extend that same lesson into math, have the students do counting, set formation, greater than/equal to, less than, and/or one-to-one correspondence computations as they go along. In art, they can draw first themselves, and then the person least like them, accentuating their differences. They can analyze a story for use of personal pronouns as well as likenesses and differences as a reading skill. "Jane in the story is a girl. I am a girl. She likes dogs. I like dogs. She has brown hair. I have red hair." In this manner, one idea builds upon another, allowing an objective to be reinforced several times throughout the educational program.

Language learning and conceptual growth are facilitated by direct experiences. Language, like other subjects, grows in relation to the experiences of the individual learner. Unfortunately, most of the materials available in language allow only vicarious experiences: students are expected to learn solely through the experiences of others. Of course, it is not possible or even advisable to provide students with all the experiences available to humankind. However, unless direct connections are made between the experiences of others and one's own experiences, learning remains disconnected, vague, or meaningless.

Just recently, I observed a fifth-grade class go through a lesson designed around a story of a horse who started out as a rebel and turned into an outlaw horse. The students were asked to interpret the selection, describe how the story made them feel, critique the art work that accompanied the story, describe the author's point of view, and, finally, to write a paragraph describing the character of the author. It was a good lesson as far as it went, but to me, it was totally lacking in personal involvement. I would want to develop the lesson beyond that suggested in the teacher's guide. I would have students identify times in their lives when they felt, or feel, rebellious. I would want them to explore some of their attitudes. When should rebellion become outlawed? How far does one have the right to go in expressing one's own way before others have the right to demand conformity? What if there were no rebels in this world? I would have them describe their own character when they feel rebellious. If there were adequate interest, and there often is at that level, I might encourage students to do their own illustrations to the story, asking them to be aware of how the author and the artist influenced their own work. I might have them talk about what else they would have had the horse do, had they been the author.

Because language is a part of every subject area, it offers multiple opportunities for a teacher to develop materials which will foster personal and intellectual growth, both for him/herself and for students.

The lessons in this unit deal with several topics found in most language books. There is no attempt to "cover" the field with these lessons. They are meant to be starters, initial ideas, stimulators, examples so that others may see ways to adapt materials they have available to a confluent approach to language. Many of the ideas here were inspired by Beverly Galyean's *Language From Within,* a handbook of personal growth and awareness exercises applied to language teaching and learning. (See bibliography.)

Objectives

To correctly use verbs in various tenses and forms in order to identify actions of self and others.

To correctly use adjectives in order to describe self and others.

To correctly use pronouns in direct and interrogative forms to make clear distinctions between self and others.

To correctly use adverbs in order to describe self and others.

To correctly use comparatives and superlatives to state values and personal choices.

Lesson 1. Imperatives I

This lesson on teaching imperatives has been adapted from a standard text. In various forms, it can be found in several different language books. Students are directed to repeat the following in patterned responses:

Teacher reads:	*Students respond:*
Anyone want to watch television?	Sure! Let's watch television!
Anyone want to hear the news?	Sure! Let's hear the news!
Anyone want to play tennis?	Sure! Let's play tennis!
Anyone want to begin?	Sure! Let's begin!
Anyone want to prepare dinner?	Sure! Let's prepare dinner!
Anyone want to go back?	Sure! Let's go back!

Students are directed in a drill: *Write the imperative:*

	(Marianne)	(work)
Tell Marianne to work!	_____,	_____!
Tell Ralph to begin!	_____,	_____!
Tell Mrs. Drurand to come in!	_____,	_____!

The following lesson demonstrates how to extend a lesson on imperatives into the realm of confluent education.

Read each of these imperatives and next to each one indicate which persons might be saying that to you. Then, indicate whether you are feeling positive or negative toward the imperative and the person issuing it.

Imperatives	*Who comes to your mind?*	*Feeling: positive or negative*
Look at television!	_____	_____
Listen to the announcements!	_____	_____
Play tennis!	_____	_____
Prepare the dinner!	_____	_____
Come back here!	_____	_____
Work!	_____	_____
Come on in!	_____	_____

Share your responses in a small group.

Now, complete these imperatives by adding whatever words come to you as you read the imperatives themselves.

	Giving or receiving	*Feelings evoked*
Look _____!	_____	_____
Listen _____!	_____	_____
Play _____!	_____	_____
Begin _____!	_____	_____
Prepare _____!	_____	_____
Work _____!	_____	_____
Study _____!	_____	_____
Be _____!	_____	_____
Do _____!	_____	_____

Once your imperatives are completed, indicate whether you are giving them to someone, or whether you are receiving them from someone. Try to recognize the feelings evoked by the imperative and indicate what those feelings seem to be. For example: Look at me! I am *receiving* that from my mother. I feel *angry.*

Listen to this! I am *giving* that to my friends. I feel *excited* and *energetic.*

Share your responses in a small group.

Lesson 2. Imperatives II

Sit in your normal places. Close your eyes. Take some deep breaths and become as relaxed as possible.

Imagine now that you are on a stage. There are many people in the audience. All of them are important persons in your life. See the stage and see the people in the audience. As you look carefully at them, they begin to give you imperatives. Listen to what they are saying. What are they telling you to do? As you imagine and listen to them, be aware of your feelings as you hear the imperatives. What do you feel as you hear each one? Some feelings may be pleasant, others not so pleasant. Which imperatives leave you feeling "uptight?" Excited? Pleased? Angry? Scared? Happy? Continue to imagine hearing imperatives from the people in your audience.

Slowly come back to us here in this room. See the people around you here and now.

In small groups, talk about what you imagined you saw and heard. Share how you felt during the fantasy.

Now, translate what you imagined in a written form. Here is a model.

Imperative	*Person who said it*	*My feeling*
Example:		
Study hard!	Father	Scared
Pick up your junk!	Brother	Mad
Kiss me!	Grandmother	Happy

By extending these lessons to include an affective component, you have an opportunity to learn much about your students. You also have an opportunity to share your life with them if you so wish. You will find that the mutual sharing of personal incidents energizes both you and your students. It causes motivation for communication. Meaningful sharing increases as vocabulary and structure continue to expand and serve the students as the medium through which important and meaningful dialogues emerge.

Lesson 3. Verbs

Words expressing an action performed by or experienced by the subjects are verbs. The following lessons allow students to be the subject of verbs.

"TO LIKE"
Make a list of ten things you like to do at home.

Make a list of ten things you like to do at school.

Make a list of ten things you like to do in general.

Choose a partner. Take turns sharing your lists. Use complete sentences stating both the place and what you like, e.g., "at home I like to watch television," or "I like to watch television at home."

After both of you have shared all three lists, talk about likes you have in common. Talk about unusual likes either of you have. Share anything else you would like to share.

"TO HEAR"
Listen to the sounds around this room. What do you hear?

Work with a partner. Take turns saying, "Now I hear _____."

Now imagine you are in a football stadium. What do you hear? Take turns saying, "In a football stadium, I hear _____."

Now imagine you are in the mountains. What do you hear? Take turns saying, "In the mountains, I hear _____."

Now imagine you are at the beach. What do you hear? Take turns saying, "At the beach, I hear _____."

Now imagine you are inside your body. What do you hear? Take turns saying, "Inside my body, I hear _____."

Now imagine being anywhere you like. What do you hear? Take turns saying, "I am _____ (name the place). I hear _____."

"TO WANT"

Think of all the things you want right now. List them. When you have done this, add the name of the person or persons who could possibly give these things to you. If you are the source, name yourself. Share your list with another person, using the phrase "I want" to begin each sentence.

Now imagine it is your birthday. Your parents ask you what you want. You tell them. Practice doing this with your partner:

"It's your birthday. What do you want?"
"I want _____."

Take turns asking the question and giving the answer. Repeat several times.

Now address yourself to me, your teacher. What do you want from me? Those who want to do so, may read or tell me what they want from me.

Listen carefully to what students say or read to you. Chances are you will receive some insights into how you can match your teachings to the learning needs of the students. You might also take this occasion to tell your students what you want from them.

"TO LAUGH"

What usually makes you laugh? When do you usually laugh? With whom do you usually laugh? Where are you when you laugh the most? How often do you laugh? How do you feel when you laugh? Work with a partner in answering these questions:

When do you laugh?
I laugh when _____.

With whom do you usually laugh?
I laugh when I am with _____.

How often do you laugh?
I laugh _____.

How do you feel when you laugh?
When I laugh, I feel _____.

Work in a small group and share your answers to these questions.

When was the last time you laughed at a film? At a song? At a joke? At a person?

When was the last time you laughed and wished you hadn't?

When was the last time you only pretended to laugh?

When have you been hurt by laughter?

When have you hurt someone with your laughter?

Make a group list of all that could be meant by laughter.

Lesson 4. Adjectives I

Words which give more specific and precise information about a noun or noun equivalent are adjectives. They denote a quality, attribute, range of application, or specify distinction.

Give the students a list of the following adjectives:

Adjective	Image	Adjective	Image
beautiful	_____	easy	_____
ugly	_____	difficult	_____
heavy	_____	relaxed	_____
light	_____	tense	_____
tall	_____	ideal	_____
short	_____	real	_____
high	_____	excited	_____
low	_____	calm	_____
happy	_____	angry	_____
sad	_____	peaceful	_____
wonderful	_____	responsible	_____
horrible	_____	irresponsible	_____
delightful	_____	interesting	_____
painful	_____	boring	_____
helpful	_____	important	_____
harmful	_____	wasteful	_____

I will read this list of adjectives. When I do, let an image come into your mind that in some way relates to the adjective. Write an image that corresponds to the adjectives as I read them. For example: Beautiful, sunset; ugly, littered street; heavy, cement truck. Share your list of images with a partner.

Go through the complete list of adjectives and choose the 10 that are the most meaningful to you. Rank them in their order of importance to you.

Now, take this list of adjectives and imagine you are communicating with someone who doesn't know you very well. Which adjectives would this person select for you? Which adjectives do you hope they select for you?

Find a partner. You may speak to this person by using only one of your select list of adjectives. Try to make a meaningful conversation using only adjectives.

Lesson 5. Adjectives II

Here is a list of certain persons for you to consider. When you think of these persons, imagine adjectives they would use to describe you.

Person	Would describe me as
mother	_____
father	_____
brother	_____
sister	_____
aunt	_____
uncle	_____
stranger	_____
classmate	_____
friend of same sex	_____
friend of opposite sex	_____
teacher	_____

Add persons to your list and continue to imagine them describing you with adjectives.

Of all the adjectives people might use to describe you, which adjectives would please you the most? the least? List the most and the least pleasing adjectives. Share your list with a partner. Compare your lists.

Lesson 6. Opposite Adjectives

Find a partner. One of you call out an adjective and the other respond with the opposite form of the adjective. See how many pairs you can identify.

With your partner, join another set of partners. The two of you select adjectives and see if the other team can identify the opposite forms.

Lesson 7. Other Adjective Activities

Form groups of four to six students. Choose an adjective you can all act out for the rest of the class. Don't tell the class the name of your adjective. Let them guess what it is by your actions.

If students are unfamiliar with adjectives, they can draw slips with adjectives printed on them and then act out what they draw. Some adjectives to act out: angular, worried, nervous, tired, abnormal, joyous.

Make a class chart of frequently used adjectives. Graph the frequency of their use during class time.

If certain adjectives are "overused" by the students, make a list of others that can be used instead. Reward efforts to use alternate words through praise and recognition.

Lesson 8. Pronouns

These lessons demonstrate ways to learn the function of pronouns as well as increase self-awareness.

"DIRECT"

Here is a list of words. When you read (or hear) them, decide whether you want it. Respond either "I want it (them)," or "I don't want it (them)."

beach	motorcycle	ring
pizza	hamburger	guitar
Datsun 240Z	herb tea	drums
dictionary	mountains	cake
party	class office	water bed
new clothes	movie ticket	job
new shoes	more friends	more free time
skis	theatre tickets	television
bicycle	records	telephone
vitamins	flowers	"someone special"
authority	honey	freedom

Work in groups of four. Each of you make up your own list of things you want. When each person has done this, take turns reading your list. Each person in the group respond to each item on every other list with either "Yes, I want it (them)," or "No, I don't want it (them)."

Adapt the list to include items of interest to the particular likes and dislikes of the students in your class.

"INTERROGATIVE"

Look around this room. See how many people you know. Now answer these questions:

Who is friendly?	Who is assertive?
Who is intelligent?	Who is shy?
Who is beautiful?	Who is gentle?
Who is talkative?	Who is understanding?
Who is casual?	Who is alert?
Who is nervous?	Who is loving?

When you have decided on answers, write them down. Go to the person and say: "To me, you are _____."

Complete the following statements:

I like a person who is _____.

I fear a person who is _____.

I admire a person who is _____.

I resent a person who is _____.

I understand a person who is _____.

I prefer a person who is _____.

I identify with a person who is _____.

Variation

Repeat the same exercise substituting the words "boy," "girl," "teacher," and/or "parents," for person.

Lesson 9. Adverbs

Adverbs describe qualities, restrict, limit, or make more precise the meaning of other words. They modify 1) verbs—run *quickly*, play *quietly*; 2) adjectives—*extremely* large, *terribly* boring; 3) other adverbs—*very* swiftly.

"ADVERBS AND ME"

Complete the following statement with an adverb of your choice:

I run _____.	I play _____.
I study _____.	I work _____.
I talk _____.	I listen _____.
I think _____.	I plan _____.
I eat _____.	I sing _____.
I drive _____.	I dress _____.
I dance _____.	I write _____.

Now work in dyads. "A" ask the question: "B" answer it:

A: "How do you run?"
B: "I run _____."

When "B" has answered each question, "A" has a turn to answer each of them.

"ADVERBS AND OTHERS"

If someone were to describe you using only adverbs, which adverbs would they choose? If this person were describing you at (a) school, (b) home, (c) right now, which adverbs would they choose?

Work in dyads. Look at your partners and tell them adverbs you think describe them.

Imagine various persons who are important to you. As you imagine each person, think of an adverb that describes them.

"MORE ADVERBS"

Complete the following statements:

I want _____ quickly.
I hope _____ honestly.
I fear _____ carelessly.
I know how to _____ intelligently.
I prefer _____ secretly.

Make up five more such sentences on your own. Share your entire list with someone.

Lesson 10. Past Tense

Along with studying the use of past tense, allow students opportunities to explore their here and now.

Imagine yourself and how you were about three years ago. What grade were you in? What did you look like then? Who was your teacher? Think about yourself then and now as you answer the following:

Three years ago, I admired _____. Now I admire _____.

Three years ago, I feared _____. Now I fear _____.

Three years ago, I learned _____. Now I am learning _____.

Three years ago, I wanted _____. Now I want _____.

Three years ago, I spent time _____. Now I spend time _____.

Make up five sets of sentences on your own which describe how you were three years ago and how you are now.
Share your responses with a small group.

Lesson 11. Past Descriptive (Imperfect)

As students learn the function of various parts of speech, provide opportunities for them to use them to make meaningful statements about themselves.

Complete the following:

I was proud when I _____. Now, I am proud when I _____.

I was embarrassed when I _____. Now, I am embarrassed when I _____.

I was afraid when I _____. Now, I am afraid when I _____.

I cried when I _____. Now, I cry when I _____.

I laughed when I _____. Now, I laugh when I _____.

Make up three more sets of sentences which describe how you used to be and how you are now. Share your responses in a small group.

Lesson 12. Conditional Tense

Allow the world of imagination and fantasy to be a part of lessons on the use of conditional tense.

Complete the following statements:

If I had money, I would _____.
If I had a car, I would _____.
If I were taller, I would _____.
If I were older, I would _____.
If I were smarter, I would _____.
If I had a motorcycle, I would _____.
If I had new clothes, I would _____.
If I had a free ticket to the movies, I would _____.
If I had a stereo, I would _____.
If I were calmer, I would _____.
If I were more serious, I would _____.
If I _____.

Now work in dyads. Take turns asking and answering. What would you do if you were _____?

Lesson 13. Subjunctive

The study of the function of subjunctives can be used to help students gain awareness of how they themselves function.

Complete the following sentences:

I am happy that I _____.
I am sad that I _____.
I am surprised that I _____.
I am angry that I _____.
I must _____.
I want to _____.
I allow myself to _____.
I forbid myself to _____.
I regret that I _____.
I wish that I _____.
I am joyful that I _____.

It is enough that I _____.
It is necessary that I _____.
It is wonderful that I _____.

Review your list of responses. Are there any responses which surprise you? What kinds of statements could you make about yourself based on the information contained in your responses?

Lesson 14. Reflexive Verbs

Reflexive verbs denote an action that is directed back upon the agent or subject—the athlete *disciplined* himself; the witness *perjured* himself. Use them to encourage students to consider what they do to themselves.

"I WONDER"

List ten things you wonder about. Say: "I wonder about _____
_____." When you have done this, compare your "wondering" with three other people. Find which are your common "wonderings."

Obtain a list of "common wonderings" solicited from the entire class. Let the students see what they have in common. Try to incorporate some of their "wondering" into future lessons.

"OTHERS WONDER"

Imagine you are:

    a) Your father: What does he wonder about?
    b) Your mother: What does she wonder about?
    c) Your brother: What does he wonder about?
    d) Your sister: What does she wonder about?
    e) The principal: What does he/she wonder about?
    f) The President: What does he/she wonder about?
    g) Me, your teacher: What do I wonder about?

Choose a partner. Role play being one of the above people. Tell your partner who you are, and while each of you are in a role, have a conversation with one another. Tell each other what you wonder about.

After the role play, talk about how it felt to role play another person. Discuss ways you and the person you role played are alike and different from one another.

"TO COMPLAIN"

List ten complaints you have right now. In doing this, indicate if these complaints are directed at:

    a) family (F)
    b) school (S)
    c) this class (C)
    d) friends (Fr)
    e) others (O)

Use your list to decide the answers to the following questions:

    1) If you could make one complaint at home and knew it would elicit a change of some sort, what complaint would you make?

    2) If you could make one complaint to the principal of this school and knew changes would definitely take place, what complaint would you make?

    3) If you could make one complaint to me and knew I would at least listen to your complaint, what complaint would you make?

Now choose a partner. Share what you wish to share.

This might provide an occasion to "air grievances" which may have been accumulating for a while in the classroom. If so, help students to air their complaints in ways which encourage growth and cooperation. "Jean, when you talk in a loud voice and I am trying to do math, I can't concentrate." Instead of "Jean, you've got a big mouth." "Larry, I want you to tell me when you need a pencil instead of just grabbing mine," instead of "Larry, you steal stuff." "Gloria, give me a five-minute warning before I have to change activities," instead of "You're always butting in."

If students do offer complaints to you, listen carefully. If there is anything you can do about them, do it as soon as possible.

Lesson 15. Comparisons

Comparisons can be used to help clarify values, to provide decision making opportunities and to allow students ways to discover how they are similar to and different from others in class.

Complete the following statements:

    Money is more important than _____.
    Time is more important than _____.

Cars are more important than _____.
Books are more important than _____.
Television is more important than _____.
People are more important than _____.
Classes are more important than _____.
Friends are more important than _____.
Family is more important than _____.

Now repeat the exercises, only this time fill in both words or phrases:

_____ is more important than _____.

Repeat the above exercises, only this time add the phrase:
. . . because I want _____.

Have students make up comparison lists using other words; beautiful, valuable, useful. Have them compare their lists with others and discuss the similarities and differences.

Lesson 16. Superlatives

Like comparatives, superlatives allow opportunities for values clarification and decision making. Students can use them to discover their own uniqueness as well as the individuality of others.

I will read a series of phrases. As you hear each one, allow an image to come into your mind. Identify persons or events you relate to these phrases:

The best looking _____.
The best tasting _____.
The heaviest _____.
The lightest _____.
The funniest _____.
The most exciting _____.
The most obvious _____.
The hardest _____.
The most wonderful _____.
The most terrifying _____.
The most intelligent _____.
The biggest waste _____.
The most interesting _____.

The biggest bore ————————.
The most helpful ————————.
The most painful ————————.

Now use these phrases in a complete sentence: "The best looking animal is a horse. Home made bread is the best tasting." Share your ideas in a small group.

UNIT TWO
Science

In the past, science curricula have been dominated by problem-solving methods which led teachers to believe that merely by teaching children five ordered steps, they could solve problems by the "scientific" method. Recently, there has been a trend away from teaching strictly by that method. First of all, it has been recognized that scientists do not use one exclusive method for solving problems. Secondly, it has been recognized that the problems students are confronted with in science texts can be solved without strict adherence to the five ordered steps of the problem solving method.

Another factor which seems to be influencing today's science curricula is the movement from rural to urban living. Many students today are raised in environments which appear to be entirely human-made. Air comes from air conditioners and heaters. Water comes from hot and cold taps. Food comes from supermarkets. Clothing comes from department stores. Homes, buildings, and streets are just there. To counteract this, new science materials are designed to lead students to consciously *observe* natural phenomena, *wonder* about them, and ask *their* questions about them. Good science curricula today urge teachers to provide learning environments that allow students to 1) find important ideas themselves, 2) explore the environment and their ideas as thoroughly as they are able, and 3) do things for themselves. Guidance is given to enable students first to ask questions and then seek answers, both by following the procedures described in the texts and by formulating hypotheses using information they have acquired from previous life experiences. Questions and experiences are suggested which will help students test the validity of their hypotheses.

These new science curricula offer teachers many new opportunities for the development of confluent lessons. Authors of different texts present excellent rationales for a discovery or inquiry approach for learning. The cognitive materials are well developed and offer stimulating ideas for all grade levels. To make these materials confluent teachers need to add the affective dimension, the realm of emotions, attitudes, imagination, and values to the lessons, and provide opportunities for students to relate their learning to themselves as unique individuals.

As in other subjects, teachers should look for ways to focus learning in science on personal and direct, rather than just on textbook and vicarious experiences. Beyond reading about life in a pond, visit a pond to actually see, touch, and smell the pond. If that is not possible, create a small pond environment within the classroom, using a large glass container such as an aquarium or large glass jar. (A gallon jar is large enough for two small fish and some plants.) Students can then actually observe the necessary balance between air, water, plants, and animals. If students are studying the formation of the earth, explore the area surrounding the school to discover which earth formations can be found in the immediate area. If there are no longer any natural formations to be found near the school, have the students talk about where they might go to find some, or have them describe places they have been where they observed them. It might not be possible to see the effects of wind and water erosion on the scale of the Grand Canyon near the school or community, but perhaps there is a nearby highway cut, river bank, or building excavation which will allow students first hand observations of those effects. If nothing else is available, after a rainfall, go out and find silt in gutters and drainage ditches. Have the students wonder about how far it traveled to get there. Or take a garden hose and spray it on one spot and observe what happens to the spot. Watch the water rise and fall in a puddle, creek, stream, or river. Have the students find out where the water came from and where it went. See if there is a place on the school ground where the class can dig a big deep hole. As they dig, have them observe, classify, identify, and/or measure the stratification of the earth.

One way to give students a richer experience and increased involvement in and responsibility for a science program is to allow them to make their own materials, equipment, science kits. While it may be necessary to purchase some science equipment, particularly at advanced levels, I personally object to students being presented with materials they can easily secure for themselves. Read the teacher's guide to find out how students are expected to use commercially developed equipment. Then let them find objects in their environment that will provide the same learning experiences. For example, rather than use uniform, plastic items from a commercially prepared science kit to work on the process of classification, have the students go for a short walk and gather several items on their own. When they return to the classroom, have them work together in small groups and use those items to develop a classification system. This provides them with opportunities to explore several ideas as they work out a system. It allows them to explore their environment with the objective of finding objects that can be classified and, best of all, it allows them to do things for themselves.

The lessons in this unit are meant to be a supplement to a regular science program. The ideas offered here cover a wide range of topics found in many science texts. Many lessons, such as "Discoveries and Wonderings" can be done repeatedly. Wonderings can be done at the outset of each new science topic so that the teacher can make certain the curriculum deals with what the students are wondering about and interested in.

Many lessons in other chapters of this book can be applied to science curriculum. All the lessons in Unit 8: Nature, relate to science. Other lessons can be adapted. For example, when exploring the concept of life systems, the students can do activities like "Body Building," "Machines," and "Working Together."

Objectives

To observe natural phenomena and human-made articles and be
    able to state what is observed.
To wonder about natural phenomena and human-made articles
    and state what one wonders.
To identify the process of changes in one's self, in others, and in
    things.
To identify ways of learning, habit formation, and changing habits.
To verbalize and demonstrate care and use of one's body.
To verbalize and demonstrate the concepts of dependence and
    interdependence.

Lesson 1. Sexism in Science

Before starting to read your science text, look through it and see what the pictures are about. Pay particular attention to the pictures that show boys and girls, men and women. Place a marker on the pages with pictures of people on them so you can easily find them again.

Work in a small group. Together, make a list of all the things you found men, women, boys, and girls doing in the pictures in your book:

Men are:	Women are:	Boys are:	Girls are:
Building a house.	Holding a baby.	Walking in woods.	Reading a book.
Driving a tractor.	Holding a baby.	Picking corn.	Making cookies.

Discuss the results of your lists. How many different things are men shown doing? How many different tools are men working with? How many different things are women shown doing? How many tools are they shown working with? What are boys mostly doing? How are you like the men, women, boys, and girls, shown in the book? Do you know any men like the men shown in the book? Do you know any women like the women shown in the book?

Today there is a growing concern about sexism as it is perpetuated through textbooks. While sexism exists in varying degrees in most textbooks, it seems particularly strong in science materials. In every science text I recently surveyed, men were shown in multiple roles: doctors, farmers, astronauts, carpenters, musicians, policemen, construction workers. They were shown using a wide variety of tools, equipment, and machinery. They were involved in several leisure time activities: fishing, skiing, surfing, growing flowers, hiking. Women, on the other hand, were portrayed only as mothers, teachers, librarians, or nurses. The only tools, equipment, and machinery shown with women were those which could be found in the kitchen or nursery. For leisure time, women were shown caring for children and working in the garden. I feel it is imperative for each and every teacher to counteract these stereotypical influences on our young boys and girls, our future men and women. The very least one can do is point them out.

Lesson 2. Discoveries and Wonderings

Science is a subject based on the discoveries of people. Some scientific discoveries, such as the first use of fire, have been made by accident. Others have been made by experience. Before we discovered how to travel into outer space, we had to first discover how to travel through air. Still other discoveries have been made through observation. By watching the movements of stars and planets, scientists discovered that the earth revolves around the sun.

Work in small groups, and discuss the following questions:

What have you learned by accident?

What have you learned by experience?

What have you learned by observation?

What have you learned through combining accident and experience, accident and observation, experience and observation?

What have you learned by combining all three of them?

If scientists and other people never wondered about things, what might our world be like today? Have you ever wondered about things? Share your wonderings with one another. What are the things you wonder about?

Make a list of the things you wonder about most. Share your list with other groups. Make a class list of the wonderings of our class.

Observe a natural phenomenon and develop as many "wonders" about it as you can. For example, observe a set of clouds. Let different wonderings come to your mind and write them down.

I wonder how high up they are.

I wonder how fast they are moving.

I wonder if they will bring rain. If so, I wonder how long before it will rain.

I wonder why some are moving one way, while others are moving another way.

Wonder while watching a stream, a tree, a bird, a rock, a fly. If you discover an important wonder, see if you can solve the mystery of the wonder. For example, I discovered why some clouds move one way while others move another way. Air, like water, moves in streams. At times I can observe the streams by observing clouds move in them.

Lesson 3. Blindfolds and Science

MATTER

Use the blindfolds and allow the students to go on a blind "feeling matter" walk. As they are presented with different sensory experiences, have them classify what they are feeling into living or non-living, natural or human-made, greater than or less than in weight (compared to last item experienced).

While the students are wearing blindfolds, pass around various objects and have them identify the objects according to specifics, such as weight, smell, shape, texture.

While students are blindfolded, pass around objects of varying temperatures. For example: ice cubes (be prepared with extras for when they begin to melt in the passing), a jar of milk that has been heated, a carton of cold milk.

Lesson 4. Changes I Have Seen

Form into small groups. Take turns describing the sequence of events in a change you have seen. Some changes you might describe are:

A storm you have seen come and go.

The changing of the seasons if you have experienced living through distinct seasons. (It is difficult to do this in areas where there are only slight or subtle seasonal changes.)

Changes in a female's body if you have experienced watching a pregnancy (this could be a parent, a friend, or a pet).

Changes in a baby during its first year of life.

Changes caused by the sun: sun-tanned skin, bleaching or changing color of hair, weather-worn houses, drying of a creek bed.

Changes caused by the wind: leaves blowing off trees, waves dashing, trees moving or breaking.

Changes caused by water: tidal action, flooding, drying.

CHANGES IN ME

Three years ago I was _____ feet, _____ inches. Now I am _____ feet, _____ inches.

Three years ago my hair was _____ (describe in length and color). Now my hair is _____ and _____.

Three years ago I had a scar _____. Now I have scars _____ and _____.

Three years ago I had _____ teeth (number). Now I have _____ teeth.

Three years ago my favorite color was _____. Now my favorite color is _____.

Three years ago my best friend was _____. Now my best friend is _____.

If you do not know the answers to these questions, who might help you get the answers? (Parents, older siblings, past teachers).

With primary students three years ago might be too distant to be easily recalled. Use a time span they can recall in some detail. With older students, it might be more appropriate to compare how they are now with how they were when they were one year old in order to emphasize a growth and change sequence. Feel free to experiment with letting the students fill out the questions based on different time spans. Let them discover which time span has the most meaning for them.

TIME CHANGES THINGS

Bring in a photograph which shows how you looked when you were much younger. Talk about the changes between now and then, not just height and weight, but strengths, likes and dislikes, preferences for foods, shape changes, etc.

Make a list of the things you can do now that you could not do when the picture was taken. Which learnings are common to everyone in the class? Have you learned anything which is unique? Which things have you learned that are common to all humans? Have you learned something that no animal has learned? Have you learned something that no other person has learned? If you haven't yet, might you in the future? What kinds of things might you know about in the future that we don't know much about today?

Bring pictures of different products as they looked several years ago: cars, radios, washing machines, television sets, telephones.

How might those products have performed when they looked like that? What kinds of changes have they gone through? How do they perform differently today than they did when the picture was taken?

Imagine what these products will look like 50 years from now. What might they look like? How might their performance be affected by the change in their appearance? How might the change in their appearance affect their performance?

Imagine what you might look like 50 years from now. What might you be able to do then that you can't do now? What can you do now that you might not be able to do then? Imagine all the things you will know about 50 years from now that you don't know about now.

Draw pictures of what products might look like 50 years from now. Make a list of what you might know about 50 years from now.

Variation

List all the tools, products, and machinery you know of that you use which were not available to your great grandparents. List tools, products, and machinery you have now that were not available to your grandparents. List tools, products, and machinery available now that your parents didn't have when they were young.

Great grandparents	*Grandparents*	*Parents*
Radio	Television	
Electric washing machine	Electric dishwasher	Micro-wave ovens
	Jet planes	10-speed bikes
Phonographs	Stereophonic sound	Quadrophonic sound

Lesson 5. Learning

How many times do you fail at a task before you give up? At what point do you become more determined than ever to complete a task? How quickly do you learn to do new things? What kinds of things are easiest for you to learn? Do you learn most by observing, experiencing, or listening to directions?

Learn to tie a knot, such as a square knot, bowline, or half-hitch. As you go about learning to tie it, make some scientific observations about yourself. Record the source of your learning. Did you learn from watching someone tie it? Did you learn from following verbal or written directions? Record the number of times you attempt a knot before you are successful at tying it. Once you tie it correctly, record successive correct knots before you make another mistake. At what number do you believe you know how to tie it correctly? Record any information you think interesting as you go about learning to tie the knot.

Record the same information while learning to tie at least three different knots. Use that information to make a statement about the way you learn to tie knots. For example: on the average, I make six attempts before I successfully learn to tie a knot from illustrated, written directions. Once I know how to tie a knot, I make one mistake in every fourth knot for the next 20 knots. After that, I do not make any more mistakes. Once I tie a knot correctly 25 times, I can remember how to tie it seven days later.

Use the knots you have learned to make a plant hanger, a wall hanging, or something useful or decorative. Imagine giving it to someone. Imagine keeping it. Do whatever you want with it.

Lesson 6. Classroom Habits

Lead the class in a discussion about the habits they have acquired which help them get things done easily and quickly. For example, how many of them automatically get dressed in the morning? What are some of the things they have learned which allow them to dress that way? How many of them are able to prepare their own breakfast? What have they learned that allows them to do that? How many of them just walk, or ride, to school and don't even think much about how to get there? What have they learned in order for that to happen?

Then have the students explore what happens in the classroom almost by habit. What activities occur so regularly they know to do them almost without thinking? With the students offering their ideas, choose something within the classroom schedule that occurs regularly at a given time and decide on a change in time for it to happen. For example, if you regularly read aloud to the class just after lunch, change to reading to them just before lunch. If there is a regular discussion session at the end of each day, have it at the beginning of each day, or just after lunch. Or decide to change a classroom routine: if there are two doors to the class and they only use one of them, have them begin to use the other door. Be sure you are willing to go along with a change they suggest before deciding to change it. For example, they might suggest using the other door, but if you know that would be impossible because of the need to share hall space with other classes, let them know why you would not be willing to have them do that.

Make a chart to demonstrate the length of time needed to have the change in schedule or routine become a habit. Record the number of correct responses to the change as well as the number of incorrect responses. Use that information to demonstrate "scientific" vocabulary. Words will vary, depending on the grade level and outcomes, but it should be possible to illustrate such terms as stimulus-response, trial and error, conditioning, positive reward, negative reward, regression, habit formation, learning. Use the chart to stimulate thinking and language in general. How long did it take to form the new habit? Was that a long time or a short time? How does one measure that kind of time? How did we feel when we forgot and regressed back to the old habit? Did everyone feel the same way? What contributes to successful habit changes? What makes it difficult to change habits?

Lesson 7. Habits at Home

Think of some habits you have which cause someone at home to be annoyed with you. For example, perhaps your mother is always asking you to pick up your clothes. For her, you have an annoying habit of leaving your clothes lying around. Or perhaps you leave the cap off the toothpaste tube, and that annoys your sister who uses it after you. Write your annoying habits in this form:

When I _____(identify habit)_____, _____(name person)_____ gets annoyed with me.

Do that for any habits you have which you know annoy those you live with. Write each on a separate index card.

Choose an annoying habit you would be willing to change. Write that in a sentence:

I will try to change the habit of _____.

Tell someone at home that you are going to work on changing a habit. If you wish to do so, ask them to help you to change the habit in ways you imagine will help you: gently remind you, give you a clue, praise you when you have done it. Make a contract with that person to work with you to change that habit.

Keep a record of your attempts to change your habit. Once it is changed, read the record and make some statements about yourself and how you change your habits.

Work with a small group of classmates. Each of you bring your index cards of annoying habits to the group. Together, brainstorm all the things you might do with your cards. Make a list of all the things you might do with your cards. Choose one thing to do from your "might do" list. Do it. Evaluate the outcome of what you did. What did you learn by doing what you did?

Lesson 8. Your Body: Cells, Models, and Energy

Scientific discoveries are made by a variety of investigations. In this lesson, three different investigations are suggested. First, students are asked to respond in a traditional manner using real cells and a microscope. Then they are asked to use their imaginations to translate scientific information in a creative manner. Lastly, they are asked to consider the effects of energy from both a scientific and a psychological perspective.

CELLS

All living things are comprised of cells. You can see some real cells with the help of a toothpick, some iodine, a glass slide, a cover slip, and a microscope.

Gently rub the flat end of a toothpick against the inside of your cheek. Some of the cells of your cheek will come off on the toothpick.

Put a drop of iodine on the glass slide. Carefully dip the end of the toothpick into the drop of iodine. Some skin cells will come off in the iodine. Cover the glass slide with a cover slip.

Look through the microscope at the skin cells. Draw a picture of what you see. Do your skin cells look like anything else you have seen? If so, what? What are you reminded of when you see your skin cells under a microscope? What do you imagine when you see the cells? What do you wonder about when you see the cells?

SCIENCE MODELS

Scientists make models to demonstrate how things work. Make a model of your body to show the digestive system. Show the mouth and stomach. Show the intestines. You can use a funnel for the mouth. You can have a rubber hose go from the funnel to the stomach. What can you use for a stomach? What can you use for the intestines? Can you think of any way you can show the heart? Can you think of any way you can show the blood? Is there any way you can show the cells in your model? Use your brain, your imagination, your hands, and whatever else you need to make a model.

ENERGY

When you do hard work, your cells work hard. When your cells work hard, they need energy. You can see what happens when your cells need more energy. You can see what happens when you work hard.

Count the number of times in one minute that you breathe air in through your nose. Then jump up and down 10 times. Again count the number of times in one minute that you breathe air through your nose. When did you breathe more? Can you tell why? Can you tell how your cells get the energy they need?

After reading about how cells get the energy they need in one or more science books, try describing the process to a friend, a parent, a younger child, an older child.

Working in a small group, talk about the things you experience as energizing you. You might think of energizing things as those things which "turn you on." What foods energize you? What music energizes you? What art? What television shows? What books? Make a list of different things you experience as energizing. Make a group list. Compare it with other group lists. Are there some things that everyone in the class experiences as energizing? If so, what? Using that information, see if you can invent some class activities which everyone, or nearly everyone, would experience as being energizing.

If at all possible, allow the students to carry out their inventions.

Lesson 9. Your Working Heart

Stick a thumb tack into the middle of a wooden match. Hold your hand out, with the underside of your wrist up and flat. Place the head of the tack on your wrist so you can see the match move each time your blood is pumped by your heart.

Count the number of times your blood is pumped by your heart in one minute.

Create some scientific or mathematical problems, using the match and the pumping of your blood. For example, count the number of times your heart pumps normally in one minute. Then count the number after you jump up and down 10 times. Do that at the same time on consecutive days, keeping a record over five days. Compare your recordings. Make some guesses (hypotheses) about the differences recorded. Record the rate of your heart beat for various kinds of work: how many heart beats per minute for mowing a lawn? How many for doing the dishes? How many for making a bed? Compare the different rates. Make some statements about the differences.

Lesson 10. Care of Self

What gives your body energy? What "fuel" does the most good for your body? What fuel is not very good for your body? When do you experience yourself as having the most energy? What do you do when you feel as if you have little energy, but you have something you must do? What things do you do that you feel energize you? What do you do that calms you? What do you do that upsets or irritates you? How do you change from being irritable to being calm? To being energized?

When does your body need to rest? How do you know that? What do you do that you experience as restful, other than sleep? Are there people in your life who are restful for you to be with? How do you experience that restfulness?

How do you keep your body clean? How do you avoid getting infections in open cuts? How do you avoid getting infections inside of you? How do you care for yourself when you are sick?

How is that different from when you are well? Is it possible to care for yourself as if you were sick when you are well? What does getting sick do for you and for your body?

When do you experience your body as becoming diseased? What things make you "dis-eased" (not at ease)? Where in your body do you first become dis-eased? If you don't do something to ease that, what happens next? Next? Next? At what point does your body become so dis-eased that you have to do something about it? (Take a rest, take a pill, become really ill, etc.)

Write or tape-record a story about a time when you became sick. What caused you to be sick? What did you experience while being sick? How did you and others take care of you when you were sick? How did you get well again? How do you stay well? How do you feel when you are well?

Lesson 11. Body Tools

Explore the ways your body is like a tool:

Tool	Body part which will do similar task
Scissors	Incissor teeth
Tweezers	Thumb and middle finger nails
Hammer	Fist, foot
Lever	Hand, forearm, and elbow
_____	_____
_____	_____

Make a list of expressions to describe body actions in terms of tools:

I wedged myself into that group.

He moved through the room like a steam roller.

I feel as if I am on a teeter-totter.

I just slid through that assignment (inclined grade).

How could you perform the following tasks just with parts of your body and no tools?

Sharpen a pencil.

Clean your teeth.

Tidy your hair.

Wash the dishes.

Make a cross-country ski trail.

Remove a splinter.

What tasks would you find impossible to do if you could never use tools?

Make up imaginary stories about how people invented tools. How was the potato peeler invented? How was the electric toothbrush invented? How was the hoe invented? How was the vacuum cleaner invented? (Imagination, rather than accuracy, counts here. If you find you are interested in discovering how a tool really was invented, then accuracy will be important.)

Lesson 12. Interdependence

Divide a piece of paper into three sections. In the middle section, write: "I do." To the left of the things you enter here, write who depends upon you to do that. To the right, write who you are dependent upon to be able to do that. For example:

Depend on me	*I do*	*I depend on*
The rest of the family when they sit down to eat.	Set the dinner table.	Mother or father to have dinner to set on the table.
Teacher to have someone to teach.	Come to school.	Teacher to provide new experiences.
People I am with depend on me to be clean.	Take a bath.	City planners so that there is water for my bath.

Discuss multiple situations of dependence and interdependence: children-parent(s), parent(s)-boss, boss-owner of business, student-teacher, teacher-student, student-principal, principal-student, grass-sun and water, cow-grass, people-cow, seed-sun, water and soil, plant-animals, animals-man, man-sun, water and soil.

Lesson 13. Natural Resources

Work in small groups. Make a list of as many natural resources of the earth as you can think of and write them down in 20 minutes.

Read your list to the other groups. When you are through reading your list, they will have three minutes to add anything they want from your list to theirs. When they are through reading their list to you, you will have three minutes to add on to your list.

For the next 10 minutes talk about the natural resources of the state you live in. Listen to each other's ideas. Try to add new ideas rather than repeat what someone else has already said.

For the next five minutes, make a list of everything in this room you consider to be a "natural resource." It might be a natural resource in the same sense as the natural resources you have just been talking about, or it might be a natural resource because it is "naturally" a resource in the classroom. Read your list to the other groups. They will again have three minutes to take any ideas they want from you. You will be able to take three minutes of ideas from them after they read theirs to you.

While still in your group, but by yourself, take the next five minutes to list your own "natural resources." Again, those "natural resources" can be natural resources, or they can be resources which are "naturally" yours. Read your list to the people in your group. They now have five minutes to tell you other things they see as being natural resources in you. You can add to your list any you want (if you do not want a particular resource, you do not have to add it to your list). Listen to others read their lists of natural resources and add to their lists as you desire.

Lesson 14. Solar System Conversations

Be the sun. Talk as if you are the sun. Example: "I am the sun. I am a very large star. I have a great deal of heat. My heat gives energy to the earth."

Now, be the earth. Talk as if you are the earth. Example: "I am the earth. I have air, water, plants, and animals."

One person be the sun and another be the earth. Create a conversation between the sun and the earth. What do you have to say to one another?

Let this be an activity in improvisational theatre as well as in science. Do not correct the students if they should offer incorrect statements. After the "play," you can clarify points, give additional information, or assign further readings. Use this activity to assess what the students do and do not know about the sun and the earth.

With advanced students, add other planets of our solar system to the "play."

Dance around as if you are the earth. Circle the room once to represent one day. Choose a partner. One be the earth, the other the moon. Earth and moon dance together, in time to one another. Now both join another partnership. Two of you become the sun. All of you dance together as if you are the sun (two students), moon, and earth dancing together.

Depending on the ability of the class to do this, continue to add students to represent other solar bodies. Create a solar system dance.

Reading

An entire world of "out there" is available to me right here, through books. By reading words, looking at pictures, and creating my own imaginary scenes, my world is enriched through the experience of reading. Through books I can learn more about myself, more about others, more about the world I live in. Many critics of education state that if we just knew how to think and to read, we would be masters of our world. I would disagree with that because I believe we also need good communication and interpersonal skills in order to make the world of books come alive for us as individuals. Just to understand and think about the ideas of others is not enough. I need to be more involved than that. I need to test out my ideas with others. I need opportunities to apply my reading and thinking to the environment I live in so that I can test the soundness of my interpretations.

As a teacher, reading is at once the most exciting and the most anxiety-producing subject I have to teach. It is exciting because I love to read, because I am stimulated by the ideas others present, because for me, reading is usually a pleasurable experience. It is anxiety producing because of the pressure to succeed at teaching reading. Much of my "success" as a teacher, as rated by others, was determined by how well the students in my class learned to read. It was permissible to be weak in other subject areas, but in order to be a "good" teacher, I *had* to be good at teaching reading.

Students, too, are excited and afraid of reading. At the end of the very first day of school, a five-year-old began to cry when she was told it was time to get ready to go home. When asked what was troubling her, she replied, "I can't go home yet. I haven't learned to read!" Long before they enter a formal reading program, students are conditioned to know that reading is vital to their success in school.

How does one go about becoming a good teacher of reading, especially today when there are so many materials available and so many different experts offering theirs as "the" best idea? First, it is important to know what is available. What texts do I have to use? What concepts should be covered at the level I am teaching? Where are the students in relation to that? Which ones have already mastered those concepts and require more than is offered? Which ones will have to begin at earlier stages? Which materials do the best possible in what areas? For example, one reading series may have an excellent listening program, but a weak comprehension program. How can I use the strong parts and find alternatives for the weak ones? Are there people available to me—teachers or reading consultants—more familiar with particular reading programs than I? How can I make good use of them? Most importantly, what skills, interests, and abilities do *I* bring to the subject? What do I believe to be most important about learning to read?

My foremost goal is to have students enjoy reading. One of the most useful devices I happened upon in trying to reach that goal was to separate the teaching of reading skills from reading for the sake of reading. During skill development, understanding concepts of reading is important. Students might find some concepts difficult to grasp, but that should in no way interfere with their enjoyment of reading. Students might get frustrated when trying to correctly divide a word into syllables, defining new words, or searching for new meanings in a paragraph. But during reading time, they should be free to enjoy their books in any way they can. They can skip over words they do not know. They can derive pleasure and meaning from looking at pictures. They can help each other pick and choose books that are interesting to them. That is how adults read. It makes good sense to allow students that kind of freedom in their reading time.

I take responsibility for the development of reading skills. Using the teacher's text and the conceptual framework offered, I take the students through concept development step by step. When students do not perform as I might expect them to, I look for ways to discover what is causing that to happen. Sometimes it is that the material is already known and they resent having to do it over again.

Sometimes important preceding concepts have not been developed, and so the lesson is simply beyond their ability. Either way, I feel it is my responsibility to match materials with the abilities of the students. At times this can be a frustrating experience, especially if the class is large and covers a wide range of abilities. But as the students' needs become known to me, I prefer to work with them one-to-one or in small groups, rather than present a lesson to the entire class which meets the needs of no one.

I insist on having the students take responsibility for designing the format of the reading time, the time they sit with their books and read. How long is a reasonable reading time? How do you know that? Let's try it and see how it works. How does one go about choosing a good book? Make a list of all the ways you can choose a book. Keep adding to it as you discover new ways. Is our room to be completely quiet as we read, or is quiet talking to be allowed? Do we sit at our desks and read, or are there other places, other ways we wish to sit and read? Try some new ideas and choose the ones that work well for this class.

It has been my experience that when students feel they have an active part in designing at least part of their reading program, their interest in reading increases. With increased interest, they read more and the more they read, the more able they are to read.

Sometimes letting students design their reading program can be chaotic, particularly for the teacher. One year my first grade class adopted an "anything goes" policy—read where and what you want, talk when you want. The only rule was that I was not to interfere with them for the 15 minute period. As might be imagined, I was terribly uncomfortable with the noise level and with seeing students reading in various strange places and positions—under their desks, under my desk, at the art center, in corners. I worried about what the principal might think if he were to pass by and see students on their stomachs, on their backs, with their feet resting on the wall, or crouched in the corners. However, at the end of six weeks, through individual interviews with each student, I discovered that they were reading far more than had my students of previous years. Even the "non-readers" were reading more picture stories. Beyond that, later in the year, the results of a standardized test showed the skill development of the class was well above the average of my past classes. Letting the students be responsible for all they can reasonably cope with and providing individualized programs for skill development produced happier, better readers and a happier, better teacher—me.

Another important function of the teacher is to teach the students to make connections between what they read in books and what happens in their own lives. It is not enough for students just to read and understand the content of the stories they read. They must be given multiple opportunities to wonder about what they read: What did the story have to say to me? What did I learn about myself by reading it? What did I learn about other people, places or things? How might I use that information? The books and stories they read should be used to increase their awareness not only of things outside their environment, but also to increase their awareness of what the experience of reading is doing to and for them personally.

The lessons in this unit center around themes commonly found in classroom readers. To begin, the lessons focus on getting the students to relate their own personal experiences to activities usually called for in readers. In readers, students are usually asked to interpret the feelings, thinking, and actions of the characters in the stories. In these lessons, they are asked to interpret their own experiences. In the middle section, there are some word games. Since reading is dependent on being able to recognize printed words, I feel it is equally important for students to have multiple opportunities to play with words as it is for them to seriously study them. Learning should be full of fun. In the last section, there are several lessons with a traditional appearance and a confluent dimension.

Objectives

To compare and contrast personal experiences with experiences
   read about or seen in books.
To identify feelings in self and others evoked by specific stories.
To create various moods through voice tones, use of words, and
   written expressions.
To invent and play games with words.
To gain meaningful information about one's self through reading
   materials.

Lesson 1. Introducing Books

Here the students are first asked to be involved in a lesson that stimulates their language and their imagination. Then they are given new books to explore. It is important to provide multiple opportunities for students to develop their own language while being exposed to the language in books. This is particularly true when students are using controlled vocabulary books for reading development.

Bring in pictures of different kinds of doors: barn doors, tent
doors, all kinds of doors, from apartments, houses, industrial buildings, busy buildings, abandoned buildings.
   Where would you find these doors?
   What kinds of sounds might these doors make?
   How would you enter one of these doors? How would you
feel as you come up to it? How do you get it opened? How should

the door feel to you? How would it be on the other side of the door? Open the door. Where does it take you?

Become one of the doors. Tell or write your story. How old are you? What do you feel like? What are some of the important things that have happened to you? When are you sad? When are you happy? Are you ever frightened or lonely? What else are you?

How is a book similar to a door? (You open it. You "go through" it. It can be an opening to adventure, information, humor, mystery.)

Give each student a book that is unfamiliar to them.

Don't open your book yet. Imagine it is like a door. What kind of door might your book be? What kinds of places do you imagine that the book will take you? What do you see that makes you think that?

Open the book and go through it, looking at the pictures, reading some of the words. Is it the kind of book you imagined it would be? Find a page that looks particularly interesting to you. Read that page.

Form small groups and share what you know about your book with one another.

Lesson 2. Being Alone

Many of the stories students read are illustrated with drawings or pictures. These often influence what the reader thinks, feels, and imagines as much as the words of the story. This lesson and the next one explore ways in which students are influenced by pictures. They also provide opportunities for verbal and written story forms to be created by the students.

Bring in pictures which depict a solitary figure in several different settings: a farmer plowing a field, a boy walking in the woods, a woman on a beach at sunset, a girl at a bus stop. Have enough pictures so that the students can select the ones which interest them.

Present a set of questions for the students to think about while looking at their pictures. Do not have them answer out loud. Spoken answers can influence other students' responses and may lead to confusion or stereotyped responses.

What time of day is it in your picture? How do you know that?

Where was the picture taken? Have you ever been there or to a place like that?

Who is in your picture? Do you know that person or someone like that person?

Imagine that person has been in that place for a long time. Imagine what they are thinking. Imagine what they are feeling.

Write those thoughts and feelings in a stream of consciousness technique: words, phrases, or sentences separated by dashes.

Now look at the picture again. Imagine that the person in your picture is suddenly joined by another person. This might be a friend or a stranger. Will they talk? What will each of them feel about the other? Will the person in the picture be concerned with the new person, or will they go on as you imagined them before? Write more stream of consciousness thoughts and feelings for the persons in the picture.

Imagine that you are alone. What are your thoughts and feelings when you are alone and doing the following (allow a pause after each one): walking around your neighborhood; looking for something you lost; waiting for someone to come to you; watching other people from a distance; working on something that is difficult. What are your thoughts and feelings when you are alone and somewhere frightening? Alone and somewhere noisy? Alone and somewhere very peaceful and quiet?

Now imagine you are alone somewhere. Imagine how you are feeling there. Write down where you are and how you feel, then write stream of consciousness statements that describe where and how you are. For example: "I am in my campsite. I am peaceful and still. How beautiful—warmer than yesterday—I'm getting hot—maybe sunburned—should get hat—too lazy—maybe when hungry—ahh, so nice."

Variations

Make up stream of consciousness writings for the following alone scenes: being sick in bed with mumps, listening to people inside while you are outside, running second in a race, being trapped in an elevator, being on a bucking bronco, reading that you have won a million dollars in a contest.

Lesson 3. Being Alone Versus Being Lost

Many exciting reading stories are about a person or an animal being lost. Students quickly identify with these stories because of their personal experiences of being lost at one time or another. Allow the students to relate their personal experiences and to read the experiences of others as well.

Have the students talk about their experiences of being lost, or having known someone who has been lost. They may mention their own neighborhood, a strange city, the woods, an exhibition or fun-fair, a shopping plaza, a lake. Have them discuss the hazards connected with each place. Discuss what they did to solve the problem of being lost. Who helped them solve the problem? How did they feel when they were lost? How did they feel when they were found again? What did they learn from that experience?

As a class, small group, or individually, fill out the following chart:

Where I got lost: Name of place	Hazard of that place	How I felt while lost	How I felt when found
shopping plaza	too big too many people	confused frightened small	relief happy secure

Now look at the pictures of the alone people (see Lesson 2). Imagine those people are lost. How did they become lost in those places? How do they feel about being lost there? How will they solve the problem of being lost? Who might help them there? How might they feel about having someone find them when they are lost?

Recall what you imagined those people were thinking and feeling when they were alone. Now imagine what they are thinking and feeling when they are lost. Fill out the following chart:

Alone, one might feel _____. Lost ___(name a place)_____, one might feel _____.

Example: Alone in the mountains, one might feel peaceful and quiet. Lost in the mountains, one might feel frightened and panicky.

Lesson 4. Family Writing

When reading stories about families, let the students talk about their own unique family experiences. To help get their ideas organized, the following may provide some starting points—first for talking, then for writing—or the students may develop a list of their own story starters.

I'll never forget the time my family . . .
Everyone in the family was really excited when . . .
The biggest surprise my family ever had . . .
Even the house seemed gloomy the day . . .
The worst thing our family experienced was . . .
My parents were really frightened the time . . .
The best day of all for my family was the day . . .

It is wise to be aware of the composition of the "families" of your students. If your students do not experience a nuclear family as their family unit, great emphasis on nuclear families can alienate and isolate them. Provide them multiple opportunities to compare and contrast real family settings (nuclear or otherwise) with the fictional families they read about. Compare and contrast the family members: the story mother, father, sister, brother, compared to the student's reality. Compare and contrast the time and setting of the story with the student's reality. Compare and contrast what the story family seems to value with what the student's family seems to value. (Be careful not to become judgmental in comparing values. Compare values in terms of likeness and differences rather than in terms of "better" or "worse.")

Lesson 5. Tone of Voice

Encourage the students to explore the possibility of tone of voice changing a message from attracting to driving away a listener. They can explore saying a sentence such as "I want to take you there" in different ways. Say it over and over, accenting a different word each time. Say it and imagine being angry, excited, in a hurry, bored. Say it with different tones of voice and let others tell what is imagined by the tone of voice used.

This is a good way to provide drill and repetition for students who need it for certain words. Create a sentence containing the drill word, and have the student repeat it several times, using different tones of voice. This activity can also help students become aware of how moods are created in stories. Practice a sentence several ways and decide which way fits the story's mood.

Variation

Have the students select a word or phrase, and experiment with different meanings they can give to it by changing their tone of voice. Try using slang expressions: "far out," "looking good," "for sure," "yeah, man."

Try using phrases of nature: "oh, spring," "dry leaves," "ill wind." Try using family role names: "mother," "father," "brother," "sister."

Lesson 6. Words Make and Break Contact

Have the students work in small groups. Recall how something someone said made it difficult to get near him/her, or a remark which made for a closer tie. After discussing in groups, have each group write up a list of words and short phrases which make contact, and a list of words which break contact.

Compare the two lists. Are there any words or phrases on both lists? If so, how could that be explained?

Compare the two lists with lists made by other small groups. What is the most common word or phrase used to break contact? What is most commonly used to make contact? Are there some words and phrases which are seen as both making and breaking contact? If so, how could that be explained?

As you go through the rest of the day, be aware of how you use words to make contact. Be aware of how you use words to break contact. Be aware of how others use words to make and break contact with you.

When you are reading a story, discover how the characters make and break contact with one another.

Lesson 7. Group Story Telling

Many stories in readers depict how the main characters deal with some type of emergency situation. Allow students opportunities to relate their own experiences of dealing with emergencies.

What emergency procedures do you know about at school? In our class? At your home?

Describe a real emergency you have experienced. What happened? What did you do? What feelings did you experience during the emergency? After it?

Work with a small group (four to six) of classmates and develop the story which begins "It was the first emergency we'd faced since landing on Mars . . ." When you have your story completed, put it on tape. Play the tape for the rest of the class.

Lesson 8. Predicting Outcomes

After reading part way through a story or a book, have students describe what they think the outcome of the story will be. Have them describe how they have arrived at that prediction.

Is the story like something personally experienced? Is it like other stories read? Is it like a film or T.V. story?

When the students have finished reading the story, compare their prediction with the actual ending. How are the two alike? How are they different? Which ending do the students prefer, their own or the author's?

Lesson 9. Misunderstandings

Have the students work in small groups and share times when others have misunderstood them. What didn't the other person know about them that caused the misunderstanding? Have them complete such statements as, "If they had known _____ about me, they would not have misunderstood me."

Talk about times when they have misunderstood others in their lives. What didn't they know about the other person which might have caused the misunderstanding?

Make up a list of reasons why messages do not get through to others:

"I tried to tell him/her/them, but . . ."

they weren't listening.

they weren't interested.

they didn't believe me.

it was hard to explain.

Make up a list of reasons why messages do not get through to you:

"I know I was told, but . . ."

I didn't understand what was said.

I couldn't hear what was being said.

I was nervous, and I didn't remember what was said.

When reading, discover how the characters in stories misunderstand one another. Make a list of reasons why their messages did not get through to one another.

Lesson 10. Word Games

You will each need a set of four index cards and a pencil. On each
of two cards, write one or two words about a positive aspect of
you or your personality. For example, say several people have told
me I am a good friend of theirs. I can simply write "good friend"
on one card.

Now, on each of the other two cards, write one or two words
about a negative aspect of you or your personality. For example,
say several people have talked to me about my bad temper. I can
simply write "temper" on my card.

Now form two equal groups. Each of you place your four
cards in the center, face down so no one knows what is written on
them. Choose a person in your group to be "dealer." Dealer, pick
up all the cards, without reading any of them.

As a group, make up a card game to play, using the cards
you have just made. Play the game.

Evaluate your game. Was it fun to play? Did everyone have
a fair chance to play? What did you like about the game? What
did you like least? What could you do to improve the game? Do it,
and play the game again. Revise it as many times as you want in
order to make it as much fun as possible.

Once it is revised and you are sure you do not want to make
more changes, write out the rules of the game. Read the rules to
another in your group, being sure they are clear and explicit. Make
sure they say what you want them to say.

Now give your rules and cards to the other group. Take their
rules and cards. Read their rules. Be sure you understand them.
Play the game. See if you are playing the game they think you are
playing. Have one of them come and observe you play the game.
If there are differences between the way you are playing and the
way they think you should play, discover the reason(s) for the
differences.

WORD ASSOCIATIONS

Let students experiment with word associations—words that come
to mind. Work in dyads. One be A, the other be B. A asks B to tell what
word comes to mind when he/she says a certain word. A can either repeat the same word several times, eliciting several responses to it, or can
use a different word for B to respond to each time. The associations might
be shown visually as links in a chain (made from construction paper
strips) or on word-mobiles where the stimulus word has the associated
words suspended from it.

CHOOSE A MEDIUM

Encourage students to think about how the medium they choose affects the message they send.

Experiment with presenting a single statement in a variety of mediums. For example, write "I'm afraid of the dark" in large letters on white paper. Now write it again in little letters on black paper. Which message seems more correct? How could "I'm afraid of the dark" seem even more frightening?

Some starting ideas:

Write happy messages on blown-up balloons.

Write "painful" messages on band-aids.

Write a "cool" message on something you think is cool.

Lesson 11. Twenty Questions

Read a story or an excerpt of a story to the entire class. Have the class form two groups, Team A and Team B. Each team is to choose ten unusual, interesting, or emotional words from the story or excerpt and write each of them on a separate index card.

Team A then selects one of their ten words. Team B tries to guess which word Team A has chosen by asking questions which can only be answered by "yes" or "no." Team B can ask up to 20 questions trying to guess the word. If Team B correctly guesses within 20 questions, they get to keep the card with the word on it. If they do not correctly guess, Team A gets to keep the card, after showing it to Team B. Then Team B chooses a card, and Team A tries to guess what is on it. The object of the game is to get as many cards as possible.

At the end of the game, discuss who were the leaders in the game? How did they become leaders? How did the teams decide which words would be used? How did the students cooperate with one another? How did they contribute to one another's thinking? What did they learn from playing the game? What other games might they invent to play with those 20 cards?

Lesson 12. Degrees of Emotions

Have the students explore words that describe degrees of a certain feeling. Have them work in small groups to make up a chart which shows several different emotions in at least three degrees. Example:

First degree	Second degree	Third degree
frightened	panic-stricken	terrified
irritated	provoked	aggravated
contented	relaxed	drowsy
happy	delighted	ecstatic

Responses will vary from group to group. Not all students will have the same vocabulary development, and not all students will choose the same words for different degrees. Encourage their differences.

When reading, discover the words authors use to indicate different degrees of emotions in order to create the moods of a story.

Lesson 13. My Multiple Meanings

Words with multiple meanings can be taken from a reader and developed into a worksheet which elicits personal responses from the student. This allows students practice in using multiple meanings as well as in identifying things about themselves.

Have the student choose a correct word or phrase to complete each sentence:

1. Stick with me and you'll soon learn that I _____. I can _____ with a stick.

2. I like to watch _____ fall from the sky. When I fall on my _____, it hurts.

3. I like to loaf around when _____. My favorite bread is a loaf of _____.

4. To get to my house from the school, I have to bear _____ more than _____. If I saw a bear in the woods, I would probably _____. I could not bear to see _____.

5. If I hiked to the top of a rise, I would like to be able to see_____. The sunrise makes me think of _____.

6. If I came to a fork in an unknown trail, I would probably _____. Knives and forks are great inventions, but I like to eat _____ with my fingers.

7. From the back, you might think I am _____, but I really am _____. When I get back home after being in school, I like to _____.

8. If I left my _____ on a bus, I would be very upset. I like to _____ with my left hand.

Lesson 14. Cause and Effect

Have the students reread a story and complete sentences from the story which show cause and effect. Have some of the sentences deal with their real world of here and now.

Examples:
1. That July the land was bare and ugly because _____.
   Here and now, where we live, it is _____ because _____.
2. Pa had to go away to earn money because _____. My mother and/or my father earn money because _____.
3. The danger (in the story) kept increasing because _____.
   The danger of _____ keeps increasing today.

Lesson 15. Word Structure

In the first sentence of each set, have the students use the root word and add a suffix to fill in the blank. (These can be sentences based on a particular story or they can be general.) In the second sentence, have the students use the root word and suffix to fill the first blank and then go on to make a true statement about themselves by filling in the second blank.

Cease: 1. The _____ rain caused hazardous driving.
      2. The _____ _____ is irritating to me.

Event: 1. So much happened, it was truly an _____ night.
      2. The most _____ day of my life was ____ _____.

Occasion: 1. There was nothing to see except an _____ light.
      2. I have had an _____ taste of _____.

Interrupt: 1. For a while, Ann's thoughts were _____ by a sound.
      2. I hate to be _____ when _____.

Disturb: 1. There was a complaint of a rowdy _____.
      2. The last time I saw a _____, I _____.

Rue: 1. "O.K., you can borrow my long dress," she said _____.

2. _____, I loaned my _____ to a friend.

Forgot: 1. Bill had _____ his old idea now.

2. Unless he had reminded me, I would have _____ that Gary _____.

Routine: 1. Police _____ check stalled and parked cars.

2. I _____ attend to _____.

Slack: 1. The rain had begun to _____ off.

2. When I _____ off doing _____, I always get disgusted with myself.

Happy: 1. John is _____ when he is camping in the mountains.

2. I am _____ when I _____.

Lesson 16. Recall and Relate Details

Choose a story for the students to read. Prepare a sentence completion paper which has them recall and relate details of the story, but ask only half the number of questions you would normally ask. For each question you ask which requires recalling information from the story, ask one which requires them to relate some information about themselves. Example paper (numbered questions adapted from standard text):

1. _____ complained because he was upset about a school assignment.

    A school assignment which upset me was one which required me to _____.

2. _____ was glad of an excuse to avoid doing his math homework.

    I would be glad of an excuse to avoid doing _____.

3. _____ and _____ fought with each other. _____ and I often fight with each other.

4. _____ was annoyed at the two boys for fighting. My mother gets annoyed at me when I _____.

5. _____ was so panic-stricken she hid and cried. I would be panic-stricken if _____.

6. _____ tried to reassure himself by suggesting the game be played by twos.

    I reassure myself by _____.

7. _____ was troubled because she couldn't cook dinner for the family.

My favorite dinner is _____.

Lesson 17. Beginning Paragraph Writing

Close your eyes now and I will lead you in a guided fantasy. Go back to some time in your life when you felt really happy. Where are you? Who is with you? What are you doing? How are you feeling? Take time to enjoy this scene. When you are ready, come back to the room and look at us here and now.

Use this model to write an account of what you just imagined:

I was ___(name place)___. The place looked ___(description)___. I was with _____. We were doing _____. I was feeling _____.

Now, write this again in the present tense and see if your feelings change as you switch from past to present:

I am _____. The place looks _____. I am with _____. We are doing _____. I am feeling _____.

If you were going to make this into a story, what would be the next sentence?

Lesson 18. Compound Words

When working with compound words in readers, allow small groups of students to work together to invent new words and create their definitions using the parts of compound words. Example:

tooth	bed
coast	board
witch	weed
chess	bare
sea	lights
head	craft
road	line
thread	west
north	men
marks	ache

First match the words in column A with those in column B to make known compounds. Then match one word at a time from column A with all the words in column B: toothbed, toothboard, toothweed, toothbare, toothlights, toothcraft, toothline, toothwest, toothmen, toothache. Make up definitions to the words you have invented. Make up definitions for only those words which are interesting to you and your group. For example: Toothbare: what people become if they don't take good care of their teeth. Toothlights: small battery-charged lights which can easily be inserted into molars so people can see in the dark when they open their mouths.

Variation

Have the students cut out words from magazines or print words on cards and place them in two separate boxes. Draw out the words, one from each box, and see how many compound words are created which seem to have meaning. Really unusual combinations may be used as names of creatures, as titles of stories, or as the basis for cartoons. Where the occasional combination has established meaning, students may see that words have been invented not at random, but by design, to serve a purpose.

Mathematics

It wasn't until after I had learned to use a confluent approach in other subject areas that I was able to apply it to the subject of mathematics. It was not that mathematics was so difficult to adapt, it was just that I felt hesitant and reluctant to attempt it. As in reading, I felt there was much pressure to have my students do well in math, but I did not have the background, skill, or confidence in math that I had in reading. My personal feelings about my abilities to teach the subject did more to inhibit my development in it than did the subject matter itself.

Then we entered the era of "new math," and all of that began to change. Because of the new texts, concepts, and methods I was required to teach, professional in-service classes were made available. I attended math classes which covered the entire elementary mathematics program. I began to understand math in ways I had never understood it before. Perhaps that was because of the new methods I was experiencing, but having been involved in teaching for the previous two years had certainly helped my awareness of math and had increased my need to know more about it. I was particularly interested in the progression of skills from one level to the next as a way to assess my own mathematical readiness/ awareness. As I applied that to myself, I began to identify what I knew as well as identify areas of weakness. By starting with what I knew, I was able to build out and into unknowns. I became excited about math and about my ability to learn. It was as much a thrill for me to correctly solve a complicated problem, create a graph, or translate statistics as it was for any of my first graders to realize that two and two is four.

With the new math, there came an emphasis on the inquiry or discovery approach to that subject. New materials encouraged teachers to provide a rich and stimulating learning environment so that students' natural curiosity could lead them to make discoveries appropriate for their age and level of ability and so learn mathematics from self-interests and self-experiences.

Now it has been recognized that an inquiry approach to mathematics is more interesting for students than a teacher- or textbook-centered program. Many texts now available give multiple ideas on how to change from a teacher- or textbook-centered program to a student-centered program. Math centers, or areas where students can go and experiment with mathematical concepts on their own, now have a place in classrooms everywhere. Not all students are expected to excel in mathematics, but teachers are expected to maintain their enthusiasm for math so that they can learn what they are capable of learning, and not "give up" as so many students have done in the past. Mathematical materials, such as number lines and geo-boards, which do not depend upon polished skills in computation, are available. Students are able to use these materials to demonstrate an understanding of a concept before they are able to verbalize the understanding. Oral language opportunities are encouraged, and only gradually are students taught to write down their discoveries. The inquiry approach not only allows for individual differences, it encourages them. When there is an emphasis on solving a real problem, students can examine it and pursue it at their own level of ability. Students should at all times be allowed to keep their self-respect, to appreciate the fact that some things cause them difficulty, but that this is no disgrace.

It is not necessary for a teacher to develop the cognitive aspects of teaching mathematics. As in other subject areas, there are a number of excellent math programs available. What a teacher does need to develop are more ways to emphasize the affective dimensions of learning mathematics. For me, the greatest opportunity for doing that is by capitalizing upon the self-interests and life experiences of the students.

One way to do that is to look for mathematical concepts in other activities of the students. For example, a science lesson that engages the students in the process of classification is not far removed from a mathematical lesson on structure and properties. Once they classify objects according to a scientific principle, they can go on to explore greater than, less than, or equal. They can look for patterns in numbers in the treatment of scientific data. Scientific prediction and hypothesis formation is not far removed from mathematical estimation. By helping the students discover the close connections between two or more subject areas, their understanding of all the areas is increased. Skills become useful tools which can be applied in several subjects, allowing several opportunities for their use and improvement. Learning becomes more integrated, more connected, more meaningful.

Another way to increase the self-interests and self-experiences of the student in mathematics is to provide opportunities for them to make their own materials. As in other subjects, the overuse of commercial products tends to make our students passive learners. They come to depreciate, or even ignore, their own ideas of how to make learning rich and meaningful for them. Besides that, many opportunities for learning through doing are lost when students are constantly presented with ready-made materials. Allow them to make up their own math worksheets. Have them make their own number lines, geo-boards, counting boards, multiplication cards. It has been my experience that the students not only learn more by making their own materials, but they tend to take better care of, and have more pride in, materials into which they have invested some of their own time and energy. Students are much more responsible for and responsive to a math program that allows them to have a part in its development than they are to a commercial package which is presented to (or laid on) them. Allow the uniqueness of the individual to show in the materials he or she uses.

Still another way to enrich math is to imagine that the entire school program is a mathematical experience with the student right in the middle of it. By using the students themselves—for measurements, for counting units, for making various sets—they "become" mathematics. We live in a mathematical world. Both natural and human-made phenomena contain multiple opportunities for mathematical explorations. By using things within their environment—clocks, money, time—they are able to become aware of mathematical relationships between themselves and their environment.

Because this is the last unit, the format is somewhat different from the others. To begin with, lessons are written as most others have been throughout the book, but then an idea for a math worksheet, using students as the source of all information, is presented. The next three lessons have the students use themselves, their environment, and others to consider mathematical concepts. The final part of the unit presents a variety of ideas on concepts which are contained in many math texts. It is hoped that individual teachers using this book will adapt those ideas into lessons that will reflect their own particular teaching styles.

Objectives

To experience being a part of a mathematical sentence.
To experience body parts as units of measure.
To create math materials.

To identify mathematical concepts in daily activities.
To play with mathematical concepts.
To experience multiple ways of estimating very large numbers.

Lesson 1. Counting Sets of Students

Will all the students with brown eyes please stand up? How many students have brown eyes? Write the number. All students with brown eyes can now sit down. Now, let's have all students wearing white socks stand up. How many students are wearing white socks? Write the number.

Continue making a variety of sets of students. Demonstrate the empty set and zero by asking something like "Will the students with pink hair please stand up?"

Begin by having all the students in one group. Once they get the idea of the game, allow them to work in small groups, letting them take turns identifying ways to form sets.

Lesson 2. Joining Sets of Students

Will all the students with blue eyes stand up? How many students are there? Write the number. Now, let's have all the students with brown eyes stand up. How many students with brown eyes are there? Write that number. In all, how many students are standing?

Write what we just did in a mathematical sentence: the number of blue eyed students (5), plus (+) the number of brown eyed students (7), equals (=) the total (12) of the two sets (5 + 7 = 12).

Repeat several times with the whole group, then allow the students to work in small groups. Encourage them to make sets in as many different ways as possible. Have them write their set formations in mathematical sentences.

Variation

Use sets of students to demonstrate subtraction as well as sets which are more, less, and equal.

Lesson 3. Objects Around Us

Go for a short walk around the school grounds. Pick up three hard objects and three soft objects.

Return to the classroom, and form small groups. First, share your objects with one another. Now, put all of your objects together in one pile. Sort them into soft and hard objects again. Now see how many other ways you can sort them. For example, you can sort them according to size, shape, or color.

Make a chart to show how you sorted your objects and how many objects there were in each set:

hard = 18	brown = 11
soft = 18	yellow = 6
big = 21	white = 7
little = 15	green = 12

Sort these things any way you wish. Write down how you sorted them and tell why you sorted them as you did.

Variations

Have the students use their objects to join sets, partition sets, and find more than, less than, and equal sets.

Use the numbers on their charts to make graphs.

If students have had no experience in making graphs, start by having them compare first just two sets of information. Use activities of the class to do this. For example, have them compare the set of students who are buying their lunch to the set of students who are not buying their lunch. Once they are familiar with that, have them compare more than two sets of information. For example, compare the set of students who are buying their lunch, the set of students who have brought their lunch, and the set of students who are going home for lunch. Once they understand a one-to-one correspondence on graphs, introduce them to the concept of one graph unit equaling more than one.

Lesson 4. My Age

Write your age at the top of your paper. Use that number to make up as many math sentences as you can. For example, say my age is six. I put that at the top of my page. I can write $5 + 1 = 6$, $3 + 3 = 6$, $10 - 4 = 6$, $12 - 6 = 6$, etc.

Make a set of math problems, leaving a missing number in each problem, and give it to someone else to complete. You complete the math problems made by someone else.

This lesson can be adapted for students of various levels. For example, for a very beginner, it might be that he or she is just expected to do addition problems up to six. Advanced math students can create more complicated problems such as having the remainder of a long division problem equaling their age.

Lesson 5. My Hand String

Open your hand and spread out all the fingers. Place it on a blank piece of paper. Use a pencil and carefully outline your hand, going up and around each finger from the bone on one side of your wrist to the bone on the other side. Make a dot to show where that bone is on each side.

Make an estimate of the length of that line. Write that number somewhere on your paper.

Take a long piece of string and tie a knot at one end. Place the knot on one of the dots on the outline of your hand. Carefully place the string all along the line you made, going from one dot to the other. Mark your string at the second dot and tie a knot at that end.

Remove the string from the outline and use a yard stick or meter rule to carefully measure its length. Write the exact measurement of the string next to your estimate of the length of that line. Compare the two numbers. Are there any surprises? If so, what surprised you?

1) How large a square can you make with your hand string? What is the perimeter of that square?

2) Make an equilateral triangle by dividing your string into three equal sections. What is the perimeter of the triangle?

3) How large a circle can you make with your string? What is the circumference of that circle?

4) What other shapes can you make?

Primary students may find it too difficult to trace around their open hand. If so, have them keep their fingers closed while they trace around their hand. If they have difficulty tying knots at each end of the string, simply have them mark the spot with a crayon, pen, or pencil.

Once they have their piece of string, have them compare it with others in the classroom. Who has the longest one? Who has the shortest

one? What is the difference, in inches or centimeters between the two? Measure many things in the room with the string. Record the findings on a sheet of paper. Find things that are less than one string length. Find things that are more than one, but less than two lengths. Find things that are more than two, but less than three. Have the students continue in this activity as long as they are curious and interested.

Lesson 6. Height and Weight

Arrange to have scales and an accurate measuring rod in the room. (In many schools, the school nurse visits classrooms annually to weigh and measure all the students. If this is the case, it might be possible to get recordings of previous years for at least some of the students.) Accurately weigh and measure each student.

Pose several problems for students to solve, using their own weight and height to get the answers:

My weight is _____.

My height is _____ feet, _____ inches.

If I gained 8 pounds, I would weigh _____ pounds.

If I lost 5 pounds, I would weigh _____ pounds.

Three people who weigh less than I do are _____, _____ and _____. Three people who weigh more than I do are _____, _____ and _____.

The person whose weight is most like mine is _____.

If I grew two inches, I would be _____ feet, _____ inches.

If I shrank four inches, I would be _____ feet, _____ inches.

_____ is one inch taller than I am.

_____ is two inches shorter than I am.

_____ is the same height as I am.

Lesson 7. Body Measurements

Span: The distance from the tip of the little finger to the tip of the thumb when the hand is spread open.

Cubit: The distance from the end of the elbow to the tip of the fingers.

Pace: The distance of one normal walking step.

Stride: The distance of one long and sweeping step (a "giant" step).

Introduce the students to the above body units of measure. Have them practice each one several times, using the correct word to identify each. Then have them measure different things around the classroom or school, using just those measures. Have them determine which one is most appropriate for measuring several different things. Which one is most appropriate for measuring a book? Which one is most appropriate for measuring a table? Which one is most appropriate for measuring from the chalkboard to halfway across the room? Which one is most appropriate for measuring the playground?

Have the students find specific things which measure evenly into span, cubit, pace, and stride. Have them compare their findings with others. Lead them to realize that because of differences in size, different students will have different answers. This can lead to a discussion of the need for standardized measures and the use of rulers. However, even when the students use rulers for accurate answers, do not ignore chances to let them estimate distances by using their body measurements.

Lesson 8. Lines

Have primary students identify parallel lines in the classroom. The top of the chalkboard is parallel to the bottom of the chalkboard. The top of a table is parallel to the bottom. Have them identify books, doors, windows, as having parallel lines. Go for a walk around the school. Find other parallel lines. Record the findings on a sheet of paper. When back in the class, share what was found to be parallel.

After they are familiar with parallel lines, have them find intersecting lines. Have them go on an "intersecting line hunt." Explore the school grounds and perhaps even the nearby neighborhood.

For advanced students, bring in pictures of buildings, such as hospitals, apartment complexes, commercial buildings, with parallel and intersecting lines that clearly show floors and rooms. Have them count the horizontal lines and the vertical lines. Multiply those numbers in order to approximate the number of rooms showing in the pictures. If they can tell how many rooms comprise the width of the building, they can calculate that number too, and approximate the total number of rooms in the building. For example, say the picture is of a building which shows it is 17 floors high, with 21 suites going across each floor. From the side of the building it appears that there are two sets of rooms across each floor. The total number of rooms might be 17x21x2. Of course, this would be an approximate number due to lack of knowledge of the exact interior layout of the building. But this activity gives some practice in identifying parallel and intersecting lines, as well as some practice in working with larger numbers.

Lesson 9. Rotation and Angle Exploration

Have the students choose a partner. One be A, the other B. A stands, facing B. A places his or her right hand on B's shoulder. B lightly touches A's shoulder with his or her left hand, inside the extended arm. A turns completely in a clockwise direction until returned to the original position, keeping his or her right arm extended while turning. B stands still, lightly maintaining contact with A. Then B turns completely around while A maintains light contact.

Once the students can easily move around in a full circle, let them experiment with turning half or semicircles. Have them observe the angles their arms make in a semicircle.

Then, have them demonstrate turning just one quarter of the way around. Again, have them observe the "angles" their arms make in relation to one another as a student rotates.

Have them freely explore all different kinds of "angles," sometimes turning less than one quarter of the way around, more than one quarter of the way but less than half way, more than half way.

Variation

Students can show angle rotation by themselves, using both of their arms to make the rays of the "angles."

Have the student stand with both arms extended, palms and fingertips touching. Have them touch a mark on some firm surface, such as a wall. Keeping one arm still, have them describe an arc with the other arm. In this way, they will be able to show a "quarter-turn," and a "half-turn."

This is a good "exercise" for fidgety students. If you see someone becoming restless, fidgety, bored, or fatigued, have him or her stand and do 15 "half-turns" to the right, then 15 "half-turns" to the left. The activity will increase breathing, release some tensions, and allow the student to return to work more alert and capable.

Lesson 10. Calendars

On the first day of each month, make a calendar. Have the students mark all the special days in the month. Mark holidays, their birthdays, and special upcoming events.

Make up math problems with the calendars: Look for the patterns of seven. How many days from John's birthday to Susan's birthday? How many weeks from the first day of the month to Valentine's Day?

Older students might enjoy making up different types of calendars each month. For example, make a calendar that shows the phases of the moon. Make one based on information from *Poor Richard's Almanac*. Make up an astrological calendar indicating "shoulds" and "should nots" for the month based on their zodiac signs.

Lesson 11. Temperature

Have primary students do a temperature "reading" once in the morning and once after lunch in terms of comfortable, hot, or cold. Keep an ongoing chart. At the end of the month, graph the data. How many comfortable readings? How many hot readings? How many cold readings? From that data, what might be said about last month's temperatures?

Advanced students can take accurate temperature readings from a thermometer. At the end of a month, they can make up a variety of math problems: What was the average temperature? What was the mean temperature? What was the highest temperature? What was the lowest? What was the greatest difference in one day?

Use the newspaper to get daily highs and lows for a month. After collecting that data, pose several math questions around it. What was the highest temperature? On what date did it occur? What was the lowest temperature? On what date did it occur? What is the difference between the high and the low temperatures? How many weeks, days were between those two extremes? How might the data be represented by a graph?

If the students are studying a foreign country in a social studies unit, see if it is possible to get a temperature reading from a city in that country. Compare and contrast those temperatures with the temperaures of their town or city. Again, pose a series of math questions that deal with that information.

Lesson 12. Time

With primary students, allow multiple opportunities for oral development of time concepts. Have them talk about how they spend their time. What can they do in a short time? What takes a long time? If certain classroom activities occur regularly at set times, teach them to read that time on the clock. Ask them about other times they know. Do they watch T.V. shows? If so, at what time do they watch those shows? How do they know when it is time to watch the show? If someone else tells them the time, can they learn to tell it for themselves? What time do they eat? What time do they go to bed? How long do they sleep?

Advanced students can develop time studies by recording the activities of their own days over a period of time. Give them sheets of paper with 24 squares on them. Have them record their activities by the hour, one square for each of the 24 hours of the day. After they have a set of papers completed, have them make a graph depicting how they spend their time. How much time do they spend in school? How much time do they study out of school? How much time is spent eating? Playing? Watching T.V.? Sleeping? Looking at that data, what might one say about how that person spends his or her time? Are there differences between the ways boys spend their time and the ways girls spend their time? If so, what might account for that?

Lesson 13. Money

Primary students may have several opportunities to develop their understanding of coins and their value within normal classroom activities. If they bring money to school to buy things, that money can be used as a part of their math lessons. Allow the students multiple opportunities to add up their milk or lunch money: How many students have to combine their milk money to make it add up to one dollar? How many have to combine their lunch money to make a dollar? If milk costs 10¢ and you bring a quarter, how much change will you get? Name the coins that could add up to 15¢. If lunch is 40¢ and you bring a dollar, name all the possible ways you could receive the correct change.

Advanced students can make up math problems for lunch and milk money: If 18 students are buying one carton of milk at 10¢ each, how much money will they spend? If each of those 18 students buy two cartons of milk, how much will they spend?

Have them discuss how they receive and spend money. How many students receive a regular allowance? How much do they get? Are there things they do to earn money? If so, what do they do and how much do they get? How do they spend their money? Have them keep track of the money they receive and how they spend it over a month. Have them discuss their results at the end of the month. Look for common items as well as unique items for which they spent their money. Is there something everyone bought? Are there items only one person bought? What was the most expensive purchase? What was the least expensive?

Allow the students to collect data in order to make different kinds of graphs. Graph the number of students who receive allowances, the number of students who earn money, and the number of students who get money both by allowances and earnings. Graph the items which students bought over a month. Graph the prices of the items.

Lesson 14. Combining Math Experiences with Other Experiences

Look for ways to enrich students' experiences with math through various other subject activities. In a primary class, if the students are going to make bread as a part of a health or social studies unit, create a set of math problems to go along with the activity of making bread. Have them figure out the total cost of the ingredients. Have them figure out some time problems such as, "If it takes an hour to bake the bread and we put it in the oven at 1:00, what time will it be when it is baked?" Have them talk about the temperature needed to bake the bread. How hot is 375 degrees? What other things, beside stoves, get that hot? What else, besides bread, might be cooked at that temperature?

If advanced students are going on a field trip, pose multiple math problems around the trip. How far will they be going? How can they measure that distance? If the bus goes at various speeds, what will be the average speed? How long will it take to get there and back if the bus goes at an average speed of 30 mph? 40 mph? If the bus gets 10 mpg, how much gas will it use to get there and back again? At the current price of gasoline, how much will that cost? Counting the time it takes to go there and to return, plus the time required there, how long will the trip be? If there is an admission fee, or other money required for the trip, how much money will the whole class need?

If advanced students are studying a foreign country, have them work out some math problems converting their currency into the foreign currency. Have them work out details of a visit to that country. How would they get from the school to a specific destination in that country? What would the return trip distance be? What transportation would they use? How does one read airline, bus, and train timetables? What clothing and other personal items would they want to take? How much would that weigh? What weight limitations might they have to conform to? Estimate the cost of the adventure, including transportation, food, lodging, and entertainment. Make up an itinerary, showing how they would spend their time while on the trip. Have them indicate the time changes from one place to another.

Lesson 15. Sports and Games

Many students are interested and involved in sports programs outside of school hours. Provide opportunities for them to bring that interest into the math period. Put up charts for them to post scores of professional, amateur, or personal teams they know about. Have them figure out averages, both of teams and individual performers. Have them figure out ratios of competitions against particular opposing teams. This need not be an activity for the entire class. Let just those who are interested participate.

Encourage students to bring their favorite games to school for use during math and free time activities. Have them teach one another how to play the game. When they have played a game, lead them to discuss how they worked together, how they learned to take turns, how they helped each other, and what they learned from each other. Through games, students often learn new ways of cooperation while working with a variety of math concepts.

Lesson 16. Color the Squares

Teach students to make "color the squares" puzzles for each other. To begin with, have them make a grid containing 25 squares, or give them a ditto sheet with the grid on it:

1	2	3	4	5
6	7	8	9	10
11	12	13	14	15
16	17	18	19	20
21	22	23	24	25

The students then color some of the squares in order to make a pattern. Next they make up a math problem for each of the numbers in the squares they have colored. Then they give their math problems and an uncolored grid to a friend. Here is a set of math problems to get started:

$$3+2=\qquad 12+2=\qquad 11+1=$$
$$16+3=\qquad 21+2=\qquad 7+3=$$
$$6+0=\qquad 1+0=\qquad 16+1=$$

In order to keep this at its simplest level, this puzzle requires only addition skills, and all sums are to be found by counting in the same row. To increase its complexity, have addition cross lines. For example, instead of asking for $16 + 1$ in order to get to 17, ask for $7 + 9$. More complicated still, use multiplication or division to get to the desired numbers, i.e., 4×4 to get to 16, $15 \div 3$ to get to 5. Once the children master puzzles up to 25, increase the grid to 100.

Here is a sample of a more complicated "color the squares" puzzle:

$8 \times 8 =$	$100 - 1 =$	$87 + 4 =$	$3 \times 5 =$	$67 + 6 =$
$90 + 5 =$	$3 \times 4 =$	$66 - 5 =$	$12 + 7 =$	$10 \times 7 =$
$30 \div 6 =$	$48 + 4 =$	$7 \times 7 =$	$91 - 5 =$	$73 - 7 =$
$2 \times 8 =$	$63 - 4 =$	$63 + 4 =$	$4 \times 5 -$	$78 + 7 =$
$71 + 7 =$	$6 \times 6 =$	$37 - 6 =$	$18 + 5 =$	$3 \times 6 =$
$96 - 4 =$	$47 + 8 =$	$60 \div 6 =$	$42 \div 7 =$	$100 - 4 =$
$7 \times 4 =$	$50 - 9 =$	$5 \times 7 =$	$90 - 7 =$	$8 \times 5 =$
$60 - 9 =$	$70 - 69 =$	$42 - 8 =$	$9 \times 5 =$	$9 + 4 =$
$59 + 7 =$	$54 - 8 =$	$91 + 9 =$	$29 + 8 =$	$6 \times 7 =$
$76 - 6 =$	$6 \times 10 =$	$71 - 6 =$	$93 - 5 =$	$7 + 4 =$

When the students finish a puzzle, have them check the pattern they drew with a master copy to see if they match. If they don't, have them discover why they don't and then make the necessary corrections. (After preparing the above puzzle, I gave it to a friend to do. He returned a different looking pattern. On checking it out, I discovered I had made two mistakes in presenting the math problems, and he had made two mistakes in computations. Thus, there were four squares which did not match the pattern I had originally made.)

Lesson 17. Large Numbers

Students in advanced levels of math are often expected to work with large numbers, but they are rarely given opportunities to deal with large numbers in a concrete form. Try to find ways to allow them experiences estimating large numbers.

1. Bring in a pail of sand. Have the students count the number of grains it takes to fill a quarter of a cup. Find the number of

quarter cups in the pail. Calculate and estimate the number of grains of sand in the pail.

2. Have the students save something in order to reach a certain large number. One class I visited was trying to gather a million bottle caps. When they got 25,000 of them, they realized they would not have room enough in their classroom to hold a million.

3. Bring in a sunflower plant. Count the number of sunflower seeds in a single sunflower. Approximate the number of sunflowers needed to produce a million seeds. How large a field would be required to grow that many sunflower plants?

4. Collect newspaper articles about events that great numbers of people attend: sports games, concerts, conventions. Using the space of the classroom as one unit for 30-35 people, have the students calculate the number of classrooms that number of people would require.

5. Bring in a box of Cheerios. Count the number in one box. How many boxes would it take to hold a million? Measure the one box. How much space would be required to hold a million cheerios? If there is enough room on the playground, measure out that space.

EPILOGUE

In having the opportunity to revise this book, I have had the chance to reflect upon the changes that have happened to me and to confluent education since beginning with the Ford-Esalen Project ten years ago. Then we were a handful of teachers exploring an unknown with not much more than our beliefs and each other for support and guidance. Today there are literally thousands of teachers in the United States, Canada, and other countries of the world who are deliberately exploring confluent or humanistic approaches in their classrooms. Then there were only theories which had to be translated into classroom applications. Today there is an ever growing number of books containing lessons specifically aimed at developing emotions and senses within the context of classroom teaching. Then we were a few teachers working in isolation. Today there are multiple organizations to help us share with one another.

I have been able personally to teach my model to a variety of persons who work in other kinds of human relations—social workers, nurses, church people, lawyers, and law enforcement officers. They have assured me of the basic soundness of the model and have taught me ways to apply it to a wider variety of situations than I had imagined possible. Current research and insights into the functions of the left–right brain split are also contributing to confluent education. That datum substantiates that it is imperative to actively include the affective domain in order to make sense

229

of and increase abilities in eidetic language, experiential outcomes, emotional thinking, intuitive outcomes, and creative procedures.

Confluent education clearly offers an alternative to orthodox procedures which may be limited just to verbal language, behavioral outcomes, rational thinking, and tangible results. It offers opportunities to develop and experience being whole, to integrate mind and body with senses and emotions. It provides ways to be willing to take risks, try new experiences, to be open, to be creative, to want to learn. It allows each of us to utilize more fully our potential to assimilate our multiple ways of learning to become an integrated being. The integrated person will have a greater love of life, be more aware of his or her feelings and thoughts, be able to use freedom responsibly, and be the kind of person who can develop realistic as well as creative answers for the future. That is the kind of person I am becoming. That is the kind of learning environment I want to provide for my students. That is why I believe in confluent education, now more than ever. It is truly a way of being. I thought so from the beginning. Now I know—affectively as well as cognitively—for sure.

BIBLIOGRAPHY

BORTON, TERRY. *Reach, Touch and Teach.* New York: McGraw-Hill, 1970. A readable, provocative, informative introduction to the development of a curriculum aimed at dealing with students' concerns. Borton believes that major emphasis should be placed on helping children understand the process of change, giving them practice in using it, and allowing them to change themselves in their own ways. The book presents numerous examples of affective techniques as used in various projects throughout the country.

BROWN, GEORGE I. *Human Teaching for Human Learning: An Introduction to Confluent Education.* New York: Viking, 1971. An account of the Ford Foundation–Esalen Institute project, containing a statement of the purposes of the project, extensive examples of affective techniques and their classroom applications, and a series of personal commentaries by teachers involved in the project. The sections on techniques and their applications are filled with practical suggestions for teachers who wish to experiment in confluent education.

BROWN, GEORGE I. *The Live Classroom.* New York: Viking, 1975. This book, edited by Lyles Grizzard and Tom Yoemans, is a list of readings from many different people who have been working in the area of confluent education. It covers an age range from elementary school to college level students. There are also articles which are not directly related to teaching. It presents a good view of the multiple uses of confluent education.

232   *Bibliography*

CANFIELD, JACK, and WELLS, HAROLD C. *100 Ways to Enhance Self Concept in the Classroom: A Handbook for Teachers and Parents.* Englewood Cliffs, N.J.: Prentice Hall Curriculum and Teaching Series, 1976. All the lesson ideas in this book are designed to enhance a student's self concept. It contains seven sections. It is well organized and easy to read. There are many activities for older students and adults. It concludes with a short annotated bibliography and a listing of curriculum materials, periodicals, organizations, and growth centers related to affective education.

CHASE, LARRY. *The Other Side of the Report Card: A How-To-Do-It Program for Affective Education.* Pacific Palisades, Calif.: Goodyear Publishing Co. Inc., 1975. This book includes a section on how to begin awareness sessions for classrooms. It is easy to read, and offers many suggestions to both a beginning and a seasoned teacher. It contains 24 awareness units, most built around a theme or concern that is meaningful for elementary school children. It contains a chapter on developing your own lesson plans, with lots of ideas to get you started, including some tips about what to do when things don't go the way you expect them to.

deMILLE, RICHARD. *Put Your Mother on the Ceiling: Children's Imagination Games.* New York: Walker, 1967. A delightful book which deals with children's fears and joys through imagination games. The introduction presents an excellent rationale for the deliberate expansion and development of imagination skills within the context of classroom learning. It also provides an exciting form that can be used by children in creative writing.

FAGEN, JOEN, and LEE SHEPHERD, eds. *Gestalt Therapy Now.* Palo Alto, Calif.: Science and Behavior Books, 1970. A useful collection of articles reporting new developments in the theory, techniques, and applications of Gestalt therapy. Of special interest to educators are "Anger and the Rocking Chair: Education of Emotionally Disturbed Children," by JANET LEDERMAN; "A Child with a Stomachache: Fusing Psychoanalytic and Gestalt Techniques," by RUTH C. COHN; and "Staff Training for a Day Care Center," by KATHERINE ENNIS and SANDRA MITCHELL.

FLUEGELMAN, ANDREW, editor. *The New Games Book.* San Francisco, Calif.: The New Games Foundation, 1976. This book is full of games that teach us all how to play hard and fair without anyone getting hurt. It is the kind of book I always wanted but didn't have until now. It is the perfect book to go along with the chapters on building trust and allowing for aggression. All of the games allow the students an equal chance for success . . . for the super star as well as for the shrinking violet when it comes to games. It is well illustrated and easy to read. Advanced students can read it themselves and teach the games on their own.

GALYEAN, BEVERLY. *Language From Within.* Santa Barbara, Calif.: CEDARC, 1976. A handbook of personal growth and awareness exercises applied to language teaching and learning. Though primarily designed for use in teaching a second language, it is also an excellent resource for ideas on how to enrich any type of language program.

GREER, MARY, and BONNIE RUBINSTEIN. *Will the Real Teacher Please Stand Up?: A Primer in Humanistic Education.* Pacific Palisades, Calif.: Goodyear Publishing Company, 1972. Presents excerpts from books and articles in humanistic education, from children's writings to statements by leaders in the field. It has questions and games for the reader to ponder and play. With this book as a guide, the reader can plan his or her own continuing reading program.

GUNTHER, BERNARD. *Sense Relaxation Below Your Mind.* New York: Collier Books, 1968. A beautiful book of poetry with accompanying pictures of exercises designed to relax and awaken the body, release the mind, and stimulate the senses. Many of the exercises can be used in the classroom, to relax or to stimulate the students.

JONES, RICHARD M. *Fantasy and Feeling in Education.* New York: New York University Press, 1968. Beginning with a perceptive critique of the Education Development Center's curriculum, "Man: A Course of Study," and focusing on its failure to deal with the students' emotions, Jones goes on to point out the importance of fantasy and creative thinking in education. He makes specific recommendations for new approaches to affective education. This book is difficult to read at times, but it is worth the effort for a theoretical base for affective education.

LEDERMAN, JANET. *Anger and the Rocking Chair: Gestalt Awareness with Children.* New York: McGraw-Hill, 1969. A dramatic, poetic account of the Gestalt methods of here and now and taking responsibility for one's self. Rather than suppress their anger, Ms. Lederman helps her pupils to transform those powerful impulses into constructive attitudes and behavior.

LYON, HAROLD C., JR. *Learning to Feel—Feeling to Learn.* Columbus, Ohio: Charles E. Merrill, 1971. A compilation of ideas in the field of affective education from different people working in many different areas. The sections on "Humanistic Education Techniques" and "Applying Humanistics to Classroom Situations" are particularly valuable.

MILLER, JOHN P. *Humanizing the Classroom.* New York: Praeger, 1976. Miller analyzes a variety of humanistic models of education in a clear and conscientious manner. By analyzing each model through his criteria, it is possible to see their various strengths and recognize the kinds of results that will emerge from their application. It is an excellent resource for people who are looking for some guidelines in selecting a humanistic program.

PERLS, FREDERICK. *Gestalt Therapy Verbatim.* LaFayette, Calif.: Real People

Press, 1969. An informative and readable introduction to the theory and process of Gestalt therapy. The first 71 pages explore the theoretical basis; the rest of the book consists of verbatim transcripts of Gestalt therapy sessions.

ROGERS, CARL. *Freedom to Learn.* Columbus, Ohio: Charles E. Merrill, 1969. An excellent book which explains in detail how and why classrooms should be organized to free students to learn. Rogers clearly points the direction of education in the years to come.

SPOLIN, VIOLA. *Improvisation for the Theater.* Evanston, Ill.: Northwestern University Press, 1963. A popular text-manual on theater games, written primarily for the teacher. It contains more than 200 games and exercises, most of them designed to develop spontaneity and release creativity.

WEINSTEIN, GERALD, and MARIO D. FANTINI, eds. *Toward Humanistic Education: A Curriculum of Affect.* New York: Praeger Publishers, 1970. Describes and illustrates a "curriculum of affect," a model for teaching based on pupils' concerns and feelings rather than on purely cognitive goals, which relates to all children, whatever their age, socio-economic level, or cultural background. The chapters "Identity Education" and "Three Diagnostic Techniques" are of particular interest to the teacher seeking to deal with pupils' feelings and concerns.